Tales of The Himalaya

Adventures of A Naturalist

Lawrence W. Swan

La Crescenta, CA 91224
USA

Tales of The Himalaya ©

Written by Lawrence W. Swan

First Edition: 2000, Original paper. Printed on demand

Text copyrighted in 1999 by Lawrence W. Swan

Published in the United States of America by
Mountain N' Air Books – P.O. Box 12540 – La Crescenta, CA 91224 USA

Phone: (800) 446-9696, (818) 951-4150

Fax: (800)303-5578

E-mail Address: books@mountain-n-air.com

Website: www.mountain-n-air.com

Cover design and book layout/design© by Gilberto d' Urso

Cover photos and all other picture from Dr. Swan's archives

This book is an original paperback, published electronically and printed on demand.

Library of Congress Card Number: 99-69267

Tales of The Himalaya — 1st edtion

Foreword by Sir Edmund Hillary

ISBN 1-879415-29-1

1. Swan, Lawrence W.

2. Himalaya—travel adventure—Natural Sciences—literature

ISBN: 1-879415-29-1

Table of Contents:

Foreword

By Sir Edmund Hillary

The world revels in mysteries—the Loch Ness Monster; the Californian Big Foot; and of course the Abominable Snowman—the Yeti. What are these creatures? Do they really exist? Everyone would like to know.

In 1960 I took an expedition to the Himalayas to try and answer one of these questions-was there such a thing as a Yeti? My party included mountaineers, physiologists, and perhaps most important of all for this purpose two experienced animal biologists. One was Dr. Lawrence W. Swan, then Associate Professor of Biology at San Francisco State University. Larry was a great asset to the expedition—not only as a scientist—but also for his energy, his sense of humor, and his extremely cheerful nature.

We followed the Yeti footprints in the snow; listened to stories from the monks in remote monasteries; and examined the pointed scalps which the Sherpa people believed came from Yetis. Our final conclusions, supported I believe by Larry Swan, were that the Yeti was a mythological creature created out of the few sightings of the rare Tibetan Blue Bear.

Nearly 40 years have passed since those days and no one has succeeded in taking a clear photograph of a Yeti. It is almost impossible to prove that something doesn't exist-so who knows? Maybe someday our theory may be proved wrong!

Sir Edmund Hillary

For the denizens
of
Cooch Nahai

Introduction

There are some magnificent books about the Himal and Alaya. It is these great snows and their abode that I find fascinating. In my youth, the world of mountains was often closed by the politics of the time but can now be visited by the many thousands who care to travel among those icy giants. The tales and descriptions about peaks and valleys, as well as the people and nature, fill my shelves. Glorious photographs burst out from my book covers, travel calendars, and wall hangings. This book is but an addition to the delicious surfeit.

I was born in the Himalaya and grew up there. My parents, Henry Marcus Swan, and Edna Lundeen Swan, worked for 30 years as Methodist missionaries in India and were primarily involved with educational enterprises in Pakur near the Raj Mahal Hills of Bihar, Calcutta and Darjeeling. All of my work in the Himalaya rests upon these beginnings, and the ferment for natural history that bubbles in my experiences and observations has its origins on the hillsides of Sikkim and Darjeeling.

I loved the wooded hills long before any current writers found their own affections. I learned the trees, insects, and birds in my own way with the help of Lepcha and Nepali associates. I let this fervor for nature blossom throughout my life. My articles in scientific journals are spilling out of their places on my shelves. But they are all about ecology, biogeography or some such similar designation. I have never written about my Sherpa associates, the thousand and more miles of walking up and down the mountains, and the emotions that come when finding the living things near the summits of the highest mountains in the world. It is difficult to share the humor of an expedition, the peculiarities of one's associates, American and otherwise. One reason for writing this book about the highlands of Asia is to elaborate on peculiar happenings, seemingly passing events that occur by chance while striving to reach the summit of a peak.

As a collector and a follower in the footprints of Charles Darwin and Joseph Hooker, I have discovered the most precarious ecosystem in the world. It is a biome beyond the alpine or the tundra where life lives on the manna donated by the wind. This Aeolian Biome is not often included in textbooks since few biologists do their research up beyond 20,000 feet, tolerating cold hands and fierce storms. They may not believe it could exist. The maps of the world still designate places where I have found little living things as "lifeless" or "glaciated" and colored to resemble ice. Text-books in microbiology do not mention the very interesting bacteria collected near the summit of Mt. Everest, collected in an environment closer to outer space than any other place on our planet. It is here the bleakness of Mars is most comparable to any other earthly zone. Oversights among scientists and geographers should be brought out and explained.

Here, too, is an account concerning the ecology of the abominable snowman or yeti — the first explanation of its sort that I know about. There is also an account of the bar-headed geese that fly over Mt. Everest and the highest peaks of the Himalaya, which exhibit a unique physiology that enable them to succeed. These geese open the way to new interpretations of the geology and geography of Tibet and Central Asia.

Beyond these reasons there is an aura of necessity that grows from a childhood of marvel about the Himalaya. I could see Chumolari, the great peak on the border between Tibet and Bhutan, from my living room in that wonderful place called "Swan's Nest" near Darjeeling. And so, when I see the Himalaya I can see it with the eyes of a child, as well as with the view of age. I can see and sense the differences. I can love the hills not only as a new and exciting mistress, but as a beautiful old friend. The analogy is, of course, inadequate and weak because I am the one who has aged, not the Himalaya. But, then, she too has lost much of her exquisite tresses of forests and has gained those balding spots of agricultural fields that brown her emerald greenness of unmolested nature. Her white snows that define her skyline are as they were before, ever beckoning, ever exciting, ever changing to the demands of sun and clouds to leave hints of allure and then hiding them like some provoking siren of the Argonauts.

There is an underlying theme that breaks through to the surface on occasion. It is my despair about the destruction of the Himalaya, its lost forests, its silting rivers, the hovels that grow in lovely valleys, the killing of wildlife, the demise of butterflies, the poisoning of the land. I yearn for more trees and not more people. My values seem anachronistic where human fecundity outweighs the morals of family planning and birth control.

I have written this book with a pleasure of memories. These memories include reading my old notes written under a flapping tent in the snow, scratched out beside a valley stream among the butterflies, or amidst the magnificence of the Barun Valley with the feel of the air above 20,000 feet. Memories like eating curry around the fire with my Sherpas, or seeing the hillsides ablaze with rhododendrons always linger.

It is my hope that some of these yearnings for the mountains, my expressions of appreciation for peaks and forests, will touch your own hopes to see these lands that still offer their pristine state. The hugeness of the mountains, their drama, their never-ending snows, their enormous cliffs, their great clefts of gorges, all these endure.

It is the software of trees and people, the ratio between green forests and brown land, that continues to change through the ages.

On Pronunciation

There is some confusion about the pronunciation of the word "Himalaya." The name comes from the Sanskrit, "Himal" meaning "snow," and "Alaya" referring to "abode," hence, "Abode of Snow." Some people, especially the British, prefer "hima-LAYA" with a stress on the "abode" while others, especially those who have been raised in the Himalaya, prefer "HIMAL'aya" with the stress on the "snow." I use the latter but could not argue that it is the correct pronunciation. Presumably, they are both adequate and I make no issue of the matter except when people try to correct me. It is only then that I show my distinct preference for "HIMAL-aya." Because of all this, I much prefer "Himalaya" to the too common "Himalayas." The plural "s"

11

does not fit Sanskrit and it would seem there is an inclination toward many "abodes of snow" when the whole Himalaya is a single "abode of snow."

There is also the word "sahib" which looks like it is pronounced like something out of the movie "Casablanca." In the region of this book "sahib" is always pronounced "sahb" and the purist may require the spelling "sah'b." I prefer "sahb" so that there is no subliminal tendency for the reader to add the mischievous "i" or "ee" to the pronunciation. Sahb is not a term of respect or honor. It is merely a term of recognition mainly used for the recognition of the white man ("memsahb" is for women). A white child is usually referred to as "chota sahb" (small sahb) and the man in charge as "burra sahb" (big sahb). My early native associates, after we became well acquainted, might venture to call me "Lawlie sahb," allowing a familiarity with my first name but including the sahb for designation. Perhaps this unusual arrangement suggests a mite of distance derived from the times of British rule. The Sherpas, however, who never acquiesced to the British still prefer "sahb" to first names.

Darjeeling

Darjeeling gets its name from the Tibetan "Dorje-ling" which translates as "The Land of the Thunderbolt." It is a finger of India that thrusts up between Nepal and Bhutan to touch Sikkim that, in turn, abuts on a southern projection of Tibet. Darjeeling centers on geographic diversity among strange lands and fascinating people. It harbors a flavor of the remote and it stands high in the Himalaya. Its history issues from the British in India, when malaria and the heat of the Indian Plains forced imperialism to acquire lands of altitude, where the sweating workers of England in their uncooled offices in Calcutta could go to recover their sense of European chill. It was, and is, what is called a "Hill Station," a place for relief from the ovens of May and the muggy airs of the Monsoon. It is pleasant in Darjeeling even though, between June and September, the clouds come in and it rains and refills the gauges. It rains about 10 feet of water in four months.

Life adjusts to rain, especially a warming rain, and, from this abundant moisture, there grows a plethora of greenery accompanied by bugs, birds and beasts. Darjeeling and its District incubate one of the world's most luxurious cultures for living things like a vast and humid greenhouse, a garden of Nature's marvels.

The town hovers along a ridge of the Himalaya with the red roofs of its houses cascading down the slopes. It is reached by road or by the miraculous little train, the "Toy Train," that puffs its way up the hills in loops and twists for 60 miles from Siliguri on tracks that are only two feet apart. It goes up and up, at first through monsoon jungles and then on through temperate forests touching places like Sukna, Tindaria, Kurseong Toong, Sonadah and Ghum. This last town is at about 8,000 feet altitude and from there the train rolls down to Darjeeling a thousand feet lower.

Darjeeling is known for its tea and if the tea is purchased at one of the many tea estates that clothe the lower slopes near the town, then anyone may well agree that no drink could be as aromatic and lovely as Darjeeling tea. The ordinary tea of the town is much better than most teas but that special stuff, saved for the few fortunates, is something out of this world.

Mt. Hermon School in Darjeeling

Darjeeling should be famous for other things besides its tea. Notably, it should stand apart as being the site that offers the most spectacular view of mountains to be seen from any civilized place. This is a hard claim for surely the people of Switzerland might object (or Coloradoans or Bolivians). There may be other spectacular sights such as that of Mt. Everest from Sola Khumbu or the Matterhorn from Zermatt, but these are places with restricted horizons and concentrated views. For a whole range of white that goes on and on across the skyline there can be nothing to compare with Kangchenjunga and its mighty cohorts which rise and fall in glistening pinnacles while attending the ice-sheathed centerpiece of the third highest peak in the world. Darjeeling can claim this supreme distinction of utter beauty. Darjeeling is a place to see.

I was born in Darjeeling and spent much of my early years in and around the town going to school and absorbing the versatility of the place. The prospect of telling about those times baffles my ability to sort them out in some sort of sequence and make them pertinent to the other tales of this book. I could simply go on and on. One beginning is to recall the road that shoved me along the route to becoming a biologist. From all my associates at my school in Darjeeling, I remained the only one who ended up with bugs, birds, snakes, frogs, and trees still with me. The others have gone their ways and I really cannot understand how, in that milieu of fulminating life where all sorts of creatures filled our existence, it was I who continued my love and commitment to forests and wildlife.

The school, Mt. Hermon School, was an optional boarding school that had been cut out of the mold of the English school and adapted to allow girls and boys to attend classes together. It was one of perhaps three or four co-educational schools in all of British India. Most students were sent to Darjeeling for nine months of the year to exist under the rules of the school and live in dormitories. The parents would try to spend a week or so during their vacations with their children and spend the rest of the year in the sometimes-grueling heat of the plains. Other students could be day scholars and live with their parents or a guardian in a cottage on the Mt. Hermon Estate. At one time or another I fit into either arrangement but during my last years, when my father was the manager of the Estate, I lived in my home "Swan's Nest."

The greatest event of the year was "Going Home Day," a day in November when nearly the whole school took off for the plains of India in the "Toy Train" or in taxis. The exceptions were those in Junior and Senior Cambridge. These students stayed on an extra two weeks to take "Cambridge Exams," examinations sent out from England for most of the students in the British Empire. These exams were designed to check on the performance of education under the Cambridge system. "Going Home Day" was like nothing else on earth. Months before the time when some of those youngsters would have the first chance to see their parents since March, when we all arrived at the school, the days were counted and displayed on calendars all over the place. Life was timed by "Going Home Day" and then the songs started. My older brother Charles, who had returned to Mt. Hermon as a teacher, now found his music and poetry run together in song after song with a new complement to be learned each year. I could fill these pages with those songs that still hum in my head and as I commute to work in the mornings, they set me singing with their lovely gusto. I constructed in my mind some stage musical, a story of Himalaya, based around those songs, which to me match the efforts of Rodgers and Hammerstein and fit a locale quite as exotic as a "South Pacific."

The following is one of those songs that have come back to me. Here are three of the verses, although there are many more.

A "Going Home Day" Song, Mt. Hermon School, Darjeeling

> Riding roads of sunshine on the wings of song,
> Lands beyond the skyline lure our hearts along.
> Heralds golden hearted, trumpets loud and gay,
> Shouting we have started, going home today!
>
> Say goodbye Mt. Hermon, woods and hills goodbye!
> Round the bend we leave it, on our way we fly
> Say goodbye Darjeeling, wintered cold and gray,
> Shouting we have started, going home today!
>
> Now we're riding homeward, on to Kurseong,
> Purple is the sunset as we roll along.
> See the plains in twilight, dark and far away,
> Calling us to hasten, going home today!

Mt. Hermon was segregated but not along lines of race. There was the practical segregation based on diet. A student had to eat what was offered and not have some religious restrictions about food. This left out the fundamentalist Hindus and Moslems who, nevertheless, could attend the school as day scholars. Thus, all sorts of nationalities came to be represented. And, for a while, the young daughters of the Prime Minister of Tibet, Kate and Tess Tsarong, were our companions. There was no segregation according to age which is the *sine qua non* of American schools. The students ranged from kindergarten to Senior Cambridge, the equivalent of the senior year in high school. In retrospect, I find this amalgam of ages among perhaps 250 students goes to the heart of the idea of education and learning. It is not only the teachers that teach but one's older friends, the young men and women you come to admire as a child and who demonstrate appropriate behavior and the direction toward meaningful goals. I have seen children get lost in American schools where several hundred youths of similar age and at the

16

same level of education are thrust together in competition or in some race for recognition. In such places, if you are good at something, you may be among dozens of others who are similarly gifted. A single child may not easily be identified as the leading performer, someone outstanding, for competition is too intense with too many individuals involved. The stage is set for getting lost. To really stand out requires supreme dedication to a single theme, and this often needs special lessons or a directed purpose that leaves much else neglected.

This was not the case in Darjeeling. Youngsters with specialties or with special loves for their hobbies were recognized. In this easy marking system a child prospered with support and a sense of status. It was this sense of status that we were offered which is so hard to acquire in the immense accumulation of students that is the norm in American schools. I must elevate this recognition of individuality to a distinctive importance in education. General acceptance of one's ability kindled further efforts towards distinction and yet all of us were involved. We all participated in sports (cricket, soccer, field hockey, track etc.), and music. We all took the same courses in school. There was no great effort to make us outstanding in any single area; we were induced to do well in all things. It was in this atmosphere that somehow I gained some acceptance as the best bug collector, the most knowledgeable about birds and as a lad who definitely had some knack in remembering the names of the trees.

If it had not been for this charmingly simple recognition of my status, even when I knew very little, I doubt if I could have maintained my interest in living things and the sense of wonder for far off places. I had very little other encouragement and there was no one in the school who could teach me what I wanted to know. Teachers know arithmetic and Latin and Shakespeare. They do not know about worms and beetles.

In my position as local authority on matters of the natural world, I spent much time perfecting my art. A wonderful local Nepalese carpenter, Kancha Rai, took me through the forests and taught me the Nepalese names of the trees and how to look for the subtle differences in the bark, leaves and flowers that distinguished closely related species. This was complemented by a local worker on the estate, a marvelous Lepcha man, Bana, who walked with me and showed me how the Lepchas used the forest products.

The Lepchas are aboriginal Himalayans. They represent the westward extension of the tribes that extend out of northern Burma and are scattered in secluded valleys along the eastern Himalaya, the Mishmis, the Abors, the Akas and so forth. All these peoples live close to nature and live off the land with minimal agriculture.

The Lepchas are nearly extinct, having been driven off by the immigrant Nepalese, and Bana represented a last link with a dying culture. He told me about his people and showed me how to strip a piece of nettle stem and to dry it to make thread. He also taught me how to easily make a cup from the right kind of rounded root of Rhododendron, how to cook rice in a large segment of bamboo and have it cook before the bamboo burned.

It was later that I read of the American "Red Indian" and how the Mohawks and others had similar ways of living off the land. It was a fascinating discovery. I became what some residents of the Estate described as a "jungle fellow" which, to me, was an endearing compliment.

Whereas I came to know the Nepalese and Lepcha names of the trees and many plants and how they were used, I did not know what an elm, oak or a laurel was. These were English names that I encountered in English stories. It was a troublesome hiatus in my knowledge that I really did not know how many of the native trees had counterparts in Europe and America.

My answers came when I found something in the library, the two volumes of Joseph Dalton Hooker's **Himalayan Journals**. Here was the Rosetta Stone. That great man, the friend of Charles Darwin and Darwin's chief advisor on things botanical, had travelled through Sikkim and the Darjeeling District from 1850 to 1851. His writings seemed to detail everything he saw. He would remark in his volumes of description about the oak *Quercus spicata*, the "arkaula" of the Nepalese or, similarly, the birch *Betula alnoides*, the "saur" of the Lepchas. It was only then that I found out what an oak or birch looked like and that Quercus included all sort of oaks and Betula, several birches. Latin started to make sense.

If someone had handed me a key to the trees of Darjeeling, published in pleasant colors, I may not have spent long learning hours pouring through Hooker's books. It would have been too easy and the challenge would not be there. Why work so hard on something that was already so well known? And so it became a sort of great game. I started to spout long Latin and Greek generic names, my status of authority merged into the hazy aura of the expert. Something of the same sort occurred with the birds of the area, but here I had that wonderful book of Hugh Whistler, **Handbook of Indian Birds**, with colorful pictures and tales of behavior that were, indeed, helpful. However, there was nothing about Himalayan insects, and they were the most intriguing of all.

The beetles of the eastern Himalaya are among the most spectacular in the world and I was not the only schoolboy who collected them. These beetles were often so large and showy, they could not help but attract attention. There were even some girls who were never supposed to like creepy things but who kept big beetles as pets. We used to cause teachers all sorts of panic when we would let a big stag beetle or rhinocerous beetle free in the classroom to buzz with a roar and smash against the window pane.

These beetles acquired local common names - lama stags (lucanids with light-colored elytrae), stone-carriers (cerambycids), saws (trictenotomids), green gages (irridescent scarabaeids), spadies (cetonids) and so forth - and when I found one that seemed to have no established name, I invented my own. I tried to keep them alive but I had no idea of what they ate, or their larval and/or pupal states. A peculiar thing that wiggled once split open and out emerged a beetle. No one could tell me about pupae. When insects died I would put a pin through them. This I had heard was done in museums. My big beetles required hairpins. In this way I accumulated quite a collection and among the miscellany that I had, I can now state, in retrospect, that there were some rare and unusual species in my boxes.

As a collector of nearly everything, I found the lovely snakes of the Himalaya fascinating and anyone who encountered a snake would usually bring it to me and, usually, it was dead and squashed. I thus amassed a considerable assemblage of snakes preserved in "spirits," methyl alcohol, and living snakes in bottles and boxes and tins. I kept them under my bed. One day, right in front of my tolerant mother, a bottle broke and released a small snake that promptly rose up and spread its hood. My mother was aghast. I was keeping cobras in the house! In retrospect it was most probably a mock cobra, *Pseudoxenodon angustipes*, a most interesting snake that mimics the poisonous cobra. I was informed in no uncertain terms that either the snakes went or she went.

My father now intervened and pointed out that there was an unused old chicken coop out back that with some fixing up might function as a museum. So I whitewashed the place and fixed it up and then covered it with hundreds of orchid plants from the nearby forest. This place in full bloom became my delight and, later on, I moved my bed in and lived among my possessions. People of all sorts would come by to see what might be new. To help discourage untimely visits, I took a large stuffed lizard and attached it to strings so that when the door was opened this beast would swing down into the face of the interloper. It was good sport.

On one occasion my father met a Forest Officer, a British official of some high standing. He was told about me and how I knew the native names of the trees. He heard I had mapped their locations so that others could go

19

out and learn to recognize them. This man (I do not remember his name) made the long trip out to the school and after talking with the Principal found me in my chicken coop lair. We had a long talk and walk through the forest. He told me that it was unusual to find a lad who knew and loved trees and, later, he sent me a small book, ***The Trees of Northern Bengal*** by A.M. and J.M. Cowan. This book still sits above my desk and I still find it very valuable. My prestige as a naturalist was enhanced when the forest officer came out to visit me.

There was a generally accepted behavior among many of us at school that when the "pujas" came, the holidays, we would find some place across the hills or far into Sikkim close to the foot of Kangchenjunga to go. Thus from about the age of 11, I was taken on long hikes lasting several days. As I got older, some of us would take off for more than a week. On one occasion, in 1936 at age 14, another lad, Maurice Gibson, and I took off on a long walk of over 100 miles to the distant mountains of Sikkim. My mother did not approve but, nevertheless, donated two whole rupees to the venture. This could buy some emergency rice. We carried our packs, our homemade packs, and set off into the wilderness hoping to use our sling shots to add to our meager commissary. When it rained too much we slept on the porches of Sikkimese houses and at other times we camped out wherever there was a convenient place beside a stream. There were nights when we had our own distinctively prepared Himalayan fruit pigeon supper, something from a lucky hit with a sling shot. We discovered little used trails in distant corners of this autonomous state where the forests were still largely untouched and the hillsides unmarred by the ravages of too many people occupying too little land.

There were many such adventures where I accompanied others and some that took me into the hills by myself. I enjoyed the warm valleys where the cicadas screamed the loudest and the butterflies or other insects swarmed. They filled the air with flutters of color and assorted themselves like jewels on the stems and leaves of the lush greenery. And during the monsoon when the skies poured out their impossible quotas of water, I walked along soaked in the pleasure of coolness and enjoyed the moisture that made it possible for this world to flourish.

I think back now and still revel. Time and again my sense of appreciation overwhelms me. I think how incredibly fortunate I have been to experience such a piece of earth's magnificence. At an innocent age, I was actually part of the Himalayan exuberance and not merely an alien observer.

I once recall a visiting missionary with an unusual interest and knowledge of snakes. A Mr. Menzel came to Darjeeling and offered to let me accompany him on a long circuit through Sikkim. My older brother John was eager to go. He had finished school and was now waiting to return to the United States. For me, being released from school for such duty was unheard of in those parts. Nevertheless, I spoke to the Principal, a rather unbending sort of person, and she recognized that this would be a vast education for me. I could leave school for over a week. We walked about thirty miles from Darjeeling to high Sandakphu, a southernpoint on a ridge that came straight down from the great peak of Kangchenjunga.

We camped overnight and in the early morning, when the stars were still out and only our clocks told us of the impending dawn, we moved out into the cold air wrapped in our blankets. Up here on Sandakphu at 12,000 feet, we would get an unobstructed view of Mount Everest and its neighbors, Lhotse and Makalu. To the north was an intimate sighting of the great peak that dominated the north, Kanchenjunga. In the dark hours before the sun, there were only vague outlines of the surrounding peaks but we could see an endless sea of clouds that seemed to cover the whole of Sikkim and much of Nepal, as well as the adjacent hills of the Darjeeling District. It was here that we witnessed a sunrise that I will never forget.

Out in the cold air, time went on slowly, then long before we had any sense of a real brightness in the east, we saw what appeared to be a red fire in the dark sky far to the west. It seemed unreal and so aloof from the earth that at first we did not recognize it. And then we understood. The sun had touched the summit of Mt. Everest and a piece of the earth glowed gold like a strange burnished star. We watched in wonder as the color very slowly spread down the distant slope. Again like a star afire, at the summit to the north, the pinnacle of Kanchenjunga, also caught the sun and flamed the signal from that direction. All else was now still in an encompassing deep indigo. But, as Mt. Everest was spreading its shroud of red glory, the high tip of Makalu caught the same fire.

Here before us, without theodolites and the instruments of the surveyors, we could easily discern the sequence of the peaks according to their heights and so in this ritual of succession, the great mountains each took their turn in exalted grandeur. It was an exhibit of the turning of the earth, something that is seldom sensed. Reaching high to touch the new rays of the sun spoke its message of geodesy. The lesson was that we were on a huge round globe in space, our home in the universe. The sun, our star, was defining our rounded form. Here, too, was the umbra and penumbra, the dark and lighter shadows that fall upon the moon during an eclipse. Here, with the light of the sun skimming the round edge of our world, there was redness on

21

the great pinnacles that reached high into space and touched the sun's rays before they spread to the ordinary world.

As the minutes went, the vast white surfaces of snow turned into hues of rose and shadowed slopes that faced the sun askance took on shades of deep purple emerging into unreflecting blackness. Soon, the colors moved to the horizon far into Sikkim and on to that isolated giant in Tibet, Chumolari, and still farther on to the eastern saw-edged ranges that lined the map between India and Bhutan. The world was glowing myriad shades of red. All this surfeit of color stood above an endless and flat sea of clouds, dark now in their valleys but white in their time. They were a rug across the lower hills to attest to a bottom, a flat floor for the world like some soft and pillowed benthos of the vast ocean of air.

Colors now touched the lower buttresses and ridges, blues and greens and the softly pink grays and they were all framed in a sky that was too dark to be mere air. More and more the sun claimed its reign over this high world and then, finally, as we watched, the nearest ridges took their color and the glow came closer. And then like some divine experiment, we were touched and gilded, too.

Now, in warmed light, we saw below an endless stratum of clouds being conquered by the sun's brilliance. Light touched the slight imperfections of the flat array and ripples of rainbows were cast on the cloud carpet. With some unseen force in the air, strands of vapor detached themselves from the matrix of white to rise magically into the air. And then some of these wisps lifted, leaving hints of rainbow edgings as they crossed favored angles with the sun. It was inevitable now. Surging clouds convened and broke from the hold of the mass and so, as we watched the fading scene on that stage that was only winged by opposite horizons, we were engulfed in an instant. The Himalayan mist won. We were lost in white. We made our way back to our camp and our fire.

Many years later, on a high rock and snow ridge of Makalu, I again witnessed a replay of that scene. It was a similar morning but now I was watching from the stage and seeing the tiered audience of low ridges standing out of a white carpet far, far to the east. The burnished star of the great summit just above me was nearly in my hand while far away a gray line in the distant clouds marked the range of Sandakphu. Once again the horizons rejoiced in red and all the shades of the spectrum that could be allowed by the physics of light and air and shadow and cloud. And once again after this morning ecstasy of nature, this rampant brush of the sun with its careless spread of emblazoned colors, once more the Himalayan mists swallowed me into their horizonless world. And this sudden end, this closing of a fantasy, was not unlike the curtains of a stage that signaled the close of a matchless performance, the end of a drama that could only live on in unassuageable memory.[1]

I often think of those mornings when nature exaggerates its pallet. I sense those mornings need more than memory. They need to have their place in writing and thought. The following endeavors to envelope those remembrances.

Once a Sikkim Dawn -

To north, the vertex peaks glow bright
Gold snows burnish the umbrad light
The ice, the cold are capped by fire
    - Anomaly

On Everest first the burning clue
A star then lights on Makalu
The sun's gauge gilds by altitude
    - Geodesy

The round earth turns and reaches higher
To glow, then beam the crimson pyre
While lesser giants take their turn
    - In glory

The snow grows rose from distant east
Rubies in jade and amethyst
Set the valley's darkened frame
    - Of filigree

And then am I on this high place
A piece among the peaks of space
Touched, warmed and gilded too
    - Finally

From Sandakphu to summits on
Horizon crags beyond Bhutan
The sea waves hues of sun-heaved clouds
    - And beauty

And then the humid monsoon mists
Air's benthos of Himalaya lifts
Its pallid curtains upward strewn
    -Obscutiry

In writing these recordings from my memories, I realize I have to leave out so much. I cannot fill the void that truly expresses my gratitude for the gift I have been given, the legacy of my young environment. I have not expressed the whole love for that place of Himalaya. It was my mold. It shaped me. But it could not last. The fatal day came. I had to leave. My mother was sick. She had had every conceivable tropical disease during her 30 years in India but now it was simple, common, western diabetes. My parents had to return to the United States and I would have to finish my last year in high school back somewhere across the ocean in a place called America, a frightening prospect. I left Mt. Hermon and Darjeeling on the 13th of May, 1937.

The night before I left, the whole school went off to celebrate the Coronation of George VI. I was left totally alone, for such festivities were far from my mind. I went up on a hill, a place I often visited. There under my trees, I watched the great range of Kangchenjunga in full moonlight. I sat for hours trying to adjust my mind to living in some other place. No one, I thought, could ever be so tied to a time and place as I was. Leaving was like tearing out some chunk of my soul. And yet I knew I had to go away - for more education. I wanted to learn more about my bugs, trees and birds.

Around me the night insects were orchestrating their myriad sounds. The chorus of frogs told of some wet place and farther away, the jackals howled. I added to these songs of the night with my sobs, great, heaping, soul-grinding sobs that came from the guts of my emotions. Finally I said goodbye to that glorious mountain that seemed to brighten the night with the moon gleaming on its immense snowfields. I should have said goodbye to my trees for the mountain would be there when I returned many times later, but the trees would go.

I went back to my room with its large windows that overlooked the valley, and the light had attracted its normal surfeit of moths that covered the window like a mosaic that changed its pattern with their movements. For those who have never seen such a display of color and form filling every square inch of lighted surface, they may not understand the analogy to a mosaic. But it is a mosaic, the incredible random array of colorful moths that are fitted together to cover the window in its frame.

In the morning, my good friend John Turner walked with me the eight miles to Ghum where I boarded a small trolley that rolled down the plains fifty miles away in what must surely be one of the greatest roller coaster rides on earth. I was alone except for the brakeman and before we finally banged up against the back of the Toy Train where the hills end, twilight had come and the thick Terai monsoon forest was alive with fireflies. They would cover banks and stumps of trees and then pulsate their lights in unison to give strange glowing shapes among the trees. I had never seen this before. It was a fitting farewell to the Himalaya.

1 After several years of promotional effort, I have, with my friend, Raj Singh Sinsinwar—a noted ornithologist, travel enthusiast and authority on India's National Parks—managed to convince the Indian Government to protect the environs of Sandakphu, as part of the Singlelah Range with its unmatched view and miles of blooming rhododendron forests (as well as other forested portions of the Darjeeling District) as a new National Park.

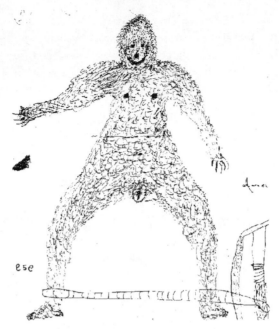

A Sherpa artistic interpretation of a female Yeti.

Sherpa's sketches of Yeti and other animals.

The Lesson of
the Abominable Snowman

In Kathmandu, Darjeeling, Kalimpong and other towns along the Himalaya, there are press agents that can easily get the attention of the world. All they have to do is to interview a mountain traveler who has some new tale about the yeti or abominable snowman. The international news services are ever alert to such stories. Similarly, the "Big Foot" of Western North America has captured the pages of newspapers. The yeti and its kin are news. A continual series of magazine articles and books feed on this publicity so that there has been an atmosphere of wonder about the creatures. As with most such things there has developed a gradient of belief from the attitude of the true believer to the doctrines of the utmost scoffers. The scoffers require the proof of a big, hairy thing lying in a box with proper tags and identification while the true believers point to all the tracks, hair, droppings, sounds, smells, photographs, sightings and personal accounts that range from murder to intimacy. Emotions peak at each end of this spread of credence and the stage is set for controversy.

My association with the abominable snowman is a long one. As a boy, I watched the expeditions headed for Mt. Everest, Kangchenjunga and other great Himalayan peaks set off for their adventures. I became friends with the Sherpas who carried the loads of these expeditions and among the earliest stories I can recall were the accounts about this strange, hairy creature that lives high among the snow fields. With each new expedition the story enlarged and finally blossomed into a wonderful tale that rivaled the narratives of Homer and had a Grecian luster of humor and pathos, virtue and vice, truth and perversity and the real and the false. I grew to love that strange beast that seemed to outwit the boldest human effort to find it and yet left its footprints clearly in the snow, like lipstick on a collar, to suggest its secret but obvious passing. The yeti had an aura of wild, cold places; it was a symbol of the glorious peaks, an ungraspable wisp that, even if it should somehow be cornered, would get away and find refuge in a far and distant mountain range where no man could ferret it out. I really don't know if I believed all this but it was a tantalizing concept for, after all, perhaps, there really could be something substantial down at the core inside its haze of implausible attributes.

Parts of the story about the yeti had some consistency. The Sherpas agreed that it had long, red hair and a pointed head. It walked on two feet but, and here we may part with logic. Its feet faced backward. Yes, backward! Now, a schism occurs between Sherpa and western reasoning. That its feet faced backward, to the Sherpa understanding, is obvious from its tracks. Do you not, when you follow the tracks, end your search without seeing the yeti? This, of course, results because you have been following the tracks in the direction from which the yeti came and not the direction in which it went. This characteristic of reversed feet is what makes the yeti so hard to find. We look at the tracks and always search in the wrong direction. All of us are fooled.

My favorite Sherpa story involves two sexes, a male Yeti that is a gentler creature that prefers yaks for food, and a more aggressive female. She, of course, as is often the case with females, prefers men and may accomplish some heinous acts when she catches them. But she is easier to fool than the male, and she is vain. Abominable Sherpa male chauvinism emerges here for it is said that when she spies a man she must stop and primp. This delay and seeming indecision allows the man to escape by running off as fast as he can. In running it is wise to go down hill for the backward facing yeti feet are not well designed for the down slope. Indeed, the female yeti has so much difficulty running down hill, where she must dig her toes into the snow instead of her heels, that she must stop and prepare herself. She must look down at her feet while she travels and in doing so, her large pendulous breasts get in her way. Thus, she must stop and laboriously fling them up and over her shoulders so they do not hang and obscure her vision. It can be noted here that the intended victim, the man, when he sees all this primping and swinging breasts becomes so transfixed with the sight that he stands in awe and is completely unable to run.

So the story goes on with a moral about being trapped by female wiles. It is charming, a delightful sample of the Sherpa ability to add a subtle touch to a tale. Yeti stories with their wily pleasantness are easily distinguished from the lurid and frightening accounts of the "Big Foot" monster in northern California. These two kinds of opposing stories emanate from two entirely different kinds of people and the difference in their tales, perhaps, reflects upon the more artistic outlook of the Sherpas as opposed to the more practical ideals of some rural Californians.

Yeti enthusiasts can point to ancient writings that suggest descriptions of the abominable snowman. They have found old paintings in monasteries that may allude to the creature and, in retrospect, they can interpret strange sightings and events of the past as being the result of yeti doings. However, the modern story emerges from the Mt. Everest expedition of 1921. Colonel C. K. Howard-Bury, the leader of that first survey of the region around Mt. Everest, found the tracks in the snow at 21,500 feet on the Lakhpa La, a pass in Tibet just northeast of Mt. Everest. His brief account in his book, "Mount Everest, The Reconnaissance 1921," is quoted in part: "Even at these heights we came across tracks in the snow. We were able to pick out tracks of hares and foxes, but the one that at first looked like a human foot puzzled us considerably. Our coolies at once jumped to the conclusion that this must be 'The Wild Man of Snows' to which they gave the name 'Metohkangmi,'" the abominable snowman who interested the newspapers so much."

Concerning the word "Metohkangmi," it should be noted that the "kangmi" part is easy to translate. "Kang" means snow, a common word, and "mi" refers to man. In "metoh," the "me" or "mi" also means man. "Ti," "te," "teh," or "toh" refers to "thing" in Tibetan; hence, "metoh" is "man thing." One can see the Tibetan porters gesturing and saying "Manthing!" "Snowman!" And Howard-Bury who was no Tibetan scholar writing down what the separate terms sounded like.

It should be noted, however, that the book came out much later than the newspaper accounts that really got the story going. It seems that Howard-Bury's letter describing the sighting of the tracks got into the hands of a journalist in Calcutta who, believing he knew some Tibetan terminology, became interested in the word "Metohkangmi." It appears, however, Howard-Bury's handwriting was not too clear and this journalist read it as "Metchkangmi." He got the "snowman" part right, but "metch" caused him trouble and this was because the word doesn't exist in the Tibetan language. Nevertheless, with perseverance noted chiefly in persevering journalists, he unearthed "metch" as the Tibetan word for "abominable." And so the abominable snowman, after a dubious gestation, was born and delivered by a columnist midwife who mistook a "c" for an "o."

The word "yeti" took me some time to decipher. It seems to come from the Sherpa variant of the Tibetan language. I asked my Sherpa friends, in Hindi, what "ye" meant, and they pointed and gestured up at the glaciers and rocks. They could not be specific, and I realized that their waving arms were denoting all the space up there, that "ye" meant the high rocky places above the yak fields, the places where no man lives. And so, "yeti" or "yeteh" means "the thing of the high places." I should also say that there are many more abominable terms, and enthusiasts of the legend can count about a dozen words to describe a menagerie of creatures. "Thelmas" and other curious denizens of forest and dale and mountain slope are, however, outside of my ecology. They confuse the main entity and they are too variable. I try to ignore them, but when and if the true high altitude yeti totters, they will presumably emerge as the next best objects of the believer's faith.

My first experience in the inner Himalaya, in the habitat of the yeti, occurred in 1954 on the expedition to climb Makalu. I was strictly an unbeliever but, curiously, I found the open honesty of the Sherpas and their forthright attitude about this creature quite infectious. They know animals very well and they knew the whereabouts and behavior of all the mammals I asked about and they mixed in the yeti with blue sheep and wolves and thar and weasels as if they were all natural inhabitants of the high places. It is easy to be anti-yeti while sitting in the comfort of a cozy living room chair. Out on the glaciers, the vastness of the place emphasizes one's own insignificance and you soon realize how little you know and how little you see. I found hundreds of tracks of the musk deer but I actually saw only three of them and animals such as snow leopards that are nocturnal are seldom seen. The snow line elevates dramatically as the inner Himalaya are approached, and near Tibet, wide areas above 20,000 feet are devoid of snow. I found plants with thick roots, tame pikas and plenty of mice. In the sun it was warm. Those high places could support many animals, even a large omnivore, especially if it was nocturnal and therefore active when it was coldest.

The high productive valleys were devoid of snow for much of the year, and the term "snowman" was obviously a misnomer. Such a creature would have to encounter snow and ice only when crossing the high passes just like the wolves and foxes that ranged between the high valleys seeking food.

Once I found the footprints of mice on a high snowfield. This was intriguing and I realized I had an extension of the story of the abominable snowman. Could it not be that in addition to abominable snowmen there were abominable snow mice? I once wrote something about this and placed these creatures into the framework of a whole abominable ecological pyramid. This had little success on the press wires for it is difficult and not very convincing to have to elaborate upon an abominable ecosystem where the food chain is founded upon an abominable herbaceous base of abominable alpine plants. However, I did collect the highest flowering plant in the world at 20,150 feet and rediscovered the highest known resident animal, a salticid spider. I mention this again because it will add to my final comments about the yeti. I would like all of us to be just as amazed at a spider that lives and eats and breeds at 22,000 feet as we are about an abominable snowman that leaves only tracks in the snow at 21,500 feet.

Some time in the early 1950s, two yeti "scalps" were found in Sherpa monasteries. They showed, appropriately, the top of a pointed head and red hair. From conversations and letters I was told that they appeared to be authentic scalps. It was said that some hairs from the scalp had been removed and there were some enigmatic results but nothing on the subject was published that I saw. However, the primary evidence for the yeti at that time was Eric Shipton's classic photograph of a footprint in the snow of the Menlung Glacier. It set the world buzzing with speculations and an uncomfortable sense that there could really be some strange beast up there among the snows. The track was 13 inches long and 8 inches wide and showed a large hallux or big toe and the impressions of three smaller toes. Most of all, it looked fresh, like a perfect casting, and it had that look about it that clearly stated that, though it was not human, it was formed by something not too distantly related to humanity.

I studied this track hoping to find how the two paws of a snow leopard could coalesce and make such a mark. I went to the San Francisco Zoo and irritated the captive snow leopards sufficiently so that they lunged and placed their paws on the protective screen, and I photographed and measured their paws. It was obvious from this that a snow leopard would make a track that was at most 4 or 5 inches in width. This realization prompted another tentative extension of the abominable story. Could it be that some huge abomi-

31

nable snow tiger with 8-inch paws was wandering around on the Himalayan glaciers? It seemed unlikely, even for the credulous press.

One day it all started to fuse together. I have in my museum of Human Anatomy and Evolution at San Francisco State University many jars containing human fetuses, preserved in formalin, representing different stages of growth. One of these, a tiny little thing about three inches long, had its tiny foot pressed against the glass. I stared. That small foot seemed a miniature of the foot that made Shipton's yeti track. For its length, it was broad and the smaller toes did not slope away from the hallux as they do in adult feet. The resemblance in outline was astonishing. So now there could be a further extension of the abominable story, something more for the newsmen of Kathmandu. I had discovered that the abominable snowman was, perhaps, a giant and red-haired fetus that leaped across the passes of the Himalaya. The press also ignored this extraordinary but highly tentative conclusion.

My fortuitous discovery did, however, open some interesting doors of conjecture and here I will wander a bit to add a biological flavor to the discussion. Late in the nineteenth century, a German biologist, Ernst Haeckel, pointed to the consideration that each individual animal, in its development or ontogeny, goes through stages that resemble the stages of its evolution or phylogeny. Haeckel wrote in a form that should be more often quoted and understood, *"Ontogenesis ist ein kleine und schnelle Wiederholung der Phylogenesis."* (Ontogeny is a small and quick recapitulation of phylogeny.) He not only showed how the human embryo goes through stages that resemble fish, amphibians and reptiles, his work inferred quite clearly that the embryos and young of animals resemble each other much more than adults. For instance, it is striking how much human babies resemble ape babies, at least much more than the adults resemble each other. A baby's foot is more ape-like than the adult human foot and some infants even have very agile big toes. The smaller toes do not slope away from the big toe. This slope that characterizes the adult human foot arises after the upright posture and walking commence in the child. With the acquisition of speech and a mastoid process and some other distinctly human traits, the child moves from an ape-like status to a human-like status. (If this presentation causes some queries concerning my reference to what some might consider old and discredited theory, I should suggest a reading of my article in the May 1990 issue of *BioScience*.) Thus, the resemblance of the yeti track to a fetal or infant foot raises a most interesting issue. One might expect that a primitive beginning type of walking primate would or could have an ancestral type of foot. This led to an investigation of the feet of creatures that are related to our ancestors, the apes. Once again I went off to the San Francisco Zoo and found, to my dismay, that the young lowland gorillas walked with their big toes spread away from the foot or abducted. They could not possibly make tracks like the yeti.

In my search for something that resembled Shipton's photograph I found a most interesting article in the October 1923 *Natural History* magazine. It was written by Carl Akeley, a noted and careful taxidermist, who had gone to Central Africa to obtain specimens of the mountain gorilla, for a display at the American Museum of Natural History in New York. He had shot a number of animals and, being a perfectionist, he had made casts of the faces, hands and feet of the gorillas and his article contained a fine picture of a cast of the foot of a mountain gorilla. (I should add here that Akeley was so moved by his experiences with gorillas, especially after he saw the facial resemblances between parent gorillas and their children, that he considered himself as something of a murderer and returned to the high Central African volcanoes to spend the rest of his life persuading the various governments to protect the animals. If it were not for Akeley's early interest, these remarkable primates would, in all likelihood, be extinct.)

Comparison of yeti, gorilla and bear track

Akeley's cast of the mountain gorilla's foot was so much like the yeti footprint that my lingering disbelief in the origins of the yeti track took some severe jostling. The gorilla foot was smaller and somewhat narrower, but the size of the hallux and the slope of the toes was near perfect and very convincing. But now there emerged a conflicting argument. Could it be that, in making the gorilla foot cast, Carl Akeley had pressed the hallux against the foot and that the adduction represented on the cast was artificial? I could not believe that the careful Carl Akeley would do such a thing, but the issue was not resolved until George Schaller made his remarkable field studies of the mountain gorilla. Indeed, adult gorillas often adduct their great toes and walk in this fashion. And so it would appear that from all the animals in the world to choose from, the yeti footprint most resembles the foot of the mountain gorilla. It was a provocative thought.

Mountain gorillas live at relatively high altitudes in Central Africa. I have followed their trails through the high forests and alpine regions of Uganda and Rwanda. Their droppings are on the summit of Muhavura at over 13,000 feet. Apes are not necessarily tropical creatures and presumably they could live high in the Himalaya. Shipton's gorilla-like yeti track could not be of an African mountain gorilla, but, presumably, it could have been made by something like it, perhaps a more bipedal ape or even some distant experiment in the upright posture. It could be some relictual species left behind in the high mountains. The Himalaya are full of such remnants that include creatures like the lesser pandas, the takins, strange shrews, odd rabbits, peculiar pigs and the scutiger frogs that I shall bring up later. Nearby, in Western China, there are the last remnant dawn redwoods and the giant pandas, isolated leftovers from a previous epoch.

Zoogeographical and paleontological considerations support the possibility that a relictual ape-like creature could exist in the Himalaya. Consider, for example, the faunal resemblances between Africa and Southeast Asia. The Ethiopian and Oriental regions have rhinoceroses, elephants, hyenas, lions, pangolins, wild cattle, and a host of other animal groups in common, including apes. The fossil record of all these animals includes northern or central Eurasia, the great Palearctic region. But, most of the northern representatives were extinguished in the late Tertiary Period or Pleistocene Epoch that saw the great glaciers cover much of that region. The present and living descendants and relatives of those extinct creatures live in Africa and Southeastern Asia and are now separated from each other by barriers of deserts. Mammoths and wooly rhinoceroses are now gone from Europe and Central Asia; elephants and the several living rhinoceroses have been left behind in their more southern refuges. However, the wild cattle tell a slightly different story. There is the widespread cape buffalo of Africa and the several wild cattle of Southeast Asia such as the banting and the gaur, but up in the Himalaya and Tibet there still exists a left-over wooly beast with an unbelievable fan for a tail and long hair that reaches the ground, a survivor of the Pleistocene extinction, a veritable abominable snow cow, the yak. There are still some wild yaks left, truly remarkable animals, big, fierce and dangerous. If such a remnant could be left behind by cattle, why not an ape or a primitive hominoid?

The Siwalik Hills in the foothills of the Himalaya hold a wide variety of extinct ape fossils, and one of these, Ramapithecus, has been proposed as something more or less between apes and man. I really don't hold to this, for Ramapithecus in its enigmatic status lived too long ago to be near human origins. Nevertheless, with Ramapithecus type fossils appearing in Africa and even Europe, the pattern of a more northern origin for this creature appears. From this and much more in the way of evidence I hold to a theory that runs counter to prevailing opinion. I support a thesis presented by William Diller Matthew (in his book *Climate and Evolution*) that successful populations of mammals have emanated from the large land masses of Eurasia and North America where they cover extensive ranges and have great genetic variability. From these northern testing grounds where the climate is highly variable, they spread south and eventually usurped the niches of less successful species.

An objective lesson in this dominance of northern mammals was the example set in a vast natural occurrence, some two million years ago. The isolated continent of South America that had nourished an endemic fauna for perhaps sixty million years and where evolution had gone its separate way, totally apart from what was going on in the rest of the world, finally joined North America. The merging of the faunas after that time must have been one of the most spectacular arenas of evolution and the fossil bones of the vanquished, as well as the living evidence of today, tell us of the consequences. We can see now that all the great predaceous marsupials (including a marsupial saber-toothed tiger-like creature) and the several orders of fascinating herbivores (some of which resembled giraffes, hippos and rhinos) that once ruled the island of South America, are gone and now there are cats, dogs, deer, raccoons, camels, pigs, tapirs and so forth that dominate the southern continent. All of these types came down from the north after that great exchange. On the other hand, the only living mammalian invaders from South America into North America are the opossum, the porcupine and the recently invading armadillo.

I see much the same sort of arrangement that could have occurred in Africa even though there has been a continuous connection between Africa and Eurasia. However, the Sahara desert lands could have acted as a periodic barrier for some of the time. Among the autochthonous faunas of Africa that have made their way out of Africa there remains only the hyrax which has expanded out as far as Syria. (Note: Even though the earliest fossils of monkeys and elephants come from the Fayum beds of Egypt, this is north of the

Saharan barrier and the major development of these groups occurred in the more northern Palearctic.)

This pattern should hold for man as well. I get dismayed when I hear the unqualified statements that insist that mankind originated in Africa. I find that anthropologists are not usually zoological geographers who may be involved with many kinds of animals, and not merely the apes and man. If they were, I should think, they would be disturbed to find all the other mammals going south, while man was going north.

It is not that mankind could not have originated in Africa which remains a possibility. It is more annoying to see the pontification about the geographical origin of mankind expounded without consideration of zoogeographical alternatives, which express an opposite direction.

On the basis of a zoogeographical pattern of distribution rather than the age of the most recent fossil discovery, I support a thesis that human origins were most likely somewhere near Central Asia, a region that has not been widely explored for its fossils. I have now seen the sites in Tibet at nearly 17,000 feet where fossil giraffes, hyenas and rhinoceroses have been uncovered in deposits that coincide in age with the origin of mankind, around five or six million years ago. Tibet was then a broad savanna and I think of no place more likely to hold, according to my hypothesis, the original fossil record of the family Hominidae.

All this seems far from the yeti and I do not wish to suggest that the yeti represents something from a deep human past. What I have in mind is to point out the possible significance of the Asian origin of hominids and imply that the presence of a relictual large primate in that part of the world is not necessarily impossible. Such a creature, in my zoogeography, is far more reasonable in the Himalaya than in California or some such place. And to add to this, I should mention the strange huge ape fossil found in south China and the Himalayan fringe; the fossil *Gigantopithecus*, and the largest of all the apes, has some earmarks of the yeti.

From all this wandering and speculating, it would seem that suggestions from zoogeography and paleontology do not rule out the presence of a yeti-like creature in the Himalaya. What now of anatomy? What creature has a pointed head? Once again the only proximity to this bizarre and demanding anatomical feature is found in apes. The male gorilla has a prominent sagittal crest on its skull. At its peak, it unites with a lateral, lambdoidal crest where the large muscles of the neck insert and at the top of this pyramid there may be some added connective tissue that contributes to a point near the back of the top of the head. What else could have a pointed

36

head? And if this were not enough to make some doubters pale, consider the impossible anatomical attribute of feet that face backward. Gorillas and chimpanzees walk in a fashion where their long arms function more like crutches than front limbs and when they move on the ground they walk on their knuckles not on their palms. Knuckle walking is characteristic of apes and when the knuckles are down, the digits face backward. Their "feet" face backward!

How could a so-called legend pick up such specific peculiarities of apes? It seems a lot for coincidence. The story seems to fit. With tracks, shape of feet, foot position, head shape, color of hair (orangs have red hair) and zoo-geography all combining and supporting the Sherpa's consistent and forthright knowledge of the animal, surely there must be some substance to the story. But congruity of this sort, no matter how compulsive, is not evidence. From the point of view of speculation, however, it is a bit hair raising.

My mind had reached this point when I was invited to accompany Sir Edmund Hillary on an expedition.[2] Marlin Perkins of TV fame was also invited and the two of us had some hopes. My equipment included some sterile glass vials. Miscellaneous droppings might reveal tell-tale ape proteins. A few molecules of yeti detected by immunological techniques would not be as good as a big hairy thing in a box but they would be better than ephemeral footprints in the snow that had no part of the actual yeti in them. Marlin was better supplied and surprised me with some gadgets that spouted tear gas just in case we came too close, and he also had some cameras equipped with trip lines that would allow the yeti to photograph itself.

The expedition headed for the Ripimu Glacier in the Rolwaling Himalaya just over the pass from the Menlung Glacier where Shipton obtained his famous photograph. One morning, our first among the high peaks, all the most avid mountain climbers were out very early full of the urge to scale some nearby summits. I was ill with the physiological qualms that come from high thin air but by late morning I had become sufficiently alive to wander about the deserted camp. Finally, the single-minded enthusiasm of the others seemed to challenge me. I noticed a small prominence nearby and it occurred to me in a moment of chicanery to go out and climb it, place a flag on the summit that could be seen from camp and then, when the others returned, have an opportunity to brag about having collected the first peak of the expedition. So I went off by myself. I climbed my "peak" of about 19,000 feet, erected a bamboo stick that I had brought along with me and

---

2. See 1962 World Book Yearbook, pp 90-110

decorated it with toilet paper, a long bluish strip that could easily be seen from the camp. I sat back satisfied to enjoy the view.

At times like this, one can become aware of the remoteness of the inner Himalaya. I could see for hundreds of miles and I knew that no one, not one single person in all history, had ever stood where I stood. It was a new place for mankind, like a little spot on the moon. I remember this emotion well for it was rudely driven from my mind by the sight of tracks in the snow. I looked at them and wondered if one of our Sherpas had strayed this far from camp.

Incredibly, I sat there pondering who it could have been and why he should care to come here and then, it finally dawned on me that there, a little down the slope, were the very tracks I had come so far to see. The broad foot—the enigmatic toes—was right there in front of me. The thought brought on a strange tingling along my back. My hair was rising. It started down near the sacrum, surged past the lumbar vertebrae and crept up to the thoracic where it stayed and prickled and thrilled. I am sure my eyes were wide open where the upper lid lifted itself above the top edge of the iris as I scrutinized the rocks and snow below and scanned the nearby slopes. Was there something big and hairy looking down on me from a nearby ridge? My insides seemed to freeze and I realized full well that the main ingredient for sighting the yeti was with me. I was alone!

But the moments of anticipation were brief. Reality supervened. I came so close! I almost found it! I moved down to the tracks below me and looked closely at the prints in the snow. The first prints were fairly good, although rather small by classic standards, but those further on seemed to change. Each footprint in the series was not sufficiently similar to its neighbor. I recognized that if I photographed only one choice track I could astound anybody. If I wished, I could scan a thousand footprints and pick out the best and most suggestive. I could select my evidence. With the confidence that I had begun to lift the curtain on the yeti's secret, I followed the tracks down the slope and across a snowfield. As I moved farther along the line, the tracks became distorted, some showing the outline of an hourglass, and then, I stood over a track that told the story. This and some succeeding tracks were clearly formed from two pug marks of a fox or small wolf.

There, before me, was the evidence. But how could it be? A fox making tracks like a yeti? It was all too unbelievable and also too prosaic. One cannot destroy such a magnificent and elaborate tale with such an ordinary solution. The yeti needed much more than this dull and heavy club of an explanation; it needed something subtle to match its own quality, something like a rapier, a thing of finesse. I wondered, as anyone may wonder, how a fox-like creature could produce humanoid yeti tracks complete with toes.

The answer emerged while I followed the tracks around a half circle. It was apparent that the "toes" tended to face in one direction, away from the sun. As the tracks progressed around the half circle, the footprints made it appear as if the yeti gradually started to walk sideways and then, yes, backward. The legend had never mentioned that the yeti not only had feet that faced backward, it had feet that were reversible! Perhaps here was that fine sword, the rapier that cut to the heart of the tale of the yeti. The explanation had that quality of art and refinement, enough to fit the elegant quality of the legend itself.

The peculiarity of this phenomenon can be attributed to altitude. Above 18,000 feet, the snow sublimates rapidly. I have been taken to task and even slandered by yeti enthusiasts who claim my explanation involves melting of snow. They do not seem to understand sublimation, or at least they ignore this crucial ingredient. Snow when laid on a rock may disappear and hardly leave a wet spot. With sublimation there is little of the sloppy, watery deterioration of a track in the snow so that it changes into a formless depression. With sublimation where the solid of snow disappears into the air as a vapor, bypassing the liquid phase, the edges of the track remain sharp and clean and, as the track alters its shape, it looks as if it had been freshly made, an unblemished cast.

The formation of the toe-like impressions on one side of the track is also a fascinating product of sublimation. A depression in the snow, even a small one, leaves one side of the depression exposed to the sun and the other in shadow. The sun-exposed side sublimates more rapidly and thus the track elongates and, to a lesser extent, widens. On the sun-exposed side where the "toes" form, sublimation occurs unevenly. No sun-exposed snow or ice sublimates evenly. The ice on a glacier sublimates to produce wave-like mounds that may, with enough exposure and age, erode or ablate into seracs, those tall towers that often grace high altitude glaciers that are often grotesquely sculptured. A rock on a glacier that protects the ice from sublimation may eventually end up on the summit of a pinnacle, sometimes 20 feet high, when the surrounding, unprotected ice has turned to vapor. The great peaks themselves are marvels of fluted snow and ice the result of uneven sublimation. And so it is that the sun-exposed side of a depression in the snow develops flutings, sometimes sharp and sometimes rounded. The expanded, sharply defined, fluted and fantastic track does not have to be formed from the pugs of a fox or wolf or snow leopard; it can be made by a raven, a falling rock or the point of an ice axe. I can make a mark in the snow with my fist or heel and within a day see the beginnings of a yeti track. Marlin Perkins and I experimented with these remarkable formations in the snow and all the other members of the expedition helped to demonstrate the reality of the explanation. It seems that such sublimation is chiefly a quality of high, thin, cold air with the best results coming from the lower sun of October and November when, also, the Himalayan air is dry and clear and the snow is usually old and crisp.

Through the courtesy of John Napier, the anthropologist who wrote the book *Big Foot*, which, in my estimation is the fairest account on the subject of the yeti and the "big foot" of western North America, I have obtained a photograph printed from Shipton's original negative. The illustration from Shipton's book, *The Mount Everest Reconnaissance Expedition*, was not clear. Part of the footprint that preceded the famous track had been removed, but the original photograph shows more of this revealing, preceding footprint. This newly revealed track has a different shape than its partner and is at least ten inches wide. It is clearly unlike the main feature which is eight inches wide. Even though the new footprint is somewhat at an angle to the main footprint, its pointed, fluted "toes" tend to align in the same direction as the "toes" of the classic track. Furthermore, the shape of small, miscellaneous holes in the snow are each expanding in the same direction as the "toes." It would appear that the classic yeti track is one of a kind, a selected, dramatic, suggestive, unique item, the chance product of sublimation and sunshine. I feel secure that no primate could have snowshoe-like feet eight inches wide and I rest content that no bipedal creature could have feet so strangely different in shape. The best conclusion is surely one that implies that the tracks could not be fresh and reflect the actual shape of the foot of some animal and that they have sublimated and grown to their suggestive proportions. Their large size points to an origin from large pug marks, perhaps, a snow leopard after all.

Part of the lesson of the abominable snowman now emerges. Consider the line of overwhelming coincidence that not only suggested an affiliation between the yeti and some strange ape, or human-like primate, the feet of the gorilla, the scalp shape, the strange toes that faced backward and even the legitimate speculations concerning zoogeography and paleontology, and recognize that they did not work out. All that suggestive logic was lost in the explanation of the real thing, the actual tracks in the snow. It was hard for me to dismiss all my intricate conjectures and the snowballing effect of accumulating inference. But I had the advantage of actually being there and seeing the evidence and I could use this personal experience to lever my mind toward reality. I have found that other lovers of the yeti have had more problems accepting this explanation. They refuse to admit the demise of all those convincing arguments and they object to the sometimes painful admittance that remarkable coincidence, the matching of seemingly impossible events, does not warrant the stature of evidence. Intense feelings of wishing, hoping and knowing do not make things real. Human insistence cannot transform Nature and its laws.

One may consider all this as prosaic and self-evident but one may also be reminded that much of the world, in both low and high places of society, runs on the premise that wishing will make it so. It is a widespread human frailty, almost a trait of our agile minds. In this case, we may love the yeti and its promise of wildness, its symbolism of high remote aretes, and be assured that I too have these sentiments abundantly, but these emotions that may be fulminating and genuine do not by their intensity and strength change the weak and simple truth.

After satisfying ourselves about the yeti footprints, there still remained the problem of the peculiar pointed head and the strong beliefs of the Sherpas. I had to leave the main part of the expedition for a month to wander over the passes with a few Sherpas, collecting and examining the flora and fauna of these great mountains, a tale I shall relate later on. When I returned to the Sherpa villages near the foot of Mt. Everest, I found Marlin Perkins hot on the trail of the yeti scalp. He had managed to make a duplicate of the original scalp that was kept in the Khumjung Monastery. It was an exact copy but the color was wrong; it was brownish instead of reddish. It had been made from the back skin of a serow, *Capricornis sumatraensis*, a rupicaprine goat of the Himalaya, a relative of the mountain goat of North America and the chamois of Europe.

A helpful Sherpa had suggested the serow skin and further directed the stretching of the skin over an appropriately shaped block of wood, a sort of cast made from the dimensions of the original scalp in the Khumjung Monastery. The pointed "head," to my utter astonishment, came from the convenience of chopping and shaping a cylinder of wood from a tree trunk, with an adze. This axe, with a blade that lies sideways, chops away at a cylinder in such a way that it leaves a natural, rather pointed product (as if a beaver had gnawed on the thing) and, with the color awry, this Sherpa offered the suggestion of dyeing it. This he accomplished with some ground-up roots. To our surprise, indeed, to our bewildered amazement, he came in one morning to view the dry and completed object, the impressively accurate, fresh,

41

red facsimile of the real thing, and approached it in awe with palms appressed as if this obvious fake was a true and holy object. Here he was, the very man who had conceived and designed the model and was involved in all its construction, now bowing to this manifest artifact as if it were something beyond the work of man, something of worshipful status.

Marlin Perkins holding a skin from a Blue Bear of Tibet

My amazement changed to wonder, for a new level of Sherpa doctrine and belief seemed to be revealed to me. It appeared that the real and the unreal were here, mingling imperceptibly together, where the things of religion and near religion were becoming continuous with that of ordinary life. The teachings of the lamas, the educated leaders, can move from devils and miracles to yaks and potatoes without whispering that the guise of these tangibles and intangibles come from entirely different realms of reality. I thought, at first, that I had uncovered some new symptom of obscure Sherpa belief but, whereas the Sherpa behavior may have been simple and obvious, the same machinations of the mind are widespread in our supposedly educated and advanced society.

Superstitions, strange beliefs, adherences to subtly occult presumptions, all in the face of the obvious falsity of their nature, are not only present among us, they are common and, at times, the major theaters of our thoughts. I think of some common religious teachings of Western civilization where statements with broad rationalizations are accepted, but where others believe the nonsense because they think it is holy.

And so now, I better understand my Sherpa friends, whom I have trusted with my life on many occasions, who, in all honesty and in clear conscience, told me of their belief in the existence of the yeti. Why should they confront the teachings of the lamas? Why should the yeti be less believable than people swallowed by whales, women constructed out of a male's rib or a fallen angel with wings of a bat?

The ability to see things and believe things that do not exist represents one of the curious paradoxes of human behavior. It has a pervasive character that involves such diverse things as flying saucers and the edicts of religion.

There may be something real that seeds this syndrome which feeds on hallucinations, lies, misinterpretations, spurious vision, faulted memory. or the need to make some things holy. Perhaps, beliefs come from the susceptibility to add meaning to curious natural events. This syndrome demands belief in the unnatural. In my view, this demeans the beauty and wonder of the natural. There are real things around us. Things that do exist are fully as worthy of our appreciation, awe and reverence. It would seem that the real world itself is miracle enough.

From the appendix written by A.F.R.Wollaston, the able and observing biologist of that early expedition, I believe I can support his judgment. He says: "Wolves were seen at about 19,000 feet and those tracks seen at 21,500 feet, which gave rise to so much discussion, were almost certainly those of a wolf." So, after all these years, I too, one of the few biologists to witness the tracks at high altitude, support him and reassure his observation. The official book of that expedition claims that the tracks were made by a wolf, while the newspapers stretched it all into something unreal. Scores of yeti hunters have affirmed their belief in the creature, thousands of articles have been written about the yeti, and no one has remembered the wolf that was really there. And now I would like to point out that those same tracks at 21,500 feet still represent the highest evidence in the whole world for a wild mammal. What was the wolf doing there? Isn't such a wolf remarkable and worthy of wonder? Apparently not. It seems we must search for something less mundane, something with the odor of drama, the smell of the occult. Why can't we truly appreciate what is real?

Actually there is something like the yeti that lives on those high mountains of Central Africa, the mountain gorilla. The yeti could not be much more spectacular. Yet we are letting this magnificent creature die; we are extinguishing it for the needs of farmers and hunters and too many people who need land. Is this because it is real, it does exist, it is not fantasy?

There was in northern Asia, during the Pleistocene, a remarkable wooly rhinoceros. If that huge hairy beast were discovered today in some lost valley, it would cause a sensation. Along with that wooly rhinoceros, there was another animal that was even more bizarre. It had a strange curved neck that grew out of its chest, long slender eyelashes, peculiar splayed, flat feet and, the epitome of oddity, two big humps on its reddish, hairy back. But this outlandish beast still lives. It is the Bactrian camel that must take some sort of prize for unusual animal design. But, once again, because it exists, it has become ordinary and relegated to the back compounds of zoos. If the yeti were real, it would lose its immortal soul of fantasy to become ordinary and to have to face the powers of doom without the necessary defenses supplied by rarity, and thus have to contend with the irreversible prospect of extinction. It would seem that a beautiful and distant hope is better than extinction.

I submit we are victims of fairy tales. We are nurtured on Cinderella, talking mice, goblins and angels. Any lack of appreciation for these bulwarks of our youthful entertainment is taken as a symptom of a lack of imagination, an essential human trait. Those lovely people in the Humanities tell us we must use our vital emotions and let our imaginations run. We grow up to want to believe in make-believe. The best stories must be contrived to fit in some ethereal never-never-land that prompts our hopes and gives us direction. The biologist in me objects. I object with mildness because I, too, am such a dreamer. But I want to believe that the best stories are real, the things worth knowing are real, and in all our exaggerations, imagination and wondering, the real should be the model not the image of avoidance. What could be more fantastic than the real affair between a spider and a wasp, the cuckoo and a nest, the dodo and the sailor, the crocodile and the Ganges corpses, the wolf and Pasteur and a thousand other tales of biology. Why are they not part of our repertoire of children's stories? Perhaps it is because reality requires knowledge as well as imagination and the first of these ingredients is too often deficient.

I must admit that despite this, I love mythical creatures, especially the yeti, and I must caution the scoffer that science with all its powers and arse-

Hillary with an "Yeti Scalp," Khumijung Monastery.

nals of machines is still a limited thing. There is a phrase that comes to me more and more that seems to fit these circumstances. Since it is my own I cherish it for it explains so clearly what seems to be the state of affairs in all those matters of belief that plague the world. It is simply "Science cannot prove the nonexistence of the nonexistent." And so it is that a whole slice of the world thrives where science cannot tread. Finally, and here I demonstrate the vulnerability of my argument, it happens that some select representatives of that world of myth sometimes spill over across that threshold that separates the real from the unreal. There really are things like the coelacanth, the nautilus, the tuatara, the giant panda, the okapi. I shall be chagrined if the yeti slips over into the real, sometime, and I have to examine a real, hairy, giant thing with a real pointed head, lying in a real box. At that point, I would wonder whether I should have written all this. I would have to apologize with embarrassment to those enthusiasts, those indomitable, persistent, brave, honorable people, my friends, the stalwart and true yeti believers. Science cannot prove the nonexistence of the nonexistent but what if the nonexistent actually exists? It goes on and on.

The Curse of the Yeti

It was October 1960, at the high camp near the head of the Ripimu Glacier in the Rolwaling Himalaya. In the few days we had been in this remote area along the Tibetan frontier, our radios were often disrupted by martial music coming from a Chinese encampment across the border, monitoring our every word. We had a council of war. It was not the Chinese who were bothering us, it was the logistics of the expedition. The problem was some unanticipated delay in getting loads carried from Kathmandu to the Everest area. There was equipment needed by the wintering party that might not be easy to transport to the high country because of the impending weather of the winter. We had had great success in deciphering the origin of the yeti tracks and now it was time to move on. The problem was put to me. Would I be willing to return to Kathmandu and lead a hundred porters up to the Everest area while the rest of the group continued eastward across the Tesi Lapcha pass towards Mount Everest? It was an interesting alternative. I agreed and so one morning Sir Edmund Hillary, Peter Mulgrew and I set out down the Ripimu Glacier. The others would follow later.

    Among the many stories that surround the yeti is the one about actually seeing a yeti. A sighting of the yeti can mean you are doomed. Most Sherpas claim they have never seen the yeti. They generally report that some lost uncle or some dead father saw the creature and witnessed the strange qualities of the beast. Now it so happened that I had not seen one, but had been very close. The hair had stood up on my back and I had felt tingles run up my spine. I did not know, and neither did the legend appreciate the inference, that even a near sighting or near presence of the yeti also had its aftermath curse. You were not necessarily doomed but you could be scared out of your wits. I started down the glacier with Hillary and Mulgrew in all innocence of the impending events. I had no idea that the aura of the yeti was setting a trap for me and that during the next few days a series of adventures and misadventures would supervene upon my innocence. I blame the yeti for what happened. It seemed that no sequential days could, by chance, gather together such a bounty of calamities.

We had just left camp and we were on our way down. We were walking on a narrow terrace that overlooked the crevasses and rock-covered ice of the glacier. The great cliffs of this glacier-cut valley went up for several thousand feet. And then, our terrace disappeared. Before us, and impeding our progress, was a huge landslide that came off the wall to our right. We were capable of crossing this loose earth and boulders but as we tried and each time we started out, some loose rocks would come pouring down. We waited and decided to cross one at a time. We anticipated our chances and when it appeared that there was a temporary lull in the falling debris, one of us would try to race across. Hillary went first and he made it without any difficulty. Then Mulgrew got across but he had to dodge a good-sized rock that whizzed by. And then it was my turn. Each time I started out, as if on cue, some falling boulders would set me back. This continued and sensing that my companions were getting impatient, I decided that the prudent thing to do was to descend the slope to the glacier and, since most of the falling rock seemed to stop near the edge of the glacier, try to walk out on the ice some safe distance from the base of the landslide. I went down and started out on the glacier with a sense that if I didn't fall into a crevasse, I would be safe.

I was out on the ice among fallen rocks that littered the place and about one-third to half the distance across to safety when I heard a thud. Almost simultaneously I heard the voices of my companions. I looked up and up. It seemed that the mountain was falling. It shook me to see that some rocks, a small cloud of rocks, were directly above me and falling straight down from an enormous height. Most of the smaller rocks, about head size, were slightly ahead of my position while slightly behind me were what appeared to be a few huge pianos rotating slowly in the air.

In such a moment the mind does strange things. Furthermore, these strange things can be vividly remembered. There was an instant decision in my mind. I decided to go forward the way I had been heading as fast as I could which, unfortunately, on the glacier, could not be very fast. Not only were there rocks and crevasses scattered about, but we were near 18,000 feet of altitude. I went as fast as I could knowing full well that it was futile to outrun the falling sky.

It was surprising how long it seemed to take but I could not look up for even a moment and waste a precious fraction of time. All my energy, and I mean all of it, was directed to moving on the glacier away from my threat which, all along, I knew was an impossible maneuver. It was like one of those excruciating dreams where, perhaps, some vicious beast is chasing you and breathing at your heels and you find that your feet stick or they slip on some frictionless sand. Such was my glacier terrain. But this was not any dream. My state of awareness was acute and honed to exquisite sharpness.

It is a strange sense that tells you that you are going to die. No part of your active mind, when it is reached and probed for the faint possibility of a favorable answer, returns with a zero approximation of chance, a nil iota of hope, no distant mathematical probability of expectation, no ratio of survival comparisons to suggest anything other than your quick demise. There is a word for this. It is called "terror."

Events during such moments occur in discrete fractions of a second and they seem clearly distinguished in sequence. First there is the knowledge that the rocks must be hitting very soon, then there is a crescendo up the slope where they have already arrived, then the recognition that you can go no farther, then the realization in that last fraction of a second that there is a rock beside you that is half your size and therefore quite inadequate for protection but that it is all you have and it may help deflect rocks from one side. You know full well that there is a hopeless opening up above you and that is the direction from which the killing things will come. You cannot waste that moment to look up and watch the approach of your final view on earth. Your body contracts to its smallest surface and you squeeze against that too-small rock just as the world seems to end in a roar around you.

My first realization was that for the first fraction of a second I had not been hit and then I was free in the next fraction of a second. There were bangs and crashes and thuds and clatters in a huge thunder all around me and some rebounding stones hit my side and back. Rocks seemed everywhere but not on me. In a sense I could not hope to live and I almost wished they would hurry up and crush my leg and maybe now, maybe now, avoid my head. On and on it went and then there came the incredible hope that I might survive.

It seemed to quiet down a little but then one last rock smashed into my savior rock near my head and sent slivers of granite onto my neck and face. I could smell the sparks of this collision. But this last chance of fate was not enough. The rocks had fallen and I was alive. Incredibly, I was alive.

But now I could do nothing but breathe very hard. Exerting oneself at 18,000 feet and then, as it would seem, hold one's breath, is a strain on the respiratory system. I could only gasp for air. I could not call out. My companions had watched all this. They had seen me crouch and then the rocks obliterated my position in a cloud of dust. And now they couldn't see me. They called and I could not call back to them. I wanted to call out and relieve their anxiety. I could only breathe hard and with the dust they could not see my feeble effort to wave my ice axe. It is interesting to actually hear the emotions around your own personal death.

Finally, I did call out much to their relief and surprise. They had started down the slope to retrieve a body and now they continued to see if they could be of aid. All I had on me from this escape from the grave was the dust and some chips of rock and after some shaky moments we found the terrace again and were on our way.

Strangely, I had always been overly apprehensive of falling rock. At night when the roar of rockfalls nearby or far off had awakened me, I often wondered if I had pitched my tent in a safe enough place. And, wherever I walked, I always noted the telltale signs of newly fallen rock, the signs of shattering, the indentations in the earth, the lack of windblown dust under a stray boulder. Now it seemed that some of that apprehension was over. It seemed that one could survive a falling mountain. My worst dreams did not match the reality. I should have thought that such an experience would heighten fear. My experience in the Great Bihar Earthquake of 1934, a holocaust that accompanied the figure 8.6, one of those enigmatic numbers that really don't seem to mean much more than give a sense of terrible intensity, was different. At that time, when the earth seemed to be grabbed and shaken like a rattle I experienced the birth of a lasting and persistent fear, an abject dread of earthquakes. But I was twelve years old at the time and all those horrors were very impressive especially when something like 20,000 people died and our world that we always assume to be reliable and constant, seemed, in a few minutes of pique, to have ignored the necessity that we may live on its surface. Anyway, I count that October day, the nineteenth of October 1960, as the beginning of another life, the life I live now, that has been a donation, a bounty, of over thirty years beyond a time when I should have ended on the Ripimu Glacier. A gift indeed!

After the rockfall, we continued down to the 16,000-foot camp beside a glacier pond. In another day or two the others would come down the Ripimu to get ready to go on to the Mt. Everest area. I would be on my way to Kathmandu for the porters and their loads.

It was decided that we needed fresh meat and now another duty was assigned to me. I should go on down with my Sherpa, Pemba Norbu, and with four other Sherpas who had just arrived, find a sheep and get it slaughtered. The four Sherpas would then return to the lake camp with half the animal and I would take the other half for my long journey back to Kathmandu. I wondered why the Sherpas insisted that five Sherpas were needed for this job. It soon became apparent.

When we arrived at the now deserted, summer encampment at Na at 14,000 feet we set up a shelter and the Sherpas went off to find their animal. In an hour or so they came back leading a good-sized sheep that seemed rather too gentle and pleasant to end up the way we had planned. They tied the sheep to a rock where it went about its innocent business of cropping the short grass. The Sherpas got busy getting ready. But first there had to be an assignment of jobs, who was to do what in this little drama of sheep murder. It became apparent that the killing of a sheep was not exactly relished by Sherpas. They are ostensibly Buddhists and, whereas they have to kill animals, they do so reluctantly and always out of sight of any gompa, the local monastery.

And now this tale begins. To my utter surprise the Sherpas borrowed my hat and put a number of pieces of paper into it on which were marked various signs, a sort of writing for these men were generally illiterate. I now held the hat while each of them reached in and, without looking, picked out a piece of paper. The first Sherpa feigning fear and reluctance, pulled out his piece, looked at it and then gave out a whoop. He danced around showing his lucky paper to the others. He said to me in Hindi, "Yes, I shall make the chili! Atcha! Atcha! Good! Good!"

The next Sherpa reached in and looked at his paper and he too started shouting up a great joy. I realized then that this was really a huge game as if the unpleasantry of slaughter was being manipulated into some sort of frolic. "I will hold the hind legs!" he said to me.

The next Sherpa was Pemba Norbu, the man in charge of the proceedings, and so the others stood around hoping that he would get the nasty job. As Pemba Norbu's hand groped the inside of the hat they were all giving advice as to which piece of paper he should pick. Finally he grabbed a piece of paper as if he did not care what he obtained, but when he looked at the symbol he too, a rather sedate man, gave out a cheer. He would hold the sheep's head.

That left only two men and two pieces of paper on one of which was the sign for death. Tension was high and the three men on the safe side started a playful betting game on which of the two remaining men would be the victim of fate.

The next drawing was the fatal one. The man looked at the symbol and said nothing. He threw down the paper and walked away playing to the hilt his role as the dejected loser. He simply went over and sat down on a rock. He would play no part in the ensuing preparations. His job was single, precise and uncomplicated. He would cut off the head. The last man became the man who would do the miscellaneous chores. He would, for instance, sharpen the kukri, that maliciously curved knife of the Nepalese. And so they started preparations. A large degchi or cooking pot emerged from the loads and chili peppers were finely chopped into it until it was half full. The kukri sharpening proceeded on and on as if a razor's edge was not enough.

One of the Sherpas was off to the side doing something or other while another was singing some weird Tibetan chant but on his rock the duped Sherpa watched quietly and played his act of sullenness. Eventually he came up to me and as if it was all surreptitious on his part, he pulled some dirty rupee notes out of his pocket. "Sahb" he said "please let it be known to Pemba Norbu that I will pay this money to any of the others who may wish to exchange positions with me." Pemba Norbu saw this encounter and told the others. They all laughed and laughed. An effort at bribery was piquant sauce for this drama, this play that was going on very well. The actors were feeling their parts with an abundant sense of the stage giving performances worthy of a Barrymore or Sid Caesar. Finally the last chilis had been sliced and added to the degchi and the kukri honed to perfection. A Sherpa went and fetched the sheep and one man grabbed the hind legs and another the horns. Another brought the degchi and its red chilis near to the animal and another took the kukri over to the despondent figure sitting on his rock. All was ready. The knife was raised high now and there was no hesitation. The deed had to be done and without delay or any feigned fear. Slash! Just one mighty cut and the whole head separated into the hands of Pemba Norbu.

Now the activity was intense. The blood shooting from the severed carotids squirted across the field but was quickly directed into the degchi with the chilis and there, one man, as quickly, started stirring the mixture. The blood came on and on and finally slowed to a drip and then the abdomen was slit down the middle and fast hands severed the stomach from its connection to the esophagus. More hands scooped out the grass that had so recently been consumed and when the stomach was clear a man held the aperture at the esophageal end and stretched it wide.

The intestines were pulled out and arrayed over the grass. There was still a hint of movement in whatever corresponds to the jejunum of a sheep. All this happened in mere seconds and now the man with the chilis and blood was ready. It had to be poured before any appreciable amount of co-agulation took place. The chili-blood was poured into the stomach. The man holding the stomach closed the opening and holding the stomach against his chest proceeded to squeeze. A dark red current now could be seen to shoot past the pyloric sphincter and down into the duodenum. The intestine swelled and writhed as the blood was forced down through it. With each mighty squeeze there was a surge of dark red down the intestine which swelled full as it was filled with blood. On and on the red tide continued. The stomach was filled again and again and blood coursed through most of twenty feet of the small intestine. Finally there was no more chili-blood to squeeze. It was time for a rest. The blood had to harden. It would take about ten minutes.

Now to go back to the bloody perpetrator of this deed. He was back on his seat on the rock. He had slashed, thrown the kukri down and departed from the resulting fray. Back at the bloody scene, a Sherpa tested the blood intestine. He sliced the gut gently with a knife and it seemed solid enough. He took a slice and carried it, rather deliberately, over to the man on the rock and handed it to him. The piece was tasted by this outcast and a big smile appeared on his face. It tasted good. The onerous task was worth it after all. The gift was there to assuage and now he could return and join in the remainder of the festivities of sheep dismemberment.

Another piece was sliced off and with all eyes upon me, it was handed to me. I smelled the rawness of gut and blood and something turned inside of me. This was not really my sort of food but living with Sherpas lowers the normal constraints of the western diet. I nibbled and then ate the whole thing. It tasted rather good. Indeed, it was a spicy, tasty, meaty wonder for the tongue that could easily grace a plate of hors d'oeuvres at a fancy San Francisco reception. It is conceivable that some of those fragments that are served to those nice people went through even more terrible preparations than this innocent looking blood sausage from our recently departed sheep.

People such as Sherpas are notable for their conservation of every por-tion of a slaughtered animal. Nothing or very little is wasted. In the absence of refrigeration this is not always easily accomplished and the Sherpas have experience and knowledge about which parts of an animal last a long time and which parts do not. Lungs, for instance, go fast whereas meat, good muscle, can dry out slowly and even when it has acquired a veneer of grayish green fungus, it can still pass the mouth. Indeed, the flavor of meat can improve with age and it is almost wasteful to eat newly butchered meat. A week or more of hanging can do wonders for the tongue and toughness can yield to a gentle tenderness that delights the palate. When, finally, the nose gets too sensitive or conditioned, or when real odors begin, that is the time for additional supplies of curry powder, onion and cardamom. If one is not used to this sort of thing, it can take courage to learn. It always helps to have a ravenous hunger.

When the sheep had completely disappeared and there was scarcely a trace of the events that had taken place on the arena of slaughter, some cooking began. I wondered what we would have for supper. Later, after sundown had left only the outline of the steep ridges that surrounded us, we sat down on the grass around a congenial fire. There, in that dim light, a soupy curry was poured into my bowl to which I added some rice. It was largely liquid and so I noticed that something kept floating up to the surface unlike what real pieces of curry are supposed to do. I brought one of these errant pieces up close to my eyes and diagnosed a section of boiled lung. It was not bad; it was just sort of airy. My teeth didn't seem to grab it with gusto and it was like chewing on a sponge.

Another try after this first tidbit from our late sheep yielded a section of bronchus, complete with hyaline cartilage rings in sequence. This required fingers. It is strange that of all the memories of food from exotic sources that range through my mind, it is those several inches of bronchus, cut just as they emerged from the trachea, that hold my memory most vividly. The thought of chewing on this ringed organ which, even in the cooking pot, clearly revealed its precise anatomical origin, still remains etched to this day. I have eaten much worse but it seems that that discrete and obvious bronchus holds first place. Lungs, frothy floating lungs, that challenge the teeth and still hold the last air of a departed sheep also come in quite high on this list.

The next day, the stripped carcass was chopped in half right down the middle of the vertebral column. Each half was bent on itself and the foreleg was stuck under the sheep's equivalent of an Achilles tendon. This union of fore- and hindlegs functioned as a handle and one Sherpa went off with a half for the camp by the lake. The other Sherpas helped me carry my loads down to the village of Beding where we intended to hire two local Sherpas to carry our loads back to Kathmandu. At Beding we found that all the men were off gathering hay for the winter while the women who, after all, did all the really hard work, could not be spared. My pleas for help didn't seem to work, but finally, a man emerged from a house with a bloody bandage around his head. I knew him. Some days before when we had been passing through Beding he had been involved in a monstrous drunken brawl and his split head had poured blood onto the gompa, the monastery, steps. Some attention from our physician had seemed to work for now he was up and around. Before we knew his name as Pasang, he acquired the descriptive tag of "Old Blood on the Gompa Steps."

"Old Bloody" now informed me that he would be willing to carry a load back to Kathmandu and he thought he could persuade his friend Nu Phutar to come with us. Sure enough, he did come back with his friend, a man who had a permanent smile on his face and seemed on the verge of hysterical laughter every waking moment. He was the complete opposite of Old Bloody who was singularly dour. I sensed some dread for this team that I would have to rely on for many days on the road to Kathmandu but they were all that was available. The three expedition Sherpas now took off back to the lake camp and Pemba Norbu and I loaded up the newcomers. They were dressed completely in the standard Tibetan clothing without any trait of items from Hong Kong or the bazaars of India. These Sherpas were pure, they were right out of the hills and I loved them for their simplicity and genuineness. It was obvious that Pemba Norbu harbored some disdain for their unworldliness and he made very sure that they understood that he was boss. It was thus that we set out down the gorge for distant Kathmandu.

I had accepted the duty to return to Kathmandu with a pleasant objective in mind. I much prefer traveling alone with a few Sherpas where we can investigate new routes, live simply and camp where we please. My intention was to explore new paths and unknown routes across the mountains and as we left Beding, we put this scheme to work right away. Old Bloody and Nu Phutar knew of a path that would take us straight down the gorge of the Rolwaling instead of over the high pass that had brought us into the valley. So down we went. Very soon the size and spectacular dimensions of the gorge became evident. Great slabs of sheer rock formed an angle of over 70 degrees and shot straight down to the river, far, far below. Our path, if that is what it could be called with some sense of jest, clung to the middle of the precipice. It was narrow and at times, nonexistent, but its main feature was it was merely a cleft in the rock, a slight rifting in the sheer slabs. It led us farther and farther over an abyss. We had to stop occasionally to maneuver the wider loads around vertical walls where the angle of the rock was so sheer that it was necessary to fudge sideways. It was an incredible passage which, if it was on some wall of Yosemite, would demand careful roping with firm belays. I wondered who would dare discover such a hazardous way to get anywhere and surely flocks of sheep could not manage this precarious crossing. It was a challenge to the finest instincts of a mountain goat. I wondered why such an exquisitely exposed route should exist at all and to this day I cannot guess as to the real function of that "path." My best thought at the time of our passage was that it had something to do with suicide.

When I thought the worst was over, I went ahead trying to reconnoiter and get some reassurance that there was an end to this balancing exercise above oblivion. I came up short. There in front of our precious rift in the rock upon which all our hopes depended, our foothold on survival ended. A deep cleft in the rock slab, a vertical slice like the work of some galactic sabre, had rent the precipice from top to bottom. Our way ended abruptly over a chasm. In front of me, where I should find my next step was air, air that seemed to go on and on forever below me.

But then I saw a place to put one foot and then the other. It led slightly downward into the vertical cleft in the rock wall. A scarce reminder that someone had been here before led to a section of a tree trunk, about eight feet long and partly sectioned longways. It straddled the abyss below the cleft. Some brave soul had carried that log here; how, I do not know. I carefully moved from my airy position and found my way to this flimsy bridge that hung over clear space and the river some two or three thousand feet below. I was about to test my courage on a crossing when the biologist part of me held me back. I noticed the tiny holes of scolytid beetles and some frass, the digested reminders that wood boring insects, perhaps the larvae of cerambycid beetles, had been here. I balked. How long had this raw tree trunk been there to experience the ravages of xylophagous insects? I decided to wait and perhaps my Sherpas could belay me on a rope while I tried the awful crossing. If I did not wait, they might never know. My body could be half a mile down below, down by the river, straight down.

I waited. Soon Nu Phutar came around the corner, smiling always smiling. He quickly negotiated the precarious steps down to the tree trunk where I stood somewhat to one side and before I could explain the reason for my pause, he casually balanced his way across the bridge that had all my suspicions heaped upon it. It was as quick as that. He gave no apparent thought of possible disaster. Faith ruled the day. Impossible fears that a log might collapse should be confined, it would seem, to apprehensions about unseen spirits and devils. This sliver of wood above eternity had apparently not yet

55

acquired its appropriate demon fiend. Sherpas have a notion of the world that our textbooks are unable to fathom. The rules for their survival in their world of perils and threats seem like a droll farce when contrasted with our own structured codes of safety and care. Yet if we should impose some of our rules upon them, I doubt that anything would be accomplished. Sherpas would stay home and die in their beds. It is better to have unpredictable demons than to try to control fate.

On and on we went, and eventually a sort of path emerged that led us down and down toward the river. But there was one more hurdle. We were confronted by a wall some fifty feet high that seemed to have no way around it. I judged that my simple guides had lost the way and that we should go back and find a passable route. The Sherpas would have no dealings with retreat and they insisted they could climb the wall. Two of them started up the sheer face but they had to give up. Their effort had given me time to assess a possible route up on one side where some bamboo shoots were hanging from cracks. I tied on a rope and started up. There seemed to be enough handholds and if not, I found the twigs of bamboo held my weight. Finally, I neared the top and, reaching high, I groped for something to hold on to and I found it with my fingertips. It was the stolon of a bamboo, the root-like stem that has many short sections and rings on it, and I slowly hauled myself up with one arm. As I pulled and the piece of bamboo came closer to my face I could see what I was holding. I looked at this saving thing and I had to pause and laugh while my feet hung over the cliff. That precious handful of bamboo was ringed and sized and so very much like the bronchus of a sheep.

Beyond that last barrier, we made our way down to the river and set up our first camp beside the stream and under the enormous cliffs of Gaurishankar that rose some 17,000 feet almost straight above us in a sheer, magnificent crescendo of rock. It became dark around us, but hours later there was still a red glow on that white snow far above. The peak seemed to hang like a giant glowing ember in the sky and it hovered in dull redness almost directly above us. Such is the exaggerated grandeur of the Himalaya. No mountains can be so enormous and spectacular, no cliffs so seemingly unending, and in the crease of its great gorges, no place can offer such an aura of isolation, remoteness and separation from the rest of the world. There was a touch of the uncanny in the red glow that hovered around our camp between the stupendous walls of the gorge and Old Bloody went over to the stream. In Tibetan fashion, he splashed some water into the air and chanted in his lowest gutteral, "Om! Om! Om!"

56

Early the next morning we were on our way over a ridge toward a Sherpa village. It was a long steep haul through thickets that seemed to have forgotten the passage of any living thing. It was a pushing and shoving through rhododendron branches and bamboo growths that would defy the best intentions of a musk deer. It would seem, however, that we were actually on a trail left by these small animals who are being decimated because of their anal pods of musk, musk used in perfumes to carry molecules of pleasant odors to the noses of the western world. Two lesser pandas scurried ahead of me for some distance. Up and up we went and then down and down. There are no straight lines in the Himalaya for human legs. For the first few months across the hills this fact is annoying but after enough of it, the true essence of this vertical world sinks in with all its impracticalities, ups and downs do not make much difference.

It was late in the day when we approached the Sherpa outpost of Simigaon. I prefer to camp far from habitation. I love those untouched forests where there are no signs of cutting and there are no distant sounds of the axes that ravage the primeval trees. I like to camp under ancient groves on a slope where I can see the distant hills and believe that I am alone with my brothers of nature, the Sherpas. But that is a western dream. A Sherpa view of such poetic needs is the simple attraction of company and gossip. Sherpas use their finest arguments to avoid seclusion and distant camps. They develop slippery tales to convince the sahb that it is necessary to spend the night in a village. They say they are out of onions or potatoes or some such thing and that the survival of all of them is dependent on some village. And through this elaborate argument you know full well what they are thinking in their hearts; they are motivated by wine and women and song.

And so it was that they talked me out of a wonderful camping location where the hills of the distance seemed to meld with the haze of the plains of India and where Japalura lizards ran over the leaves of the forest floor. Yes, I remember how they duped me with their innocent disputations of necessity. In retrospect, my mind was divided—whether to enjoy the peace of untrammeled hillsides or regret experiencing a broiling affair at Simigaon. The choice may seem as confusing to you as to me. We left my choice spot for the Sherpa village of Simigaon. As we approached, there was much shouting and gesturing. We were all received with hugging and overt affection. None of us had ever seen each other before. We were led to a sort of patio between two houses, a sort of central location reserved for guests, and this was the focus of a party that soon blossomed. The affair started informally with some jugs of chang, a fermented mess that comes from barley or millet or whatever becomes over-ripe. My Sherpas gave their hosts the ultimate compliment by stating that the chang compared with the chang of Sola Kumbu, the seat of Sherpa culture. With such subtle compliments the hosts reached ever deeper into their supplies of liquor and brought out more of the stuff. The approach to drunkenness thus became cyclic; with each new batch the compliments emerged and with the compliments new chang appeared. Seeing all this debauchery emerging I had some concerns about the necessity of getting an early start in the morning. But this notion became less and less imperative and what I first suspicioned as a thing to be avoided moved imperceptibly to a pleasure, a frustrated pleasure, for what else could I do?

In the joy of Sherpa company I found a discarded small package made of aluminum foil, something from an envelope of orange juice and, knowing that some time around now there should be some celebration of Halloween, I constructed a small mask with eyes and mouth and nose and put this device over a candle. Seeing this lighted face emerge from the darkness set the growing group of revelers into a sheer wonder of ecstasy. I was a magician, something superior, an honored guest, someone who needed vast attention and a profusion of chang. I have some experience in recognizing the beginnings of a horrendous party and this affair at Simigaon had all the symptoms of being something phenomenal.

The celebration was well along when two men emerged from the darkness, panting and at the limit of their endurance. I recognized them immediately for they were our mail runners who periodically took our letters to Kathmandu and returned to our base camp with whatever had accumulated since their last visit. They carried a leather pouch of mail that had a large and impressive lock hanging from it, a sort of a reminder that within the bag there were inestimable values. These runners had been cautioned by me and others that they were never to open the bag and no manner of emergency could warrant the breaking of the lock. They were here in Simigaon on their second last day on the road. They had made a desperate effort to get this far to feel the comforts of Simigaon. However, I realized that in their valued leather bag were my own precious letters, words from my dear wife, my little children, my friends whom I had not heard from for a very long time. I then started a game of persuasion, a test of their honesty and dedication. I, who had cautioned them originally on how valuable their burden was, was now deprecating the importance of that safety protocol. I did not have to break the lock and make it look so obvious. I could take a knife and with a little slit reach in with my tweezers and remove my letters. Perhaps, I could lift the cover and with stretching some strong hands, test the leather until an aperture appeared—and then reach in. Very well, how about sheer remorse? All my mail is in there. If I do not get it now, it will be months before I could see it. Have you no heart? The steadfast Sherpas had won again. I took the bag and sat on it. At least it could function as a seat from which I could view the proceedings of the fulminating party.

During the evening I noticed that our fire and the several lanterns were attracting insects. They started to fly in, a few at a time, and then they seemed to form clouds. An ordinary person may have suggested that they were merely obnoxious but I, a biologist, found them amazing. This was no cloud of moths or midges—this was an attack by strange Hemipterans, insects of that well-known order that contain stink bugs. In the firelight I identified them as Nabids which are predaceous and predators and should not come in such hordes. I reasoned they must be phytophagous out of their sheer numbers and that my taxonomy must be in error. They were, by this assumption, a late Fall migration from some decimated field of crops. Perhaps they were Mirids but this couldn't be for no Mirid could smell as bad as these things. These half-inch greenish creatures gave off a truly preposterous odor. Their presence permeated the place as well it might for in their omnipresence, the multitudes were being stepped on and squashed all over the place.

In the face of these inconveniences and the growing sensation that I needed some sleep, I decided to erect my small mountain tent in a corner of the patio and hope for the best. The tent might hold out some of the bugs, but I did not recognize that one of my thin tent ropes would be the cause of much tripping and cursing during the night.

Unfortunately, just before I turned in, I had the bright idea to take some flash pictures and these sudden bright lights became the focus of much new interest and much loud excitement. When I finally did get back to my tent I was too late, the bugs had beaten me. I slid in anyway and as I rolled on the smelly things my enclosed place filled with an unbelievable stench. Skunks are bad and I would not trade stink bugs for skunks but skunk odor did not seem to have the hatred of this heavy air, this permeation of skin, bone and brain. Somehow I stayed in my tent. It was all so novel an experience in spite of its discomfort. I felt that a biologist should experience one of nature's most offensive defenses.

The party went on and I dozed off. It must have been about 3:00 a.m., when a great shouting and barking of dogs awakened the roosters in pitch darkness. A group of people with torches flaming in the night came into the village. They were from Bongbong Danda, a neighboring village from across the valley, perhaps two hours away. So what could be the occasion for the visit of the whole village of Bongbong Danda, men, women, children and dogs? They had seen bright flashes in the direction of Simigaon and they wondered what sort of lightening, without apparent thunder and clouds, was striking their neighbor from across the valley. They had set off en masse and here they were after two arduous hours of stumbling around on the steep paths. They had seen my camera flashes.

So now the party flared up again. Now came more dancing and singing and drunken stumbling. Now the mugs were raised even higher, now I was rousted out of my tent, now I had to show how I could make lightning, now there was even more awe at my magic, now came the dawn.

Morning brought complete silence upon Simigaon. The place was scattered with bodies curled up in various corners, tattered rags of people in various stages of coma. All over were little windrows of dead bugs and their flattened bodies marked the places where many feet had been dancing and shuffling around. Slowly life emerged from this place that had the earmarks of a staged Nazi attack in some cheap movie. The thought of an early start had long since left my mind but I did see the body of Old Bloody and it moved. It was a relief to see that he had survived. Somewhere from the evidence of degradation that surrounded me, Pemba Norbu, appeared. He had an apologetic smile on his usually smiling Sherpa face. He came with his head erect, which was more than I could offer. He wanted to know what I wanted to do. I suggested that he go off and gently see if there was a chance that Nu Phutar was alive and whether we could get going some time during daylight.

It was not long after this that Pemba Norbu had Old Bloody and Nu Phutar in tow, twins in their drooping posture. Now there was another man with them. I was introduced to Seb Siri, a fine young man, but very quiet and entirely naive. He was a citizen of Bongbong Danda, a place that, from my brief experience with the whole village the night before, did not seem to be an origin that commanded respect for intelligence. But now I realized that the night's roistering had not been entirely wasted. Old Bloody in his droll way explained to me that the loads were too heavy and that if I would add one rupee per day to pay for Seb Siri, they would in turn each add one rupee to pay for Seb Siri. These scoundrels wanted to hire their own coolie. This would mean three rupees per day for Seb Siri while the two others would reduce their own wages to four rupees per day. When I hesitated, they made some horrendous complaints about how they had nearly fallen off the cliffs of the Rolwaling gorge and so forth. They also suggested that if I was not willing, they had been invited to stay at Bongbong Danda and I would have to find other, lesser men to carry my loads. It was an old argument. I had heard it before.

Actually, I am rather a soft touch on such issues of economics. I knew I had to stay within the bounds of the local procedures for payment, but I also realized that it is incredible for a man to sweat and work and risk his life for less than a half a dollar per day. And so I agreed to this novel procedure. There was just a touch of the unexpected on their faces. I knew they were surprised that they had pulled off this radical proposition and I had to point out to them that my generosity came only because I expected them to be vastly superior to the ordinary. I did not give a hint that I dearly loved them and I really wanted them to come with me.

I was amazed that it was only a little after noon when we were all packed and ready to go. The whole village of Simigaon had awakened to see us off and all of the folk of Bongbong Danda were there to wish their son Seb Siri a fruitful trip and see him now as part of the great sahb's entourage. But first there had to be much talking and hugging and the hearing of wild stories. Finally the farewells became more final and we shouldered our loads and I led the way out down the path. I now realized that I had acquired a new status, some kind of royalty, perhaps a baron of some sort with the Sherpas. My word was law. Behind me there was Pemba Norbu, aide de camp and chief knight. Old Bloody and Nu Phutar followed, with the former of a slightly higher position. These were knights second class. Lastly there was Seb Siri, always in the rear and well aware of his lowly status, something below knighthood, perhaps a squire of sorts since this was his first foray away from home.

This was my retinue and a true hierarchy. Seb Siri would not talk to me directly; he would make any approach to me through Nu Phutar who, if he thought it was of consequence, would pass the word on to Old Bloody who would consider consulting with Pemba Norbu. Pemba Norbu, if he should receive the word or if he should care to bust in on the sequence any time he chose, would hold judgment and decide if I should be approached or if he should suggest a solution to me. And so it went. But there was no doubt in their minds that I was dictator and that there were ranks below who must hold their places. And all this was their doing; they formed this structure themselves and with it there arose a remarkable esprit de corps for, to a man, they were proud of their role as supporters to the great baron. Around "chang" (or beer) drinkers in the villages we passed, they would brag of their association and elaborate on the great job they had and how they were important personages. They started rumors about me that seemed to thrust me into legend for all such praise reflected back on them as helpers to greatness.

For instance, one day on a long haul up a hill, I saw a lizard high on a tree branch. It was just a common *Calotes versicolor* but it was large and quite magnificent. I could not spend much time to capture it for I had many specimens of the species, so I picked up a stone and heaved it at the animal. It was perhaps forty or fifty feet up in the tree but by sheer and impossible luck it was hit square and it fell almost at my feet and so I quickly grabbed it before it could run off. Nothing was said of this at the time that I can recall, but several days later while we were spending some time in a village, a man approached me and bowing, he said,"Sahb! It is an honor to meet the great man who charms the very lizards out of the trees!"

As we passed through Nepal various young men saw our group as an opportunity to travel. Being associated with us could have been protection from occasional brigands but it was mostly the opportunity to be accepted by great personages and touch briefly upon such superior company. These men who wished to join us recognized the hierarchy immediately and always made their first inquiries with Seb Siri (who was generally happy to invite such strangers for then he would not be of lowest rank). The man would next approach Nu Phutar and so on. I would watch this formal dickering and the quiet suggestions of cash for favors and slowly the request would make its way to me and when it did, the new man would stand at the edge of the encampment, stand at attention like a Gurkha and await my decision. At first I let these men accompany us and at such times we looked more like a caravan than a scouting party. Subsequently, I would allow a stranger into the group only if he could be informative about trees or the customs or some such thing. I, like the great Frederick II, Stupor Mundi, would gather scholars around me.

This description of our way of travel has only been a digression for now it is necessary to go back to that ceremonial departure from Simigaon. With the preceding introduction, the marching out of Simigaon can more fully be appreciated. We were high class, our visit was a great honor, and furthermore Simigaon, as well as Bongbong Danda, had had the opportunity to have a party that may still be talked about. I can see some old man in a dark corner of a hut in Bongbong Danda wistfully reminding his grandchildren of the time many, many years ago, when there was a strange demon-man with fair hair on his face and whose eyes were a fierce blue, yes, blue, who came through the village and who could take lightning from the skies and drink three casks of chang at one sitting.

Our path led, once again, down toward the river and we reached the valley floor just beyond where the Rolawaling stream meets the Tamba Kosi

River on its way out of Tibet. We were back in a gorge but here we were at only about 4,000 feet and the buttresses of Guarishankar rose up and up and there, far above, was snow. There was here some 20,000 feet of difference in elevation. The river roared down through this mighty chasm with the many rapids turning the gray-green glacial water into white foam.

I could see the torrent for about half a mile upstream and as I was sitting in the shade beside the river I thought I saw two logs floating down. But they seemed to go too fast and they went too far in the air as they poured over the rapids. And then my eyes widened; those were not logs, they were otters, a pair of otters swimming full tilt down stream. They would come to a place where the water would fall a few feet and they would sail out in looping dives to land in the pools below. They were almost flying down the river. It seemed obvious that they had done this before and they knew all the rocks and rills of their route. They came rapidly toward me and I expected to see them surge past. But, right where I sat there must have been some impediment known to them and they rushed out of the water to run along the bank around the obstacle. Thus they came right up to me. They would have run right into me. They stopped and looked at me sitting there as if to wonder where I came from, what sort of a strange rock was I? And then they were off, cavorting in the wild water. I love otters and this brief encounter was a happy experience. I think of them often and I wonder what they were doing there where the roaring water of the gorges is not known for abundant fish life and where the barrier of foam effectively separates the fish faunas of Tibet and the slow rivers of the lowlands. Perhaps they were just playing around and enjoying the fun of a fast river. Otters do things like that.

After our rest by the river we continued up the slope trying to find a path that would lead us westward over the range. We camped near a few trees where the land had been otherwise wasted by overgrazing and poor farming techniques. In a standard way we soon established for camping, my box of specimens and equipment was brought to me. This acted as a desk or seat or table. My duffel bag was also laid down where I would have my little territory and then I would drag out my sleeping bag and poncho which I usually carried myself and call the place home. Sometimes I would erect my small red mountain tent. It kept out the breezes while I wrote up my notes for the day by the light of a candle.

The next morning I realized that the frightening curse of the yeti was still at hand. I got up early and it was chilly for my thermometer was registering 49° F. I reached into my duffel bag to drag out a sweater and I had just enough time to recognize that awful odor of stink bugs from the night before when I got a mighty surprise. A snake over two feet long slithered like a shot up my encroaching arm. At somewhere near my elbow it flew off onto the ground. Perhaps the snake was not traveling at its full speed for it was chilly and I had ample opportunity to diagnose it down to genus and species. It was very clear to me that this was Trimeresurus graminii, a very deadly pit viper and not a very gentle snake. I had been very lucky. I have seen wounds from this species of snake swell up a leg into a blue and reddish balloon and a life saved only because of excellent hospital care. This far-out place was not the place to be bitten by a snake of these nasty proportions.

It did not get away. My bug net was handy and I netted him. It had encountered a biologist, ostensibly a poor choice for the snake. But consider the alternatives from the point of view of snakes in general. They are hounded and killed with gusto and anger and even hysteria by most people. I actually revel at their presence and I enjoy their existence and I would not kill them except when they, by some accident, are chosen to represent their species. A specimen in some far off museum may yield some information about the species, something about their kind which, in the long run, may help all of them survive. If one does not know the animal then how is it possible to appreciate it? I consider the creatures that I catch rather fortunate. Theirs is a sacrifice for knowledge. Consider how few pit vipers are selected for eternity. Yes, that creature that scared me out of my wits was fortunate on some grander scale of things.

We went on up over the pathless mountain. Later in the day we did find a route of sorts that led up a side canyon and finally, near day's end, we found a pleasant, wide field of grass with surrounding trees and a small stream. It was ideal for the night. There were some clouds and an overcast sky so I elected to pitch my little tent.

Just at nightfall, however, a dozen or more horses ran out onto the field from some path higher up the hill. They were followed by a group of impressive-looking and swaggering Tibetans dressed in dark robes, high boots, fur hats and each of them carried a wicked-looking sword. They came up to us and I watched as there were all sorts of gestures which I could easily understand. This was their camping place, their grazing field and we should move our camp to the far side and right away. I could see that Pemba Norbu was disturbed and the first chance he got, after we swiftly moved our things to a far corner, was to come up to me and say "Sahb, these are fierce men, Khambas from eastern Tibet, a race of brigands. They are in the process of smuggling horses out of Tibet and this is their secret route where the authorities do not ask questions." He paused now and then said quietly, "Sahb, be on your guard tonight!"

My small tent was now pitched off at one corner of the field but a little to one side of where the others planned to sleep. It seemed sufficiently out of the way but the fates would rule otherwise. It was that yeti curse again. I climbed in as always, lit my candle and wrote up my notes. As always I fell off into a deep-tired sleep. Sometime during the night I was awakened with something nudging my head. My tent was small and my head often found itself pressing against the thin wall of the tent and now, something outside was pushing at my head. It took a moment for me to begin to appreciate what was going on and then I realized that a horse was nosing at my tent trying to get another bite of grass from under the tent floor.

I should note here that these horses spend all day walking across the mountains and it is only at night that they have any real chance to graze. The horse out there was obviously hungry and eager for a meal. I lay there receiving nudge after nudge and since its head was separated from my own by the thinness of a mountain tent, I was actually on very intimate terms with a Tibetan horse. Furthermore, the meeting of heads was so arranged that my ear was directly on its snout and I could clearly hear what was going on inside its head. There was the distinct clip, clip of the incisors, the grind of the molars and then the spectacular gurgling of a giant swallow - clip, clip, crunch, crunch, ggggrrump, clip, clip, crunch, crunch, ggggrrump!

As a biologist I was fascinated, but I was also an exhausted person and there was some exasperation and annoyance in all this. I tried to think of some procedure that would not only scare off the innocent creature but would discourage it from returning and waking me up repeatedly during the night. The idea that came to me in my sleepiness was to arrange a dramatic loud shout using some appropriate Tibetan epithets which would be screamed directly into its ear. I calculated that the guileless beast would respond with such surprise that it would never come back to my side of the field again.

I took a deep breath and yelled. There was an instantaneous grunt from near my nose and I knew the poor animal had been frightened out of its horse's wits. But then it did something that had never occurred to me. Instead of running away, the horse, undoubtedly surprised beyond what its senses could estimate, ran right over me. It shot out not away from the tent but directly at it as if the sound had come from its rear. There followed some seconds of pandemonium. The horse got mixed up with the guy strings of the tent which were snagging its hooves while it pranced around trying to get free. And I was inside being stepped on and rolled over and over and totally immobilized. The horse finally freed itself and galloped off snorting while I, like some carelessly wrapped mummy, lay enmeshed in the fabric of my tent. I was not hurt even though there were quite definite places where hooves had been, and my chief problem was not bruises but finding a way out of my collapsed tent to fresh air.

I squirmed and wiggled looking for the lost entrance and finally I got my nose out. It was a relief. I lay there in that mess and decided that was the way it would be for the rest of the night. This rolled up form of mine would respond to future horse investigations better than an erected tent. In the morning the Sherpas saw my strewn form and scattered belongings and wondered how it had all happened. When I described the affair with the horse they nearly died laughing. I should add that Sherpas tend to laugh at anything, boulders whizzing by your head, falls into crevasses, bridges that break, and horses that step on you. They laugh at the wonder that you are still alive. Evasion of cruel destiny is a great joy is it not? And I laughed too.

Our path now led up to a ridge that reached over 13,000 feet and we went up through the various zones of life to near timberline. On the way we visited a small isolated monastery that served the few Sherpas who lived in this unfrequented region. Here, as I have so often seen before, there were photographs in small silver frames. There was always some likeness of the Dalai Lama and some other notable individuals of Tibetan Buddhism. It would seem that these remote people were so unacquainted with photography that a simple black and white rendition, a portrait, had some special religious significance. Perhaps the only photographs they ever saw were images of holy people. Thus, whenever a photograph of anyone managed to find its way to these far corners of existence, they were considered holy or had some venerable quality. Thus it was that in that smoky chamber where burning butter sent its acrid smells and a lama was chanting in the corner and occasional bells rang, I looked at the altar and there with the Holy Lamas in silver frames was an old Hollywood publicity photograph. Joan Crawford was among the honored personages.

We had seen some unusual events take place on this journey back to Kathmandu. In the past I have had many events of some unusual quality affect my travels but I cannot remember having them occur night after night and day after day. Thus, it crossed the whims of my mind that the curse of the yeti seemed to be implicated. In sequence there was that terrifying gorge, the stink bugs, the viper and then the horses. Surely it could not go on. But, yes, it did.

We started down the long trail to Bharabise, or at least we thought so. It got later and later and our path hugged the side of a steep slope that offered no comfort for a camp. But then, almost suddenly, we emerged onto a wide and generous flat expanse, a sort of stage formed into the side of the mountain. This seemed designed for us so we camped and stretched out in splendor. But not for long.

Just as dusk was setting in, what should we see but sheep, hundreds of sheep, coming down the trail. And, just like the horses, this was their night place. Nepali shepherds led them onto the field and they set in to munch the short grass. They were starved and I could see them chewing away all night just as the horses had done. We moved our camp to the most secluded corner which we knew would not be distant enough from the sheep but that was as far as we could go. We lit our fire and the herdsmen lit theirs. We were all convivial and the sheep behaved themselves. And so to bed.

Sure enough, I was awakened by sheep all around chewing the grass to the edge of my tent. They would bump into my tent strings and the structure would shake. I reasoned that they were not as bad as horses for surely they could not knock down my little shelter. But I was wrong. My sense of security was rudely shaken when I realized that one and then another animal was nibbling on the tent ropes! It collapsed. I searched out the entrance and stuck out my nose and for the rest of the night those sheep tumbled all over me. My sleep was fitful to say the least but now my self righteous Sherpas who were so gleeful about my horse intervention were suffering too. Oh, the language I heard that night when the sheep walked over their prostrate bodies!

Morning eventually arrived and with the sun the shepherds led their flock off down the slope headed for some distant market. There was a sense of relief from the lowly Seb Siri to the haughty baron. But then something happened that was absolutely fascinating. No sooner had the sheep disappeared when coming from the path above was a family of Nepalese, about six of them. I have no idea where they could have spent the night but here they were and it soon became obvious that they were following this particular flock wherever it would lead them. What was their interest? Sheep dung! It was now scattered like coarse pepper across the grassy land.

There was evidently a father, a mother, an eldest daughter, and some younger children. They moved onto the terrace as if it were indeed a stage. They behaved like actors with every movement memorized and their performance had a practiced air to it that made the whole affair seem as something from a medieval play, like some wandering troubadours playing for the wants of royalty, like that sub-play for the king in Hamlet. Mother and father started sweeping around the periphery. The younger children, either with their bare hands or the aid of a large leaf, gathered the growing piles and ran them to center stage where the eldest daughter had her tall basket. The children would drop their loads in the center and run back for more. Handmade brooms were whisking madly away and children running back and forth and in the center the young lady was bending down and picking up and dropping the fast accumulating dung into her basket. She used her bare hands and they flicked away at the job with amazing rapidity. It was all a well-oiled machine that worked faster and faster and then even furiously. I saw the girl in the center bending and throwing and bending and throwing with such dexterity and speed that I couldn't keep my eyes off her. I couldn't see her face; a shawl of sorts was in the way and she didn't pause to look around.

There is a need here to tell of Nepalese women, before I complete this tale. It is a time honored tendency for travelers to generalize or compare the women of different parts of the earth. As far as I am concerned, no region or municipality has any monopoly or even an advantage in the matter of feminine beauty. Percentages of attractivity are generally equal wherever one may be. The variant to this assessment is the length of time the male appraiser has existed without the company of a woman or women. Thus, the longer he is away, the women he witnesses seem more and more attractive. He pays more and more attention to the sweep of a garment or some covert arc in the line of a torso or the quality of a sternocleidomastoid muscle that rims a slim neck. These subtleties, which he may not otherwise dawdle with, best come with time.

The saturated man is much more inclined to note the obvious signs of gender and neglect the qualities of femininity that hover in the background and are shaded by the more manifest features. All this I can say because I had been away a long time, long enough to note the growing symptoms of my refinement.

A further tendency, and a characteristic I have not found in the literature of sexuality that pervades our culture, is the matter of identification, the development of a fine sense of comparison between what is seen and what is remembered. This stage of mental intimacy may not be reached by many save the celibates who I do not believe should have much to say on this matter, and thus, the infrequency of the experience has not been drawn to the attention of our chief authors on such matters. They themselves, the authors, tend to show, with the overt circumstances of sexuality that they choose for their general themes, to not be, themselves, capable of reaching the insightful levels of quality that emerge from deprivation. I am talking about the development of a tendency to see a face and immediately adjust that countenance to some admired face from one's past. Such a comparison often is made with a notable face, some movie star or someone who, through use of sheer feminine attraction, becomes famous.

It goes something like this. I was standing beside the road resting while climbing up a long slope. A threesome of young Nepali ladies came down the path. Such young women are often very shy and take only quick glances at a strange foreigner. Thus they passed me with eyes elsewhere but I smiled and they saw it and I heard them titter and fly off down the road like a covey of tropical birds. At a sufficient distance away, one of them turned to take a quick glance; she was the tallest and lithest of the three. Her face was shown to me for just that slight moment but there, with her nose ring and dark hair, she was a template for Rita Hayworth back there in time of war. I am not crazy. Try it sometime. Go off into the mountains for a few months and watch how the women get prettier the longer you stay away and how they start to look like a selection from the Hollywood screen.

So let us go back to the young women stuffing dung into the basket with her blackened hands and her continual effort, a dedication to a menial task that is hard to believe. In time the accumulation of droppings started to wane and her work became less hectic. The stage had been nearly emptied of its evidence of two hundred sheep. She finally paused and leaned back and stood erect and then with a casual, and oh so feminine, sweep of her hand pushed back the sari-like cloth that had hidden her face. She now looked at me. And there was Sophia Loren.

Camp on the Barun Glacier and stationary clouds over Everest.

The Aeolian Biome

The British considered naturalists as valued members of all their voyages of exploration—Joseph Banks with Captain Cook, Charles Darwin on the "Beagle," Joseph Hooker with Sir James Ross, Thomas Huxley on the "Rattlesnake" and many others. The men of biology in England, the leaders in science, generally had experience in the wild corners of the world. The tradition did not cease with the Mount Everest expeditions, which, after many delays, finally commenced in 1921 with the reconnaissance led by Colonel Howard-Bury. That first expedition was accompanied by A.F.R. Wollaston; the second expedition in 1922 was represented by the mountaineer naturalist T.G. Longstaff and the 1924 expedition had R.W.G. Hingston. All these men added an enormous amount of information concerning high altitude biology and it grieves me to see how infrequently they are mentioned in bibliographic references today. It was the accounts of these men, their descriptions of the extreme environments of Tibet and the high Himalaya that first intrigued me, and long ago, as a child, I would collect high altitude records for various creatures. For the most part, records of the highest living things came from the observations of these three men. And so it was that Hingston's spiders became part of my early knowledge of life in the Himalaya.

It seems that some climbers of that 1924 expedition, while returning to base camp, encountered some tiny spiders at the enormous altitude of 22,000 feet. Mountaineers as a rule do not see such things or, if they do, they usually do not bother to collect them. I refer now to the purists in mountaineering (in case I may offend someone). I therefore compliment those unknown alpinists. From my own experiences with mountaineers, I envisage they stopped in an exceptional moment of insight and recognition. They saw the creatures, noted that they were in an unusual place, and did the best they could to capture them for their friend Hingston. Without any vials to hold the specimens, they most likely wrapped them up in some dirty handkerchief. Hingston recognized the two specimens as representatives of the family Attidae, the old name for what is now called Salticidae, the family of jumping spiders. He noted also that they were juveniles and he must have surely noted that they were rather badly battered. When the spiders were finally delivered to the British Museum, W.S. Bristowe, the arachnologist there, suggested that they could belong to the genus *Sitticus* and referred to them in some of his writings. Later, a succeeding spider authority, D. J. Clark, thought they would better fit in the genus *Euophrys*, but he did not get around to describing them down to species for the simple reasons that the specimens were not only immature, they were rather squashed and ragged. Nevertheless, Hingston's spiders were evidence that living things could exist where the environment appeared to consist totally of ice and snow and barren rock.

The problem in the interpretation of this existence for the spiders centered on the well-known fact that spiders are universally predaceous. There is not one spider in the whole world that does not eat some other animal and their food is chiefly directed towards insects. Therefore, Hingston's spiders must have been eating something or other up there in their frigid niche and, whatever those creatures might be, they in turn had to be eating something. It is a basic premise of biology that animals must ultimately rely on plants as a source of food. It seemed rather unlikely that plants, even austere lichens, would exist at 22,000 feet. When queried on this subject, Hingston, presumably when he was in his least lucid mood, vaguely suggested that the spiders may eat other spiders. This line of thought creates even more severe problems associated with entropy and some foundation laws of physics. The energy of life, with some remote exceptions, such as the chemotrophic bacteria of hot springs and the hot waters that emerge from the rifts in the ocean floor, must come from the sun and be fixed into organic molecules by something akin to photosynthesis. If spiders ate only spiders their meals would not last long and there would be a quick extinction.

The quandry of Hingston's spiders was also faced with the known fact that many spiders are able to balloon and travel great distances. Ballooning spiders include the family Salticidae which, shortly after they have hatched from their eggs, release a fine thread that is caught by rising air and as the thread rises, it carries the tiny spider aloft. In this way millions upon millions of spiders are scattered over the earth. Sometimes the massed threads of millions of baby spiders form a sort of sheet as they rise and such flimsy wisps of gossamer poised high in the atmosphere may reflect light in curious ways and may therefore give rise to unidentified flying object sightings. It is odd that this mode of transportation for ballooning spiders which should allow them to reach any part of the world does not seem to function as a universal distributing agent. Remote islands which must witness occasional rains of spiders from any part of the earth have their own endemic and native spiders with few if any cosmopolitan species. Since all island spiders belong to ballooning families, it can be assumed that the original spiders got to their remote homes by ballooning but that new arrivals are somehow shunned. It is perhaps a lesson in zoogeography that is not always understood by sparrow and starling conscious citizens that introduction of a foreign species requires a congenial and fitting environment and very often the helping hand of man. If it were not so, the Galapagos Islands and such places would be run over by much more than such things as the descendants of pirates' goats. I am reminded here about how the U.S. Department of Agriculture spends millions of dollars and haunts the world of aviculture with the nemesis story of Newcastle Disease among introduced birds that would wipe out our resource of chickens, while in my back yard I witness day after day new arrivals of migrant birds fresh from Mexico and places south.

The question next posed to Hingston was whether or not his spiders were casual, windblown ballooning spiders. He could not answer. His proposal that they lived up there on the mountain was largely based on his broad experience and his knowledge of how things survived in extreme lands. He had seen how creatures eked out a living on what appeared to be barren slopes and his opponents had not. He could, with his respect for life's ability to cope with what seemed to be the impossible, readily include those enigmatic spiders among the normal residents of extreme altitudes. However, as time went on, it seems his critics won. Those spiders, it was generally assumed, must have been exceptional ballooning spiders that had arrived only shortly before the climbers had found them. It was believed that life could not prosper at 22,000 feet and that the limit for resident living things was substantially lower than that incredible altitude.

Personally, I did not like this solution. I liked Hingston's writings too much to see the man defeated by the logic of scientists who had not been touched by the cold heights and had never dug out a specimen from under the rocks with freezing, dirty hands. I also considered something that the logicians had too easily overlooked. Hingston's spiders were juveniles, young spiders, but they were not babies, the kind of spiders usually associated with ballooning. I kept Hingston's spiders as my choicest record for life on earth. To me they represented resident breeding species but just how they managed to hold their own against the impossible sterile land, I did not know.

And so it was that when our expedition set out in 1954, one of the things that was near the top of my mind was a hope that I might encounter these record-breaking arachnids. Makalu is not far from Everest and even though I would be on the Nepalese side, I did not believe that a species would be so confined as to exist only on the north side of a peak.

Salticid spiders are a favorite of mine. They do some marvelous things and seem to be a step above other spiders in their agility and pouncing ways. The manner in which they can anticipate the movements of their prey and leap up to some insect's destruction is, if you have seen it done, beyond belief. During the expedition I was always on the look out for them, and I did find a few at lower altitudes, but up above the timberline the spider populations were essentially confined to the fierce and aggressive wolf spiders, the lycosids. These big spiders were well adapted to their cold habitat and in the late afternoon when the sun had moved behind the mountains and the air temperature plummeted near the freezing mark, they were still active. It was in this chill that ordinary flying insects left their air and came to the ground to squeeze near the still-warm rocks. Butterflies, bees and flies that were normally beyond the reach of the spiders were now down to their plane and as the insects searched for their protective crevices, the lycosids went to work. When the usual insect was being threatened by a cold torpor the spiders were in their element. They seemed admirably adapted and, perhaps, in the face of such success, the salticids were excluded.

As the expedition made its way up the slopes of Makalu and I had explored the lower reaches of the Barun Valley, I decided it was time to go farther north to see if I could reach the Tibetan border

However, I needed some help to carry loads and all the Sherpas were needed on the mountain. I then became fortunate on the misfortune of others. Fritz Lippman became ill as did our Sherpa cook's helper, a very young man on his first adventure to the peaks. As they recovered, I persuaded them to accompany me up the glacier. We found a site for our tents at 19,000 feet. That night I witnessed the most remarkable display of Cheyne-Stokes breathing. This is a periodic deep and fast breathing between episodes of no breathing at all and it occurs most frequently after climbing several thousand feet. It seems that the new and thinner atmosphere provokes some maladjustment

74

in one's normal cadence of breathing while sleeping. Here it was that Fritz demonstrated the ultimate extreme to which Cheyne-Stokes can go. Not only did he hold his breath longer than I could believe possible for I continually became suspicious that he had died in his sleeping bag that lay beside me, he loudly snored his rapid breathing recovery. I could not imagine how he managed to sleep through the roars he was producing that came in such gasping frequency that I wondered how a pharynx could take the strain. Needless to say, my own sleep was limited and I had little sympathy for Fritz when he complained of a sore throat in the morning.

We toured the high glacier for the next three days and as we set out on a glacial terrace that ran on one side of the glacier, I saw what I wanted to see. There it was on a rock about 40 feet ahead, the unmistakable jerky movements of a small black spider. I gave out a whoop and the others wondered about my sanity. I watched it for a few moments and then it was in my tweezers and into a vial of alcohol. One may wonder about my hurry to dispose of a creature whose behavior and ecology were a classical enigma. Dead spiders don't reveal much about their lives. This horrendous eagerness to kill needs an explanation.

Taxonomy is the classification of plants and animals, and systematics, its associated discipline, is the study of how living things are related. Systematics is an inquiry into the evolution of species and its premises are largely based upon accurate taxonomy. If any extension of knowledge is to be made in areas of behavior and ecology, it is imperative that the student knows what creature is involved in the study. In this case, the spider must be identifiable; it must be seen to be the same or different from another spider. If confusion of identity occurs, then any other information may also be confused. It would be necessary to establish that the spiders I collected were the same species or a different species from those that were obtained by Hingston. Knowledge could not be extended on the ecology of these spiders if, in fact, there were several species of spiders involved. And so, the first specimen becomes the important reference, the needed item for identification. Ecology and behavior must wait their turns as subservient extensions of the prime knowledge, taxonomy.

As it turned out, I found quite a number of salticid spiders and, although they were sometimes difficult to catch, I collected about a dozen. I saw many more but these usually escaped while I tried to find out what they were eating and where they were hiding. I saw spiders all the way up to the Tibetan border at over 20,000 feet and I found them in locations where the surroundings were devoid of plants and only rocks and gravel near old snowfields were in evidence. However, once in a while I did encounter a small black anthomyid fly, a small thing that was not too unlike an ordinary house fly. Under the rocks there were some gatherings of tiny springtails, primitive insects of the order Collembola. Occasionally too, a bee or tortoise shell butterfly sailed by. There were indeed some insects at this edge of the living world and I reveled in the thought that I had finally shown that Hingston was right. Spiders did live up here. They were not windblown derelicts. They were residents. They lived in what must surely be one of nature's most inhospitable realms.

On these high slopes I could look far to the north and see the rolling red mountains of Tibet and to the west there was the unknown east face of Everest. I could see parts of the north face of this great peak and make out the first and second steps that were so much part of stories from the early Mount Everest expeditions. I could almost see where those climbers had captured Hingston's spiders exactly 30 years earlier. To the south down the Barun Glacier, it was easy to see that the snowline ascended towards the north. On that ridge overlooking Tibet there was little snow at 19,500 feet whereas peaks to the south were clad in snow at between 15,000 and 16,000 feet. Furthermore, snowless slopes ascended to great heights on the high peaks so that exposed rock was visible up to altitudes that exceeded 22,000 feet. It seemed entirely possible that spiders and other life could be found at enormous altitudes and not be covered by perennial snow and ice.

Knowing that Wollaston had reported that the highest plant he had collected was at 20,000 feet, I ascended the slopes looking for something still higher. At 19,600 feet there were still some indications of mats of plants that had survived in favored spots where moisture could have lingered as the last snow patches disappeared but, for the most part, plants only were able to survive in a niche at the base of rocks. In such localities, where the presence of a rock hastens the melting of snow and the snow therefore becomes liquid before it sublimates to vapor, some water percolates into the soil. Rocks absorb heat even when they are beneath some inches of snow so that the snow melts fastest around the periphery of a rock and it may protrude from the snow long before the snow has disappeared. This also enhances the time when the rock base is free of snow and allows more time for the growth of plants. The rock base is also where windblown debris accumulates and so it is where flying seeds are most likely to settle. The rock base niche is so apparent at extreme altitudes all over the world that it should be more widely appreciated in the literature of the alpine biome.

One of my most successful projects had been the collection of plant specimens. I amassed over a hundred species of plants in flower above timberline, that is, above about 13,500 feet. I had watched the changes in the flora as I ascended and so now near the limit of flowering plants, I searched for the highest. Far up a slope where the occasional plants became more and more infrequent I finally stopped when my map and calibrated altimeter read 20,150 feet. Here I found a straggling specimen of *Stellaria decumbens*, one of the pinks (Caryophyllacae), and I collected its prostrate form at the base of a rock. It was and perhaps still is the highest collected plant in the world. The doubt I show here is because some climbers have reported plants somewhat higher but such travelers sometimes only mention their discovery, and thus there is the possibility of error, both as to species and altitude. These record plants seldom seem to find their way to museums.

It is curious that on these nearly barren slopes north of Makalu there appeared to be no lichens. On temperate and polar mountains lichens ascend higher than flowering plants and throughout the literature of mountain ecology there is the assumption that this is the case the world over. This was obviously not true where I was. It could be that I obtained my highest plants in an area that had only recently been freed of a covering glacier or permanent snow pack and, in such new terrain, the first pioneers were flowering plants that could reach moisture below the surface with their roots. Lichens on bare rock surfaces could not easily acquire water where this compound is usually either a gas or a solid. They could, perhaps, eventually succeed at these altitudes but they are not the pioneers that they may be at lower, moister altitudes on other mountains.

During my wanderings on these high, almost lifeless slopes, I investigated a pile of rocks that had been left from some long past glacial activity. It was here that some of my latent questions concerning the ecology of this extreme land finally seemed to reach for answers. I was lifting some boulders to see what could be beneath them and as I lifted one large granitic block, I noticed some dust on the surface of the rock that had been just below it. I looked closely and to my surprise I found some springtails (collembola) occupied the spot. These small insects had been deep within the pile of rocks and some distance above what might be considered the base of the rocks. What could they be doing among otherwise sterile rocks and far from what might be imagined as soil? What could they feed on among the rocks? I looked closer still and then I saw a tinge of yellow. There in a faint trace was the sign of pollen, pollen presumably from the juniper bushes that were covered with the stuff far below this altitude and many miles away. I looked closer still and brushed some of the dust onto my notebook and I could see small pieces of plants, feathery pieces from the dandelion type of seed of composite plants, minute seeds and other tiny particles that were not sand or powdered glacial dust. It dawned on me that the springtails were surviving on this food or, more likely, the fungi or bacteria that must be slowly consuming this small cache of organic matter. It took some time for the observation to enter those corridors of the brain where simple facts are sorted out into those neural containers that hold meanings for facts.

The recognition of the meaning of the fact that the wind had supplied this largesse for the collembola did not immediately sink in. I did not immediately realize that the dictum of biology that says with authority that animals were dependent upon plants did not explicitly state that the plants had to be nearby. I did not grasp with suddenness that there was an applicable analogy that told how creatures of the deep sea, far beyond the reach of the sun, fed in the dark depths upon food that filtered down to them from a productive surface that could be some miles away. Those creatures are supplied by gravity. These collembola were supplied by the wind.

I went back to camp that late afternoon with thoughts surging. Little pieces of evidence started to fit together. I could not rest and through some strange compulsion I started rolling great boulders off the glacial terrace and watched them bound and bounce down to the glacier that was at least 500 feet below. It was on that glacier that I had discovered some strange insects of the order Thysanura (now often included in Microcoryphia or Archaeognatha). These so-called glacier fleas lived among the glacier rocks in as hostile an environment as there could be. What could they eat? I had played with the idea that they too may have sampled the small anthomyid flies but such behavior would be entirely foreign to these machilid thysanurans. It could only be that they survived on windblown organic debris. And, under the rocks where I had found the pupae of the anthomyid flies, the flies that fed the spiders, they, as fungus feeding flies, could have been nurtured only on the fungi that decomposed windblown organic material. Similarly, the springtails that lived under some of the same rocks where the spiders found their hiding spots, and could be another source of food for the spiders, found nutrients derived from windblown organic debris. As each piece of the puzzle seemed to fit and form a picture I would find larger and larger rocks to roll down the cliff and see them crash down onto the glacier below. I think back now and wonder what possessed me. It seems that I was overwhelmed by the excitement, the overpowering captivation of a discovery that opened doors to new concepts and seemed to answer the many questions that had accumulated on the threshold waiting for the door to be opened.

My mind would not stop and my body could not stand idly by and so it took to the inane exertion of rolling rocks, huge staggering boulders, down the mountainside.

The real entrancement of that occasion was the valid synthesis that was coming together in my mind. All those enigmas of high altitude and, indeed, the polar regions, where life seemed to exist without readily apparent sources of nutrition could now find an explanation. And it was a simple and straightforward explanation that had somehow slipped by the minds of others, like Hingston. Furthermore, it was not just a mere extension of an idea or an addition to some already functioning ecological concept, it was a totally new sort of a thing that I was playing with. My elation was exploding out of the idea that I had discovered something that was beyond and quite different to what was called the alpine region, or alpine tundra, the zone of the highest life. This was a new zone, a zone based on atmospheric nutrients, a zone of the wind. I would eventually call it the Aeolian Biome. It would be a whole new category to the geography of life and not just some new variation or subsidiary ecosystem. There are those major biomes of the earth that textbooks like to list, things like the Tropical Rainforests, Tropical Savannas, Temperate Deciduous Forests, Deserts, Tundra and so forth. Here was another major realm for the earth for surely this land near the sky was not tundra or alpine. It was something new and like the benthal division of the ocean abyss it stood alone in its nutrient base. This was a whole new biome type that derived its being and its name from the wind.

It has now been over 40 years since that discovery and the concept has expanded to include the world. The Aeolian Biome can be divided into three phases; a terrestrial phase is occupied by such things as the springtails, the glacier fleas and the salticid spiders; a nival phase on the snow and ice contains animals such as the ice worms of North America (whose distribution reflects the extent of the old Pleistocene glaciers) and also plants like snow algae that derive their nitrates from organic debris. There are also many nival birds, mammals and insects that prowl the snow for its contents of food that has blown onto the sticking surface. The snow accumulates great quantities of air borne nutrients from all sorts of originating sources including, it seems, albuminoid proteins that come from the spray that is lifted into the wind by the force of ocean storms. That the ocean and the Aeolian Region should be linked is a wonderment of sorts.

This ocean-aeolian relationship needs some extension of thought. A.T.Wilson recognized that the grasses that fed the sheep of New Zealand had some nitrogen source that was inexplicable. To isolate this source, he went up to the Southern Alps of New Zealand and in the middle of winter when organic materials such as pollen would least contaminate his samples, he collected new-fallen snow. He used what may be a rather crude method for the presence of protein in terms of recent techniques, the process used in sewage analysis, and found to his amazement that he could detect, on an average, about 0.23 parts per million of protein in the snow. He assumed that this must come from the ocean but when he sampled ocean water, there was no comparison. He therefore sampled ocean foam, the stuff that blows off the ocean with winds. Here he found a close relationship between the calcium, nitrate, sodium and potassium in foam and the protein of snow.

Subsequently, oceanographers have marveled at the way the surface layer of the ocean seems to aggregate the tiny algal life in the water and where bacteria work in a synergistic way with the algal cells to produce organic materials. As one oceanographer put it, the microscopic surface of the ocean could be a "weak bouillabasse" of organic materials fully 2,000 times the concentration of the open ocean. As droplets form from wave action, the tiny bubbles adsorb these organic materials onto their surfaces and, thus removed from the water surface, are blown into the air and far off onto the land. As Wilson suggested this contribution from the ocean may amount to "several pounds per acre."

All this accretion of food continuing year after year for the centuries is packed into snow and pressed into the ice of glaciers. These eventually melt and release their age old bounty by fusing or melting into water to produce a third phase of the Aeolian Region, the aquatic phase. On a glacier, temporary ponds may form and in these brown and dirty-looking accumulations of water, there may be numbers of the fairy shrimp, *Branchinecta orientalis*, that, in the absence of much competition in these passing pools, sometimes form incredibly large populations. Their resistant eggs blow in the wind everywhere. These animals feed on the nutrients released from the ice. Where torrents emerge from the mouth of a glacier, great numbers of aquatic insects can congregate and make use of these organic materials that may be many thousands of years old. There may even be aeolian lakes. Those high tarns of mountains that are ringed in by cliffs and hold water that could be utilized as distilled water, but which still hold life in their apparently sterile environment, are seemingly aeolian. The only source of food for such creatures comes from the snow that melted to form the lake.

I have delineated the Aeolian Biome on the high volcanoes of Mexico where lizards exist some 600 feet higher than the nominal snowline at 15,200 feet and must be covered by snow for much of the year. They live among piles of rocks that allow them an opportunity to bask in the sun. They survive on wind-blown insects that are brought to them from the tropical lands of Vera Cruz many miles away. I call them abominable snow lizards. Rattlesnakes climb to 15,000 feet attracted by the lizards and mice that, like the lizards, survive on the fallout of insects. There are salamanders near 15,000 feet and these seem to lie under the rocks for protection from the dessicating air and wait for insects and spiders to come under the rocks searching for their own shelter.

My students have studied the Aeolian Biome in the Sierra Nevada of California where great piles of windblown insects supply the food for large populations of mice and some shrews. As John Spalding, one of my students, put it after spending a summer on the summit of White Mountain at over 14,000 feet, the summit area is like an "aeolian oasis." The Aeolian Biome is now widely known on Mt. Ranier in Washington and various investigators have shown how windblown nutrients supply the living things on distant arctic islands and far into the interior of Antarctica. There is a tendency on the part of biologists who prefer warmer climates for their work to believe that plants cease with the snowline and that therefore anything above that level is "nival" or virtually sterile and not worthy of categorization. And some day I shall persuade geographers and the map makers to avoid using those terms that boldly cover large parts of the world map and state things like "Glaciated," "Rock and Ice," "Barren" and even "Lifeless." Animals and plants do live in some of these mislabeled and neglected areas. And these are not tundra or alpine creatures as other maps suggest. Such designations infer the presence of flowering, vascular and rooted plants, the food base of the tundra and alpine zones. The creatures of the earth's extremes are aeolian biota that eke out their bare existences from what the air supplies to them. They are a different sort of thing and they deserve greater recognition.

During various encampments at high altitudes and especially when waves of negative ambition overcome me, I have often resorted to an activity that seems to suggest to others that I am hard at work. This is my predilection to stick thermometers into everything and see how temperatures change during the day. A series of thermometers stuck into the ground at different depths reveals information about the environment and they do not require much attention. It is curious that a thermometer placed about 12 inches into the soil yields a fairly constant temperature during a 24-hour period and this temperature rather closely approximates the monthly mean of the normal shade temperature at that altitude. (I learned this from Joseph Hooker's similar affection for thermometers in his Sikkim travels back in 1851.)

Near the surface, the temperatures achieve some huge variations and I have recorded differences amounting to about 80° F. between the surface of the soil in the sun and the air in the shade a few inches away. It occurred to me that as the altitude increased these differences could become even greater so that, for instance, if the temperature of the air near the summit of Mount Everest was near -40° F., then it would be possible that a dark rock surface in the sun could have temperatures considerably above freezing. And if that were the case, living things could exist near the summit of Everest. Those hypothetical creatures would have to survive freezing every night and for many days but that would not be unusual for even the life near 18,000 feet was subject to freezing every night of the year. The problem of survival near the summit of Everest might well be based on the availability of water, liquid water, for snow would tend to sublimate very rapidly into vapor at this extreme altitude. It should be remembered that the environmental conditions near the summit of Mount Everest begin to resemble the environment of outer space. However, near some dark rock high on Mt. Everest, melting could occur with sufficient rapidity to allow some moisture to penetrate into a granular surface on some favored ledge in some special place. A helping suggestion came from a photograph made near the summit of Mt. Everest. It showed a small icicle. How else could icicles form except from the refreezing of melted water? If water was occasionally available where temperatures were above freezing with some frequency, then, if organic nutrients were also available, life could exist.

With some of these assumptions in mind, I approached Will Siri in 1963 (Will was our expedition leader in 1954 and was now organizing the 1963 American Mount Everest Expedition) to take some sterile vials and persuade summit climbers to collect what granular soil they could find at or near the summit of Mt. Everest. I hardly expected success for Everest climbers are generally too dedicated to the climb to bother about much else. I was suggesting some sort of digressing activity and requests of this sort can too easily be ignored. Siri agreed to try and I supplied him with a boxful of sterilized vials with directions on how to scoop up granular material without contaminating the collection.

The expedition of 1963 was most remarkable. It accomplished the third successful ascent of the mountain after the British in 1953 and the Swiss in 1956, but it also managed to get three pairs of climbers to the top. In the first team there was Jim Whittaker and Sonam Gompu, a Sherpa and my good friend and champion butterfly collector of our 1954 expedition. The second team included Luther Jerstad and Barry Bishop and Barry, recently with the National Geographic Society, had been a friend since we were together in 1960. The third successful group was composed of Tom Hornbein and Willi Unsoeld. Willi was also with us in 1954 and a very close friend. This last team did the impossible. They explored a new route up the West Ridge of the mountain and made a first ascent from that side and then, beyond belief, they traversed the mountain, going down on the standard southern route. Their plan was to meet Jerstad and Bishop at the summit and descend with them. However, the trials of the new West Ridge delayed them and they arrived at the summit at sundown. Thus they started their descent onto unknown slopes in darkness, calling out and hoping the others below would hear them.

Jerstad and Bishop had stayed at the summit an overly long time waiting for the other team and had left the summit in disappointment but, high on the summit pyramid of Mt. Everest, in the dark while they themselves were stumbling and getting lost, they heard the distant calls of their friends far above. They kept calling and finally they found each other. And now the four of them were lost. There was only the drastic and frightening alternative to spend the night out on the frigid slope and this they did.

By Everest's standards it must have been a mild night for if it had been otherwise they would not have returned. But there on the unprotected slope they huddled and shivered and survived. Bishop and Unsoeld ultimately lost their toes from suffering the freezing experience but they lived. And the point of all this and why I tend to suffer with them was that on that frozen night while they fought for life, my buddy, Willi Unsoeld, had one of my precious vials in his pocket.

These climbers and some others, particularly Barry Corbet, a support climber on the West Ridge, had scraped up samples of what they could on the high slopes, gravel that would fit my vials. After it was all over, Will Siri delivered my vials back to me and I looked at labels that professed altitudes that were hard to believe. There were samples labeled 27,500 feet from both the south slope and the West Ridge. I held these things that still contained the summit air of Mt. Everest and I knew that if I unscrewed the caps I would let in air from my surroundings and possibly contaminate the specimens. In anticipation of possible success I had contacted various laboratories that may have been interested in examining the soil specimens. I finally decided that the Ames Research Laboratory in Mountain View, California, was the most appropriate. They were the leading laboratory investigating the hypothetical environment on Mars and were prepared to look at specimens from exotic places. After all my searching I found the place I wanted very nearby, within sight of my home in the hills of Redwood City.

I took the vials to the Director of the laboratory and suggested I had something for him resembling a piece of Mars. He was amused at first but when I explained that the top of Mt. Everest has only about one third of the air at sea level and approaches the conditions of outer space he started to listen. With this thin blanket of air, the radiation on the surface begins to resemble Mars. The temperatures rise high in the sun on Mt. Everest and also drop to night minima, that often exceed -60° F., very much as they do on Mars. Water, so scarce on Mars, is only a bit more available on the summit of Mt. Everest. Indeed, no place on earth resembles Mars as close as the summit of Mt. Everest.

All this persuasion and some more made the Director do the right thing. He decided to treat my specimens as if they were an approach to the real thing from Mars. He would give my vials of gravel and dust a "dry run." After all, nothing like this had ever been collected from Mt. Everest before and not even now, after 30 years, with all the teams that have gained the summit, nothing of the sort has been duplicated. Those vials would now have to face the rooms of glassware and monstrous instruments, the best the United States had to offer.

A few days later a call came suggesting that I hurry down to the laboratory. The news was a bit cryptic suggesting something strange had happened. As I hurried down to the laboratory, science fiction crossed my mind. Some blob had developed in the agar plates, some exotic new thing that could blossom into a threat to mankind, or some new "Andromeda Strain" had been found. But when I arrived, what was actually in the series of Petri plates growing in all sorts of cultures, temperatures and nutrients were crowds of bacteria with their colonies speckling the agar. The Director was amazed (I suppose as amazed as Directors can get). He said that some colonies had already been examined under the microscope and it seemed that there were really too many bacteria species for his laboratory to handle just at that time. He suggested a solution. It was a response that came in those days when finances were looser and more malleable in scientific institutions than they are now. He wondered if I would accept a sub-grant and hire my own microbiologist to determine the nature of what was developing in the Mt. Everest soil. I suggested the name of a dedicated graduate student, Edward Ishiguru, who was then working with a supervising microbiology faculty member. Ishiguru might be happy to investigate these exotic creatures for his Master's degree.

Ed Ishiguru started his studies and the months went by. It became apparent that many species of bacteria were involved along with some yeasts and fungi. They all showed a high degree of pigmentation which might be expected from microbes exposed to high solar radiation. They also showed a high resistance to freezing and thawing. If ordinary bacteria are exposed to daily bouts of freezing and thawing, some of the creatures die so that a curve of their population growth tends to indicate a pattern that resembles a series of saw-tooth-like increases and decreases. If bacteria are conditioned to freezing and thawing, they simply close up when it freezes and start growing again when it thaws. There are no irregularites in their growth curve. And the bacteria from the summit area of Mt. Everest showed all the indications that they had been exposed to freezing nights and some warmer days.

If there had been any doubt about this bacterial flora and its actual functioning and metabolizing existence near the top of Mt. Everest (there are always suggestions that the life was merely transient and in spore form so that the creature was not actually living near the summit) the question seemed settled when one of Ishiguru's cultures continually produced variant forms that were inexplicable. He could not identify the creature and as he further studied it, it changed its shape and arrangement so much that he soon realized he was dealing with a species with a very complex life cycle that had no comparable stages among known bacteria. He slowly became convinced that he had discovered what appeared to be a representative of a whole new family of microbes. To establish and prove such a radical hypothesis is not easy, and microbiologists are conservative on the matter of such revolutionary proposals. It turned out that Ed Ishiguru not only completed a Master's degree on these bacteria but went on and finished a doctorate on these elusive microbes. It would seem to me that he still has not established their true identity. After years of doubt, the bacterium can now be compared to some other Actinomycete bacteria found in strange places but, as far as I am concerned, it is quite a different thing. I do not fully appreciate the taxonomic compromise that has been made. Some unknowing microbiologists, in their obscure ways, have named this creature *Geodermatophilus obscurus everestii* (obscure skin lover from the ground of Everest.

It may also mean obscure thing that resembles skin loving bacteria that comes from the soil of Everest. Surely it deserves more respect and individuality. It should state in an outright and uncompromising way something like "wunderbarius" or "implausiblensis."

And so it seems that the Aeolian Biome reaches to the summit of the earth. Since that time different bacteria have been discovered in the remote interior of Antarctica among the barren gravels of the Beardmore Glacier at about 86° S., a relatively few miles from the South Pole (the few bacterial spores found in the South Pole snow can be considered as non-metabolizing vagrant spores).

It seems to me that if *Geodermatophilus* can live near the summit of Everest they might be able to survive on Mars. I have made some crude calculations concerning available moisture near the summit of Everest and some assumptions concerning the vapor pressure that might occur on Mars which has something like 1/100 the atmospheric pressure on earth. I find that the available water on Mars may not be too far below the level that exists on the summit of Everest. But life does not pay much attention to mean values and usually takes advantage of very special niches where local conditions are more favorable than what may be considered the average place. Thus, under some special rock or in some propitious crevice, living things could find a fortunate existence. Whereas if *Geodermatophilus* could resist the high radiation, the cold, and even somehow acquire enough water, it could not manage without organic nutrients. So if Mars never did have any life on it and there could be no legacy of organic molecules remaining from some distant time, then it would seem that *Geodermatophilus* could be doomed on those sterile surfaces. Perhaps organic materials derived from nonliving sources could be available, but I do not believe such molecules have been detected.

The failure of the Viking Landing Craft to detect life on Mars with its rather random digging in the sand and its pushing of rocks has given the general opinion that Mars is sterile. But it should be considered that if such haphazard searching, albeit fantastic efforts, were attempted on Mt. Everest, they too could yield negative results. Knowing about the capabilities of organisms such as *Geodermatophilus* which are seemingly confined to the incredibly hostile world of the highest peaks or driest land, I still harbor a distant speculation that some equivalent organism could be hiding on Mars. There is, I think, the distant possibility that the Aeolian Biome extends beyond our earthly realm and that this zone of ultimate extremes has found a place for life on the hostile surface of our neighboring planet.

There are some sequelae to this account. Hingston's spiders remained unidentified in the British Museum for many years even though they had received my mature specimens. Finally, F.R. Wanless became curator of the Department where spiders are kept and he gathered together all the collections of high altitude Salticidae. He now found that there appeared to be two species involved. One that had been collected by several other expeditions and favored some of the less extreme altitudes around glaciers was now named *Euophrys everestii*. The other species was obtained from higher altitudes and from the mature specimens I collected he was able to identify those small and ragged juveniles that Hingston had collected so long ago at 22,000 feet. Indeed, I had rediscovered the spiders. Wanless now named this species *Euophrys omnisuperstes*, a Latin species designation that means "highest of all." I wish he had chosen "hingstoni" to honor that intrepid naturalist. As far as I am concerned, they are still "Hingston's spiders."

The strange "glacier fleas" that I had collected among the barren rocks of the Barun Glacier as high as 19,000 feet also proved to be a taxonomic problem. However, P. Wygodzinski of the American Museum of Natural History has compared them with other similar organisms and has described them as a new species. He has been forthright and embarrassingly complimentary for he has named them *Machilanus swani*. I am honored to have my name associated with a most remarkable creature which survives on the ever-changing surface of the glacier, where, when it springs away from capture it often tumbles down into the unknown depths of glacier crevasses. I wonder if these accidents are final or if they somehow manage to climb out of their traps. Animals that live in moving sand dunes are comparable but even they, with all their problems of dealing with a shifting habitat, cannot compare their niche to the insecurities of moving rock and ice. Is there some other insect that has found a more inhospitable place to live?

These "glacier fleas" are representatives of the most primitive group of insects, insects that lived on earth as the first pioneers onto the land. They are closest in their morphology to other Arthropods such as the Crustacea and most like some theoretical first insect. I visualize that they adapted to the land very much as they are now adapting to the last frontier for life on earth today. Textbooks that speculate about the way in which life moved from the ancient oceans on to dry land point out how, back in Silurian times 400 million years ago, that before the land could welcome animals, there had to be plants. Biologists have assumed things like algae and moss emerged from the sea and set the stage for plant eating animals. I see it all quite otherwise. It seems to me, that at a time when the land lay barren and all life was in the water, abundant nutrients from the sea blew out on the land and that the first organisms on land were the creatures that could feed on this marine manna. Fungi, bacteria and organic detritus feeders are the ancestors of insects. These are things very much like *Machilanus*. They were aeolian then and are aeolian now as they seek their food beyond other life, beyond the realm of plants, to find existence on the hostile edge of life, the Himalayan glaciers.

In some ways, perhaps, on those parts of the earth where the Aeolian Biome reigns, there exists a biome type that is analogous to that of the ancient earth when the sterile land was first being conquered by living things (just as aeolian creatures are the first to arrive on sterilized land such as Mt. St. Helens, Paracutin and Surtsey Island). Perhaps the first aeolian organisms on land were bacteria that survived on the accumulations of wind-blown nutrients that blew off the seas during the Cambrian Period when the oceans first accumulated abundant life, followed eventually by crawling animals that could have been the ancestors of insects. Perhaps again, to paraphrase a ringing slogan introduced by Ernst Haeckel in the 19th century, "Ontogeny Recapitulates Phylogeny," pointing out the resemblances between the growing embryo and the evolution of its species through geological time, I could say that "The Aeolian Recapitulates the Cambrian." At least, it would seem, that the Aeolian Region was the original biome type and remains the oldest biome type on the face of the earth.

Goose of the Himalaya

At night there is a quietness in the high mountains. Far into the Himalaya, among the glaciers and the walls of great peaks, a stillness settles, and when the wind is gone and the torrents are frozen, there is no background of singing crickets or airplanes or distant voices. The quiet is different from that of a closed room, for against the stars the dim outlines of crests and ridges show the vastness of the space - and it is all soundless. It is as if the whole world had ceased. One seems to hear the very absence of sound. Then the roar of an avalanche or a rockfall booms across the valley, sudden and brief and then gone, echoing its way down the canyons into silence again.

On one such cold and still night in early April, I stood beside the Barun Glacier. At 16,000 feet, above nearly half of the atmosphere, the stars were brighter; and old, familiar constellations acquired new, small bits of light unseen at lower elevations. Even without a moon the peaks could still be seen, and the great dark cliffs of Makalu rising more than two miles above me to the northeast were outlined by a halo of starry brightness. Mount Everest some miles up the glacier to the northwest, Chamlang to the south-west, and Tutse to the south encircled my spot on the moraine in a dark ring against a lighted sky. I was listening to the silence. And then a sound came, a quiet hum muffled by distance. But this sound had a pitch, an alien quality in a land where sound is generally a clatter or a roar or a hiss. It grew louder, and suddenly I knew. I had heard it before. Coming from the south, the distant hum became a call. Then, as if from the stars above me, I heard the honking of bar-headed geese.

I searched for their outlines in the darkness, hoping to see a spot of light go off and on as their wings passed a star, but they were too far above me. I know that it is possible to locate an object by sound within a very few degrees of its actual position and confident of this ability, I listened and followed them across the sky. Their calls diminished, and finally, somewhere beyond the Barun-Kangshung Divide over Tibet, their sound ceased. I realized then that I had followed their movement directly over the summit of Makalu, 27,824 feet high. Later I learned that climbers had seen geese fly over the summit of Mount Everest, 29,028 feet above sea level, but that night beside the Barun Glacier I felt I had witnessed the most incredible feat of bird flight. At 16,000 feet, where I breathed heavily with every exertion and where talking while walking is seldom successful, I had witnessed birds flying more than two miles above me, where the oxygen tension is incapable of sustaining human life - and they were calling. It was as if they were ignoring the normal rules of physiology and defying the impossibility of respiration at that height by wasting their breath with honking conversation.

Thinking about the wonder of this accomplishment, three questions posed themselves. First, because it seemed so strange from my own high-altitude experience, I wondered why the geese were not silent, thereby conserving oxygen. Second, of all the places to fly across the Himalaya, why should they pick the highest spots to cross? A few miles to the east, the Arun Gorge reaches Tibet at less than 10,000 feet and this passage to the 14,000-foot Plateau would seem much easier to negotiate. Third, why should these geese, which spend the winter months in the warm waters of the Indian plains, fly to Tibet where most of the lakes are barren, salty wastes and where greenery itself is an exception? Why should they make such a seemingly poor choice and in doing so, have to cross the greatest mountain barrier in the world?

I think I may have a few answers: some obvious, others speculative. A study of the migration of the bar-headed goose (*Anser indicus*) provides much information about the history of Central Asia. It touches on the geology of mountains and tells us in rather vivid terms of the changes in the past.

A look at the map of Tibet shows a desert raised up to 14,000 feet or more, where dryness is augmented by bitter cold. The severity of the environment can scarcely be matched. For the most part its hills are barren and its valleys waterless. Nevertheless, Tibet has many lakes and it is these lakes—their positions and shapes—that are perhaps most revealing in the story of the geese. In the west the tributaries of the Indus reach into Tibet, and beyond the present limits of these rivers a series of lakes can be seen. They are generally at the same altitude along a continuous basin, and some of them reveal in their shape a long, sinuous outline as if a river valley had been filled with water. Throughout Tibet lines of connected lakes tell the story of old river valleys that somehow became dammed and separated from the main stream. It is difficult to dam a river. To the south, where the Arun and other rivers cut tremendous gorges right through the Himalaya, it is clear that the stream preceded the mountain uplift. The huge mass of the mountains rising athwart the rivers was not able to dam them. The reason lies in the amount of water carried by the stream. If the river is running full, it generally cuts down just about as fast as the mountains can build and it will not be stopped.

Geologic observations indicate that the old Tibetan rivers flowed eastward from western Tibet, the highest part of the Tibetan Plateau. Today this is a vast deserted land lying mostly above 18,000 feet. The area of the Plateau lying between elevated western Tibet and the modern sources of the Yangtse, Mekong and Salween rivers far to the east, is a land of lakes. The Tsangpo River is the only remnant of the old river system that today flows entirely across Tibet from west to east, but its course has been rudely interrupted and captured by an active tributary of the Brahmaputra River, the Dihang, which has cut its way directly through the Himalaya of Assam. The Tsangpo now flows through a huge gorge into India as the major tributary of the Brahmaputra but, in all likelihood, it was once one of several main tributaries of the Salween. Perhaps the Tsangpo remains as a relic of this old river system because it gets some water from the nearby snow-capped Himalaya, whereas the old tributaries of the Yangtse, Mekong and Salween, farther north, were not able to cut and prevent their occlusion by the uplifted land of Tibet. Without sufficient water, they degenerated into strings of lakes with no outlet to the sea. The sources of the modern rivers now lie far away on the eastern slope of the Tibetan Plateau where some moisture reaches up from China and Southeast Asia. How did the old Tibetan rivers lose most of their water and the fullness of flow that kept them active?

Precipitation in Tibet is generally less than 10 inches per year. The moisture that settles as snow on the highest peaks is a mere wisp of the monsoon. The snowmelt keeps some of the lakes fresh and also supplies the flow to the Tsangpo, which ultimately becomes the great Brahmaputra of India. South of the Himalaya, places like Cherrapunji may get 900 inches of rain annually. In 1861 a world record of 1,041 inches fell on this town in the Khasi Hills of Assam. Rainfall of more than 100 inches is commonplace on the southern slopes of the Himalaya. The monsoon reaches up the valleys and in those few gorges that traverse the range some clouds carry through and reach up to Tibet. Most of the range exceeds 20,000 feet, and little effective moisture crosses this huge barrier directly into Tibet. The dry hills of Tibet are a result of the Himalayan Range, which reaches up through most of the atmosphere and effectively throws a rain shadow across Central Asia. Because the now dead rivers of Tibet did at one time flow, the Himalaya could not have been the barrier they are today.

Recent research reveals the suddenness, in geological time, of the final upthrusts of the Himalaya. The beginnings of the range date back ten to fifteen million years into the early Miocene Epoch, but for most of the time since then, the Himalaya were insignificant and did not materially impede the movement of moist air from the south. It was only in the late Pliocene and early Pleistocene, perhaps two million years ago, that the Tibetan Plateau was uplifted to nearly its present height. This was followed in turn by the final upthrust of the highest Himalayan peaks, which must have risen 10,000 feet or more in the space of a few hundred thousand years. This last spectacular upheaval of the earth was essentially completed less than half a million years ago, and with it the climate of Central Asia must have turned from humid to arid. The rivers that were already cutting their valleys into the elevated land of Tibet ceased. Lakes formed in the river beds and, as with the desert lakes of the American West that were left after the glaciers retreated, they shrank by evaporation, concentrating their supplies of dissolved minerals. The salt lakes began, and to the accompaniment of the cold and warm phases of the Pleistocene, the environment of Tibet became a desert.

Into this picture came the bar-headed goose. When it first arrived in India is only a guess, but as the behavior of most migrating birds suggests, these geese responded to the glacial expansions and retreats of the Pleistocene glaciers, and their presence in Central Asia probably predates the beginnings of glaciation during the Pleistocene. At that time—presumably during the late Pliocene Epoch—it is likely that parts of Tibet had lush green valleys with lakes and streams in summer. The flight between India and the north was a simple adventure—from winter feeding grounds to a congenial breeding summer in the moist valleys of Tibet. Then the earth started to move and the Himalaya reached for the sky. Year after year the birds flew their annual circuit and as the thousands of years went by, the mountains rose beneath them. Higher and higher they drove the geese, which in turn met the challenge. Surely a mountain range reaching that high through the atmosphere into the frigid lower limits of the stratosphere would defeat the flight of birds? No—the birds beat the mountains. Each year they accomplish the incredible: in one majestic flight to the north in March or April and a similar return in September or October, they span the highest ramparts of the earth. Their flight, like a behavioral fossil, tells of a time when the Himalaya were small and the rivers flowed full in Tibet. The geese over Makalu are older than the hills below them.

The challenge of the Himalayan altitudes was accompanied by the forbidding threat to survival posed by the drying up of Tibet. In place of a multitude of wet marches, ponds and streams, the habitats of the geese dwindled to a few hostile valleys. The birds now congregate along the Tsangpo River, and here and there on the freshwater lakes. They are wary and elusive on the northern plains of India where they are hunted throughout the winter. From the few accounts of travelers who have encountered them in Tibet, it seems the geese are crowded and careless of their safety. I have heard that in places they are so tame, they can be clubbed. At any rate, these concentrated flocks among the rocks and arid slopes surrounding unproductive ponds are a far cry from the birds of India. But even this great change has not been enough to destroy them. It may be of significance that until recently the Tibetans were Buddhists, who generally protected life or at least did not wantonly destroy living things. Sven Hedin remarks in his great work *Transhimalaya* that Tibetans considered bar-headed geese to be particularly favored for protection inasmuch as the birds mated for life and the killing of one bird left the other in a state of humanlike remorse. Killing geese, as he learned from the objections of Tibetan hunters, was in a different moral category from killing sheep or pheasants. Perhaps the geese, in their tameness and their protected status in the vicinity of monasteries and religious preserves owe something of their survival to a considerate human population in the past. Whether this situation changes remains to be seen. Recent political and economic instabilities, and the presence of armed Indian and Chinese troops, are not conducive to the survival of edible wildlife. It would be instructive to get information on the population status of the bar-headed goose as it returns each year from Tibet. It seems to be declining. It may be that, after all the victories over mountains and climate and time, the bird will be defeated by man's callousness and its demise related in some way to the demise of Buddhism itself in Tibet.

Next there is the question of why the birds fly over the highest peaks and apparently avoid the several gorges that penetrate the Himalaya at lower altitudes. Perhaps some of them do fly at lower altitudes, but I have not heard them in the gorges. I have heard them far above Darjeeling headed directly toward the great massif of Kangchenjunga, and other reports of their presence coincide with the main mountain barriers along the eastern Himalaya.

The air over India before the monsoon is probably the dustiest in the world. Distant views are out of the question. But as an airplane rises out of the murky air of Bihar or Bengal the form of the Himalaya emerges to the north. From 200 or 300 miles away the great range is not a continuous line but can be seen only as patches of white snow scattered and separated across the northern horizon. These are the great groupings of peaks divided by lower mountains and the deep river trenches of the range. The Kangchenjunga group is discernible in far-off northern Sikkim; nearly 70 miles to the west the Everest-Makalu group stands out, and beyond that, the Rolwaling summits, then the Ganesh Himal, the Annapurna chain, and Dhaulagiri. The human observer sees the highest points, visible at enormous distances from the south. Couldn't this also be the case with the geese? The great Himalayan upthrusts can be identified and located, whereas the gorges and passes would be difficult to find and follow. Furthermore, most flights reach the mountains during the night when flying between the peaks and cliffs could be precarious.

In the matter of safety there is also the consideration of wind. In Spring the Himalayan traveler is sometimes able to see the great peaks displaying long plumes that reach out from the mountains for several miles. These long, steady, banner-like clouds are not typical. They may be likened to the contrails of jet airplanes and are undoubtedly caused by enormous winds. I know of no accurate analysis of this type of cloud. It is obviously not composed of wind-blown snow over its full length of several miles, although in the vicinity of the peak, as the flight over Mount Everest in 1933 demonstrated, there is a violent hail of ice particles. It would appear that on its lee side the sharp summit of a mountain in a high wind produces a sufficient air pressure decrement to initiate condensation, which in turn must freeze into minute ice particles that remain suspended in the air as a long and stable cloud. Typically these banners affect only the highest peaks and from Sandakphu, near Darjeeling, I have seen a trio of plumes extending from Everest, Makalu and Kangchenjunga at the same time. It is possible that these three great peaks, all over 27,000 feet, are high enough so that their summits are occasionally swept by a low jet stream of the stratosphere, with air moving at more than 200 miles per hour. I have seen a plume from fairly close on Makalu. Whereas the air below was still, the summit pyramid was boiling with white spumes of clouds, and down the ridges from the summit, twisting vortices of snow, like miniature tornadoes, gave evidence of the power of the air. Even though the peak was a mile or more away, the whole mountain seemed to moan. The roaring wind on the mountain top covered the valley below with a low, steady sound like the deep tones of an organ.

Consider a bird flying into this maelstrom. Unless it could fly higher than the highest peak, it would be hurled into the mountain. Flying high, it might be driven hundreds of miles out of its course, but it could survive.

Incidentally, as far as I know, no carcasses of bar-headed geese have been found in the high snowfields of the Himalaya. Georges Blond in his book **Great Migrations** writes poetically of graylag geese being driven by the winds into the snow slopes of Mt. Everest, but I cannot find any actual reports of such an event.

There are other geese in India, notably the graylag goose (*Anser anser*) and the white-fronted goose (*A. albifrons*). These, together with a few rare species more typical of other parts of Asia, must also cross parts of Central Asia to get to their summer breeding grounds in Siberia. The graylag goose is known to cross high mountains. Indeed, in order to fly from western Siberia to Kashmir and northwestern India it must cross, depending on its destination, the Tien Shan Range, the Takla Makan Desert, the high barrier of the Kunlun Range, the Tibetan Plateau and the far western Himalaya. Some of these geese must surely fly over the Karakoram and Pamir barriers. There is a report, which I have been unable to authenticate, of an airplane sighting of these geese flying at 26,000 feet

Another report involves a flight of geese over the western Himalaya. The geese, probably either graylag or bar-headed, were seen through a telescope as they passed in front of a full moon. Their altitude was estimated at 29,500 feet, but because it was impossible to use triangulation, the figure is subject to doubt. For the most part, however, the specific routes of these trans-Tibetan migrating geese are not known. Apparently, they do not fly over the eastern Himalaya. The migration patterns of some birds suggest that geese other than the bar-headed goose move first to northwestern India and Kashmir and then cross the mountains to the north.

It seems that many smaller birds follow the routes of river trenches such as the Indus and Sutlej in the west and the Arun and Brahmaputra in the east; however, migrant birds of many species are found deep in the Himalaya making their way across the high passes but staying close to the ground. Wollaston, during the 1921 reconnaissance of Mount Everest, recorded among migrants Temminck's stint (*Calidris temminckii*), pintail snipe (*Gallinago stenura*), house martin (Delichon urbica), Blyth's pipit (*Anthus godlewskii*), Hodgson's pipit (*A. roseatus*), and several other migrants from the plains of India at altitudes above 17,000 feet beside the glaciers on the Tibetan side of the Himalayan Range. He also records a hoopoe (*Upupa epops*) from 21,000 feet flying over the Kharta Glacier. This is a few miles directly north of the Barun Glacier, where at 19,000 feet I met a hoopoe going up while I was coming down. Both of us were walking. In the barren waste of the glacier this bird of the warm plains seemed unreal, and the power of the drive to migrate was dramatically portrayed in its steady gait as it hopped over the boulders and went doggedly on up toward the 20,000-foot pass at the head of the glacier. It must have covered a quarter of a mile while I watched. (Fortunately, Wollaston's observation of a hoopoe in flight dispels the uncomfortable and improbable possibility that this bird walks all the way to Tibet.) There may be more than 30 species of birds that regularly migrate across the high passes of the Himalaya.

The bar-headed goose, the only one known to migrate over the eastern Himalaya and the only goose known from the lakes and rivers of southern Tibet, is accompanied in its high habitats on the Plateau by several other species of Indian-wintering wildfowl. These include ruddy sheldrakes (*Tadorna ferruginea*), common teals (*Anas crecca*), pintails (*A. acuta*), gadwalls (*A. strepera*), wigeon (*A. penelope*), and several other water birds. These birds undoubtedly migrate across the Himalaya, but it is not known whether they fly over the peaks, keep to the passes, or follow the gorges. I have seen teal resting in a small glacial pond at 18,000 feet on the south side of the range, and the pintail has been seen on the Khumbu Glacier at 16,000 feet. This clearly suggests that these birds do not fly directly over the summit of the peaks. Elsewhere in the world, birds flying at 20,000 feet have been seen on radar screens. Perhaps radar studies in the Himalaya would yield information concerning the flights of birds over this highest of mountain barriers.

Lastly there is the question of why the geese keep honking while flying in high, oxygen-deficient air. Unfortunately, most extensive studies on acclimatization and the physiological responses of animals to high altitudes have been conducted almost entirely on mammals. Invertebrates and the lower exothermic vertebrates seem little affected by low pressure and oxygen tensions. To these creatures high mountains are primarily inhospitable because of low temperatures. Endothermic birds and mammals require more oxygen for survival; but it seems the physiological adaptations of birds to high altitudes has been a neglected field. It has been found that birds with a high-altitude habitat have larger hearts, and laboratory pigeons have been shown to increase their red blood cell quantity in response to lower oxygen levels, but most other knowledge seems to be inferred from mammalian physiology. However, the respiratory system of sea-level birds has been studied and something can be said about their ability to breathe. Birds do not have the diaphragm and movable rib cage that allow air to enter the chest cavity of mammals. In fact, their lungs are fixed to the ribs and are scarcely inflatable. They have, instead, a series of air sacs. Air passes through the lungs to these air sacs, then passes back through the lungs to the outside. In flight the powerful movement of the wing muscles creates a pumping device that empties and fills the air sacs and passes the air repeatedly through the lungs. A mammal must breathe with special musculature reserved for respiration, and since it has an in-and-out type of breathing, residual, oxygen-deficient air must remain in the trachea and bronchi. Birds, however, fly and breathe with the same muscles and, since the air passes entirely through their lungs, this organ does not hold a component of residual air. The breathing of a bird is essentially more efficient than that of a mammal. Conceivably, at high altitudes in thin air where flight may require a faster wingbeat, the respiration may accordingly be enhanced.

Mammals such as yaks, pikas, wolves, foxes, and sheep wander above 20,000 feet to an approximate maximum of 21,500 feet in the Himalaya, and acclimatized man with incredible perseverance has reached over 28,000 feet on Mount Everest without the use of oxygen apparatus. The early climbers on Mount Everest who were able to achieve this physiological milestone were visited by scavenging alpine choughs (*Pyrrhocorax graculus*) that wandered regularly up to the 27,000-foot camps, always on the lookout for human waste. These birds, together with the red-billed chough (*P. pyrrhocorax*) and the Tibetan raven (*Corvus corax tibetanus*) are known to follow man and his beasts and any wandering wild mammal wherever they go. The alpine chough was seen by Sir Edmund Hillary on his way to the summit of Mount Everest at 28,000 feet, and I believe it is likely that the little cache of biscuits and candy placed on the summit by Tensing Norkay in May, 1953, was visited by alpine choughs on their patrols in search of human debris.

Lammergeyers (*Gypaetus barbatus*), huge vultures of the Himalaya, have been seen flying at 25,000 feet; an eagle carcass was found on the South Col of Mount Everest at 26,000 feet; a flock of small birds, probably mountain finches, have been seen to fly over this same gap. I have seen a Himalayan griffon vulture (*Gyps himalayensis*) flying at the limit of vision directly above me, a mere speck in the blue sky, while I lay on my back in the sun at 18,000 feet. Through binoculars it seemed unbelievably high, and it flew far above the 22,000-foot peaks of the Rolwaling that surrounded me.

Since it is possible to distinguish a moving man at two miles, I believe the six- to eight-foot bird may have been flying at over 28,000 feet. All these records indicate that birds are more independent of altitude as a limiting factor than are mammals, and that it is their food supply and nesting opportunities that restrict their actual residency at lower altitudes. In this regard, alpine choughs have been seen nesting at 21,500 feet, and I have found the nest and eggs of a snowcock (*Tetraogallus tibetanus*) at nearly 19,000 feet. It should be noted, however, that the bar-headed geese begin their northward flight at nearly sea level and may reach an altitude approaching 30,000 feet in the same day, allowing no time for acclimatization. This it seems would be a challenge to any type of respiratory system. I think it is incredible. Perhaps there are preparatory changes in their hemoglobin and vascular system prior to their flight, but this would seem even more incredible.

The sound-making apparatus of birds is the syrinx, located where the bronchi join the trachea. It does not function exactly like the mammalian larynx. The syrinx is related to the unique respiratory system of birds. The call of some birds in flight may last through several wingbeats and a continuous expiration would be necessary for this to occur. This would presumably interfere with regular breathing. If the sounds of geese were made to synchronize with wingbeats, and this does not seem to be the case, then their calling should not require any alteration of their breathing rhythm or a deficiency in their oxygen supply. It would be similar to a man who merely grunts upon expiration when he breathes. Talking or longer sounds require control of the diaphragm and cessation of the breathing rhythm. Perhaps birds have evolved some method of sound production that does not interfere with breathing rhythm or has little effect upon a regular oxygen supply but, as far as I know, this speculation, which derives from the sound of birds high above Makalu, is unanswered.

Nevertheless, why should geese keep honking while flying in oxygen-deficient air? It has been suggested that they communicate with each other. From older studies and from more recent computerized calculations, the V-shaped formation of flying geese appears to be of some aerodynamic importance: if it is properly positioned, each bird gets some lift from the wingbeats of its neighbors. Conceivably, the calls of geese enable the birds to better appraise the shape of the flight and allow for distinct positions to be maintained. This may be true, but I see another function. My answer is speculative, but nevertheless, intriguing.

It is well known that some birds that live in dark caves, such as the oilbirds (*Steatornis caripensis*) and some swiftlets of the genus *Collocalia*, use echolocation, but the use of sonar by night-migrating birds is apparently unreported. The presence of an echolocating ability in a variety of nocturnal mammals other than bats and tenrecs seems a justifiable assumption inasmuch as it has been demonstrated that man himself, an almost strictly diurnal mammal, can locate relatively small objects by hearing echoes from his voice. The ears of birds, although lacking the three ossicles of the middle ear of mammals, sometimes seem to function as well with a single bone. Most birds are diurnal and would not use echolocation as a substitute for eyes, but many nocturnal birds are also prominent sound-makers. The shrill calls and flight behavior of nighthawks (*Chordeiles*) and related birds, and their ability to catch flying insects in twilight and near-darkness, suggests an echolocating ability reminiscent of bats. This would be a fine subject for research. There are other examples of bird behavior that could be investigated for information concerning echolocation. I am impressed by the clicking sounds made by my pet great horned owl (*Bubo virginianus pacificus*) when it is surprised in darkness. The sound greatly resembles the noises made by echolocating cave birds. These clicking sounds are also made by the night-flying swallow-tailed gull (*Creagrus furcatus*) of the Galapagos Islands. When they are disturbed at night in my aviary, the peculiar hovering flight of orange weaverbirds, or red bishops (*Euplectes orix*), together with a repeated, sharp call that differs from the diurnal call, further suggests echolocation by birds, especially when these strictly diurnal birds return to perches in nearly total darkness. It should be remembered that echoes are characteristic of nearly all sounds. When played backward, tape recorded sounds made in different-sized rooms or out of doors in the presence of trees or walls reveal a preceding echo that is usually ignored when the tape is played normally. The echo is generally interpreted as part of the originating sound and is sensed as a quality of the originating sound. Sound in a large room is clearly distinct from sound in a small room, yet we do not consciously attribute the difference to the echo. The ability to echolocate does not necessarily imply a highly specialized attainment such as that exhibited by bats and oilbirds. If man can echolocate and utilize this talent at night or when sightless, then it is likely that many nocturnal animals may also use some form of orientation derived from sensing echoes.

We know that man rarely flies in silence. Almost all our flying machines make noises. The glider hisses and the hot-air balloon is heated by a roaring and noisy flame; the propeller airplane drones and the jet plane roars. But the helium or hydrogen balloon is quiet, and in the flights of such craft we come closest to the birds. The air is still because the balloon moves with the wind. Far above the ground the pilot can hear dogs barking and people talking; it seems that sound from the surface moves upward aided by an echo from the earth and travels better vertically than it does horizontally. Normally we encounter few experiences that allow us to appreciate this phenomenon. It would seem that sounds made above the earth produce a returning echo, yet I know of no experiments that have been conducted to demonstrate this. It would be interesting to put sound-recording apparatus on high-flying birds, and perhaps some suggestions can come from tests while parachuting or ballooning. Could it not be that the sounds made by birds high in the air echo back to them and give them a perception of their height above the land?

I speculate that the sounds made by high flying geese are a means of determining altitude. At night this sonar over a mountain terrain would readily inform flying birds of a valley or the rising land beneath them. I like to think that the geese calling high above Makalu are getting the signal that the summit of their flight has been reached. They are honking to localize the peaks in the darkness below them, and the increasingly distant echo that they hear coming from the jagged slopes tells them that they have conquered the highest mountains of the world. I should like to know that I am right.[3]

There have been some additions to the information concerning these geese since this article was written in 1970. Notably, a British biochemist, presumably after seeing this account of the birds flying at around 30,000 feet, obtained some bar-headed geese from a zoo and in analyzing their blood found that it contained a unique hemoglobin that allowed the blood to associate with oxygen at very low concentrations. Actually, the molecule of hemoglobin with its sequences of amino acids was altered in such a way as to allow a portion of the hemoglobin molecule to flip into a new shape when oxygen levels became low so that, with this new arrangement, the hemoglobin could associate with the lower level of oxygen in the lungs. It was, it seems, a new discovery of the biochemistry of hemoglobin. Subsequently, investigators in Kansas and elsewhere, also using captive bar-headed geese, found that the cells of their lungs and cells associated with the flight muscles had increased concentrations of mitochondria, the cellular units that accomplish respiration. Indeed, when bar-headed geese were placed in an altitude chamber from which the air was evacuated to correspond with an altitude of 12,000 meters (roughly 40,000 feet) the geese remained standing and ap-

---

3. This chapter reprinted with permission from **Natural History**, December 1970. Copyright the American Museum of Natural History 1970.

peared quite unconcerned with their treatment. Other geese (except for the graylag goose that flies over the Tien Shan, Kuen Lun and far western Himalaya on its route from Siberia to India) and mammals collapsed when far below this incredible altitude. It seems that this article inspired some interesting physiological experiments and points to some recent evolutionary developments among birds that are faced with flying at extreme altitudes because their old migration routes are barred by rapidly rising mountains.

Some of the geographical statements I made in 1970 have matured into new channels. The Tsangpo River, in my newer perspective, did not join the Salween. The history of this river seems to be most unusual for in all likelihood it once flowed westward, a possibility that is suggested by the several large tributaries that approach the main river at what is now an upstream angle. This can happen without a stream reversal but, after my tour of Tibet in 1980, I discovered an empty gorge, a giant wind-gap, connecting the valley of the Tsangpo with a tributary of the Arun River near the town of Lhatze where the Tsangpo now makes its only major bend in hundreds of miles. It would appear that the Tsangpo once flowed into the Arun. When this route was obliterated by rising land, great lakes formed whose remains are now evident near Shigatse and south of Lhasa. Ultimately, it would seem the Dihang portion of the Brahmaputra cut its way back to reach these lakes and started the drainage eastward as it remains today.

Lawrence W. Swan and a string of collected frog samples.

Frogs and Their Friends

Herpetology involves the studies of amphibians and reptiles, it offers some advantages in the study of zoogeography that attempts to analyze why some animals are found where they are. There are two major subdivisions of zoo-geography: (1) ecological zoogeography that helps to explain how animals exist at the present time under the current environment and (2) historical zoogeography that tries to look back in time at past environments and past alignments of the continents to explain why animals are where they are. On ecological grounds alone, one may wonder why elephants are not browsing all over South America for they could surely survive in the Llanos savanna of Venezuela and other places. Ecological zoogeography is not sufficient to explain this absence. On historical grounds it is possible to look back a few million years and point out how the ancestors of elephants, the mastadons and mammoths, spread across Asia and the Americas—and even sent a del-egation down to South America. These once successful elephants died out all over their range during the glacial times of the Pleistocene to leave only two descendant species in Africa and southeast Asia. The real problem is why they disappeared from South America and elsewhere. Were they de-stroyed by mankind or was there some more subtle ecological reason for their extinction? Such is the realm of zoogeography.

Zoogeography is fascinating and challenging because it uses so many disciplines in its efforts of analysis. There is first some standard biology that requires collecting specimens in all parts of the world and the necessary taxonomy that requires their identification. There is, further, some understanding of their behavior and the environments in which they can succeed and prosper. This is primarily ecological zoogeography. To involve historical zoogeography there is first the requirement of understanding paleontology and the study of fossils, both plant and animal fossils. This requires some facility with geology. There follows a need to understand paleoclimatology that gives a clue to ancient ecology. Add to this some knowledge of Plate Techtonics and why, when and how the continents moved into their present configuration. Put these together with various factors that encompass the processes of evolution, add a great dose of geographical knowledge and the subject of zoogeography emerges as a unit that has its roots in all of science. It is no wonder that all sorts of disagreements arise and that conclusions about past distributions are characteristically vague or merely suggestive. There are few "proofs" in zoogeography and the students of this composite area of knowledge have to be satisfied with inferred or speculative data. But in reality, this is the beauty of zoogeography. It has all the earmarks of a discipline that should be rife with arguments and wonderfully different points of view.

Herpetology and the distribution of frogs offer some unique opportunities in the understanding of zoogeography. Unlike mammals and birds that can wander all over the place or fly where they choose, frogs are fairly fixed in their little niches. They require moist environments, rivers, ponds, swamps and so forth. Some have adapted to dry environments by burrowing into the ground and only emerging when rains produce enough puddled water that can last long enough for tadpoles to survive and grow into frogs big enough to burrow into the ground and await the next rain. Some frogs survive in rainforests where there are no ponds by carrying their tadpoles on their backs in little sacs. But such frogs need a lot of rain and forest wetness. And then there is the frog of eastern Australia that swallows its eggs and the tadpoles grow up in the moist environment of the stomach. The mother frog does not eat during this time and subdues its normal digestive enzymes which would otherwise digest the poor little tadpoles. Birth to this unusual frog is to be shot out of the mouth of the mother. Frogs can be wonderful.

Whereas many frogs are associated with the damp areas around large rivers and hence can spread over wide areas, some frogs are restricted to very local regions. This is due to either the current ecological limitations or by some past historical events that have left them isolated or very scattered in their distribution. It is these frogs that are most revealing in zoogeography and it is in mountain areas that these more isolated frogs are most likely to be found. It is the initial phase of zoogeography, collecting and discovering where frogs can be found, that becomes a fascinating enterprise. Collecting frogs in the Himalaya may not sound as irrational as it seems. I am proud to be a frog collector.

After collecting and obtaining specimens, there is the necessary business of taxonomy, the identification of the species. This is not always easy. Some creature that looks a little different from a standard description in the literature may have to be compared with the type of specimen. The first individual discovered is what the description of the species has been made upon. Sometimes this type specimen has to be obtained from the museum where it is kept and the questionable specimen is compared by some herpetologist who is trustworthy enough to receive the valued type specimen. Hence, such taxonomic work is usually done by scientists in a recognized museum and not by some maverick enthusiast. When taxonomy and the identification of the species is completed, there remains the problem of systematics. That is the evaluation of the species as a relative of other species so that its status in some evolutionary framework can be understood. No species is an island unto itself. And when some theoretical systematic arrangement is achieved, there often arises the problem of its zoogeographical status. This becomes interesting if the specimen has been found in some place that is unusual or unanticipated. The fact that it occurs in some location, as determined by its collection, opens speculation about how it got there. In addition, special ecological conditions determining this locality, or what past events allowed for its survival in its unusual place, are evaluated.

All this has been a preamble to help explain and justify the collection of frogs for frogs, with their limited means of distribution, are clues to past environments and their geography can reveal more than most animals. But a collector is not just interested in catching one or two frogs that may be particularly interesting; he or she must aspire to collect almost anything for frogs are not the only determiners of zoological speculation. Insects, spiders, lizards, snakes and plants, as well as the whole gamut of living things by their distribution, can add to the final analysis. Furthermore, collecting is fun and the prospect of catching something of interest is what drives a collector to go where less motivated people would rather stay behind. The ordinary traveler, with a limited knowledge about the identity and significance of a creature in a particular locality, can look at a butterfly, a green-mottled lizard, or lumpy old frog and comment on its artistry, or lack thereof, but seldom can remark with the enthusiasm of a collector about why that creature is where it is. Thus it is the collector who, generally knowing what to expect, flies off his decorum with expletives such as " Holy Karoo!" or simply "Yeeow" at the sight of the unexpected. Ordinary sane people sometimes wonder about this behavior.

※, ※, ※,

It is now time to tell some tales about collecting, mostly frog collecting. It was on a remote hillside in a far corner of Nepal. I had spent the night in my little tent and awoke to find a group of about a dozen Nepalese children peering in at me. I don't know how long they had been there and if they enjoyed my snoring. In far corners of the world there is constant behavior among the denizens to gather in groups to watch or follow the foreign interloper. Some people are casual about this and others act like your presence is some new phenomenon from outer space and they become very persistent and they come close enough to look into your eyes with open mouths as if blue eyes were some awesome peculiarity. They hover. You have no chance to do some of the things you must do in private. But these kids from some local village had some sense of propriety and just looking at their faces that were overwhelmed with curiosity made me like them. My awakening kindled considerable interest for now they could get a full view of that strange man with a light beard and light hair. In this remote part of Nepal I am quite sure that I was the first westerner they had ever seen. I was the object of intense but discreet attention but I made no suggestion that their peering was making me uncomfortable. I didn't want to scare them or make any gestures that they should leave. I knew from previous experience that I could use them. A biologist should know that youngsters will climb trees, wade through rice fields, slosh in the mud and do things that adults prefer to avoid. These kids could be collectors for me.

I moved over to a bush and found a few bugs. I lifted a rock and found a beetle. I pushed through some grass and pretended to collect things and then I faced them with a coin. In mixed Nepali and Hindi I suggested that if they brought me specimens of any sort, they might expect a reward. They finally caught on to my subterfuge and when the notion of money finally overcame their dwindling curiosity, they took off. Their absence gave me time to prepare something to eat and get ready to leave. Shortly, the children came back and they had various things wrapped in leaves or tucked into their clothes while their hands were full of crawling creatures. Two of them had frogs and I seemed particularly pleased with these. After awarding them all with with copper they all took off again with true belief in their eyes. We broke camp and started down a trail but after some minutes some children came rushing after me and they had a supply of slippery frogs. Perhaps I had indicated with my face some strange predilection for frogs. I gave out some more coins. It had been a successful morning.

This had occurred at about 7,000 feet so it was some distance downhill from there to reach the Arun River which roiled its way through the mountains with a roar that could be heard a mile away. Here, in the depths of the Arun Valley we basked in the warmth of the near tropics. We were at about 4,000 feet and somewhere up there in the clouds the peak of Makalu towered to 27,850 feet. This was a master chasm in the earth. It defies comparison. It probably is matched only by that untraversed gorge of the Tsangpo that winds its way in a sharp horseshoe curve around the base of that unknown peak, Namcha Barwa, as it makes its way to Assam,. where it becomes the Brahmaputra.

The forest around us was not a forest of the plains. We were in the Indo-Chinese realm and this came to me suddenly as a giant butterfly, Troides helena, sailed by. This gorgeous yellow and black jewel was known to me as a school boy as the "Burmese Princess" and I knew I was in a land where the fauna and flora stretched its way back along the Himalaya to South China and Taiwan. Many years later I caught this same species in that piece of paradise called Bantimurung near Macassar in the Celebes of Indonesia. It occurred to me that this gorge seemed large enough to accommodate even a bigger river than the mighty Arun. I did not then think that this may have been the route of a giant river that once drained Tibet at a time before the Himalaya had reached its present size. The Arun still drains a large part of southern Tibet and its course clearly exhibits the clues that suggest that its ancestor stream existed before the mountains appeared. It is an antecedent river and the Himalaya were raised under the river and the river kept its course by cutting faster than the mountains could rise. I was in an ancient valley. I was on a meander of a stream that once flowed on gently sloping ground. Geological wonders and physiographical marvels were all around.

The steep slopes beside the river were forested and untouched and scattered touches of pinkish blossoms here and there up the green slope attested to the presence of Bauhinia trees with their bi-lobed leaves that give the genus its name after the twin Bauhin brothers back in the time of Linnaeus. Tuni trees (Cedrela tuna) were here and Terminalia trees (the Saj of the Nepalese) which have been decimated in the Darjeeling area for their wood. Pandanus "pines" grew out of the cliffs where the bare rock was too steep for other vegetation. It all looked like a lower valley in Sikkim, something I had not seen farther to the west and represented, in my estimation, an isolate, a last remnant of the forest that is typical of the eastern Himalaya that extends to Burma and beyond. In a small stream beside the roaring Arun I collected two interesting torrential fish with the handful of derris root poison I had left, *Oreinus richardsoni* and *Nemacheilus rupecola*. These genera are characteristic of the Tibetan Plateau and represent the few kinds of fish that have survived the roaring rapids that separate the Nepalese lowland fish with the fish of the Plateau. And here, there was a freshwater crab that wandered through the forest near the stream. This was all about six miles from the Tibetan border.

After two days in this piece of Nirvana among lianas and butterflies I started up the steep path out of the gorge. I had ascended about 2,000 feet when I suddenly realized that I had forgotten my collecting jacket lying beside the river bank. There was nothing else to do but to go back. I started out jogging down the slope and I finally found my jacket where I had left it. Then I started up again, still jogging uphill on a considerable incline. I was now far behind my Sherpas but that wasn't the reason I kept running. It just seemed to me that I could run like this forever, higher and higher and on and on and not feel exhausted. It seemed to demonstrate to some interior part of my mind that I was remarkably fit, manifestly strong and beyond mere fatigue after some months among the snows and peaks. I was offering myself a dose of self satisfaction. I had noticed that my lower leg muscles were like rock. The gastrocnemius was a solid block of crystalline granite that stepped down to an unconformable stratum of a metamorphosed gneiss soleus that then strung itself out to the iron wire of an Achilles tendon. I actually squeezed and probed this stony mass of my leg and had to remind myself that what I had was living stuff, muscle and fascia covered by skin. It was a worship of flesh, sheer narcissism, but it felt good. I ran on defying the near vertical land to stop me. And then a boy or, perhaps, a young man stepped from the side of the way and stood directly in my path.

I stopped and he came toward me. I noticed he had something wrapped around his neck and over his shoulder like some huge necklace. He started unraveling this thing and holding it in loops as he handed it to me. "Sahb" he said, "Bulwa!" Frogs! There must have been fifty frogs of several species tied to this cord which was actually not a cord at all but a long thin vine. In this land where even empty tin cans are a rarity and containers of any sort are infrequent, how does one collect and hold slippery frogs? Why of course, you take a thin vine, wrap it around the waist of a frog and tie a knot and then take the next frog and do the same and so on. What you end up with is a long line of frogs like an endless necklace of wiggling and squirming things on one long writhing string.

How did he know I was collecting frogs? He waited specifically for me. Apparently I had been described in some detail and he could have only known about my penchant for frogs from the experience of some days earlier when I paid those children some money for their collecting efforts. How did the word get from that distant village, far off the common path? I started to visualize old movies of Africa where the jungle drums beat out messages across the voids "man wearing red shirt pays money for frogs, yes frogs!" This lad had heeded the cryptic message that came across the hills and valleys carried by some wandering tale teller. He had worked for some hours to amass his string of frogs and he was waiting, in all surety and confidence, for his coin. I was as pleased as I was dumbfounded. After all, I was making the first collection of frogs and such things in Eastern Nepal. Actually, I should not sound so sure of that last remark. Sir Joseph Hooker had gone up the Tambur Valley to the east of the Arun sometime around 1850, the only outsider to be so privileged. He was the lucky friend of Brian Houghton Hodgson who, through his associations with the Royal Family of Nepal, was able to get that unique permit. I believe I remember that Hooker had caught a frog or two. Perhaps, I was only the second. It was an honor to believe that over a hundred years separated me from my hero, Hooker, and here I was only the second biologist to have the privilege of studying this land. I would be the first naturalist to cross that great naturalist's path. All this I add to give a sense of the remoteness of the place, how unknown it was in terms of biology. A gift of 50 frogs on a string can add some measure of knowledge to the place. I paid the boy or man rather handsomely, perhaps as much as 20 cents in U.S value for the whole necklace.

On and on we went on our long, wet, monsoon journey back to the plains of India. Finally we came down that last slope nearing Dharan, the end of our long walk. As we came through the outskirts of this town that sits at the base of the Himalaya, I saw that the trees that overhung the path had bright yellow and red ripe mangos hanging down like the tempting fruit of Eden. I could not resist and since they seemed like public property, I climbed up and snagged a few. I peeled the skin and sank my teeth into the luscious stuff and expressed my raptures. My unsatiated tastes for the Indian mangos make our varieties pale in comparison. I sat there in the shade beside the path and drooled the stuff down the front of my shirt. Now, it seems, my American associates who had joined me after my solo explorations, came along the path and became interested. No one should be so irreverently pleased. What could it be that so captured the man? They too would try a sample. I offered advice and nice words to help condition them for, strangely, if you are not raised with mangos, you may consider them just ordinary. If you had never tasted mangos as was the case with some of these western novices, you may need some reassurance that it is the food of heaven.

I demonstrated the best way to eat a mango which is a method in which you dismiss all daintiness and where drippings and smears are essential and where huge and voracious bites are most satisfying. They listened and peeled and bending over forwards they set in their teeth. I did the same and immediately encountered a large black weevil. In a second there were shouts of agony, an overly loud response with a siege of spitting and blowing. One of these fellows even smashed his mango to the ground and looked at me with fiery eyes thinking that I had played a very dirty trick. So there I was still holding my precious mango while these others were acting as if they had just eaten some cockroaches. I myself would have preferred to choose another mango and search its skin a bit to find a less contaminated specimen but the time was ripe for a lesson. I continued eating and found the fruit was riddled with the beetles. I carefully ate around each one and after they were relatively free of the juicy pulp, I put them, one at a time, into my cyanide jar. Those mangos were entirely too delicious to be left to insects. Besides the weevils were of an interesting species. This is just another exhibit of the peculiarities that may develop in collectors.

We walked into Dharan, the bedraggled veterans of five months in the high, high heights. It was tropical here and I reveled in the warm air that was filled with bugs and where birds like the fascinating blue, longtailed magpies flew their sweeps across the road. We were assigned to a Rest House which should in no way be confused with a hotel. I tried to organize the children by showing them tricks of magic and then persuading them to go off and collect things for me. It didn't work. They were of a persistent species. They were much too interested in me and they followed me everywhere, noting everything I did.

I wandered around trying to seem interested in all the affairs of Dharan but my pelvic colon was being very informative about its state. I lasted. It grew dark and now with some quick footwork I evaded my followers and slipped off into the pervading tropical forest that surrounded the place. I had a flashlight but I didn't want to use it for fear my position would be disclosed. I found a hidden spot where my colon told me that all was right. I now had a quiet time to listen to the ringing of the katydids, the buzzing of things in the nearby bushes, the distant chuckling of an unknown night bird and the myriad sounds of the monsoon forest. And then, right beside me as

110

I sat there something moved and, since this was cobra country and where I had earlier seen centipedes a foot long go their incessant way across the forest floor, I turned on my flashlight. And there it was. It seemed to come right up to me as if it was requesting the honor of being saved and deified for all eternity in some museum. It was a frog, a strange and wonderful frog with yellow streaks and a compact form with an appearance and demeanor that informed me quite clearly that it was something special. I caught him while I sat there.

This frog requires a special discourse. Along with my piles of frogs and miscellany that finally ended up in the California Academy of Sciences, I took it back to the frog men of Stanford, Professor George Myers and his student, Alan Leviton. Now taxonomy took over. They looked at it and measured it and hemmed and hawed about it until they realized they didn't know what it was. There followed considerable communication and requests around the world for specimens that could be close to it. They wanted to see these specimens and not just believe the published descriptions. After many comparisons and more measurements and hunting in museum basements they decided it was a new species that belonged to a rather primitive group of ranid frogs just about the first of this group to be found near the Himalaya. Taxonomists have the privilege of naming new species and so the subject of what to name it came up. I made some suggestion about the possibility that the animal's new name could reflect the unusual locale and method of its capture. This was not approved so they did the next best thing, they named it after me. It would be *Rana swani* (now *Tomopterna swani*) and I was and am most pleased.

But that is not all there was to it. There is still the interpretation of its zoogeographical status. The huge genus *Rana* has recently been split up into several genera and one of these new designations is *Tomopterna*, a distinct group that is found in southern India as well as Madagascar and parts of Africa. This distribution immediately elicits the interpretation that these frogs are remnants of that huge extinct continent Gondwanaland and that some of these frogs remained in Madagascar while the rest went off to sea on the moving continental portion of India. When India, in turn, impinged on Asia, there was some understandable mixing of the faunas. Thus zoogeographers play games trying to figure out which groups that now populate India and its environs came from Gondwanaland or Asia or have evolved since the junction of continents. One can understand how those frogs that are adjusted to rivers can spread around quite easily but mountain frogs have more trouble getting around and have to wait for long periods before they can jump from one stream system to the other. Perhaps climates have to change as during the glacial epoch and they are driven downstream until it joins another stream or, perhaps in time, one stream system captures another system.

Now it so happens that the mountains of Peninsular India are completely separate from the mountains of the rest of Asia including the Himalaya and the hills of Assam. The broad Plains of the Ganges Valley or the Brahmaputra Valley have to be crossed to get to these extra-Peninsula mountains. This has prompted some zoogeographers to invent a lost mountain system between the Peninsula and the Himalaya or the Garo-Khasi-Mikir Hills of Assam. This causes geologists to scream for there is no evidence of such a lost range which the eminent zoogeographer Sundar Lal Hora called the Satpura Extension, the Satpura Mountains being a major range of the Peninsula that ends in the Raj Mahal Hills some 200 miles from the nearest Asian mountains. This Satpura Hypothesis of a lost range of hills would explain the multitude of mammals, birds, amphibians, reptiles, fish, insects and plants of Asian origin that have crossed into Peninsular India, a crossing that, in large part, can be explained by the change in climate during the Pleistocene Epoch of glaciers when the Plains of India could have been forested. But that doesn't explain how torrential fishes and frogs (whose tadpoles have sucker discs on their bellies to hold them to rocks) require swift, highly oxygenated, mountain streams and would not survive on even forested Plains. Here is a classic enigma of Zoogeography: the biologists insisting on a nonexistent mountain range and the geologists claiming that it is impossible. Now look with new eyes upon this little frog *Tomopterna swani* that offered itself up to me in such innocence and in such an unusual fashion as if pleading to bring new light on this classical dilemma. Here we have a mountain frog of very limited distribution that has obviously made its way from the Peninsula to the Himalaya. The problem is how? I think it has offered a final contribution to the solution of an enigma. But I can't tell you the whole story. It is just emerging and I have already encountered the wrath of geologists for even suggesting a solution. I can only hint that if you examine a map of India you may see that the Assam Hills that are composed of the same ancient granitic rocks of the basement of India are now about two hundred miles east of the Raj Mahal Hills, the terminus of the Satpura Range. I think the Assam Hills have moved. Such things can happen when continents wander all over the face of the earth. These Hills could have once linked the Satpura with the Himalaya. A little frog told me so. (For more recent information on this interesting topic see "The Satpura Hypothesis: A Biogeographical Challenge to Geology" "*Journal of the Bombay Natural*

History Society," Vol. 90, No.2 August 1993.)

There are more enigmas of distribution that hover around the Himalaya and I shall choose one more that concerns the frogs of the genus *Scutiger*. Scutigers could be called toads for they have fairly lumpy skins but I tend to call all such things frogs and leave the designation of "toad" to the family Bufonidae, the real toads. Scutigers belong to the family Pelobatidae which have vertically slit pupils in their eyes. The first scutigers were found at high altitudes in Sikkim during the last century. After the taxonomists had worked it over it was finally designated *Scutiger sikkimensis* and the one or two specimens laid unmolested in their preservative in the British Museum over the years. But they were not forgotten and although some relatives were captured in Tibet by the early Mt. Everest expeditions and some other species cropped up in western China, the originals had no friends from other places in the Himalaya to join them.

As I set out with my bottles and nets and collecting paraphanalia on the Makalu expedition of 1954, I was accosted by my taxonomist friends, from Stanford, to be sure to capture some scutigers for they stood out like a sore thumb among the Pelobatidae. Thus whenever I crossed a small stream at higher altitudes or saw a small pond down the slope I had to search and dig and scoop and try to find a scutiger of some sort. I turned over rocks by the thousands but no scutigers. It was a humbling experience to return empty handed and face the scorn of the taxonomists. The fact that I had discovered a new species did not seem to alter the tone of their taunting. So it was that on my long journeys across Nepal in 1960 I had an added incentive to find a scutiger that might subdue their jesting jeers.

In my wanderings across Nepal while crossing a pass at about 12,000 feet, I had found a tadpole in a small stream flowing among the Rhododendrons. I immediately had my Sherpas drop their loads and help me find the parents of this embryo. We searched for an hour and couldn't even find another tadpole. I knew that at this altitude that that tadpole could only be a scutiger tadpole. I explained to my Sherpa companions that where there were tadpoles there must surely be frogs but, to my amazement, these men who knew animals quite well did not believe me. Pemba Norbu, a more worldly and traveled person, disagreed with me. "Sahb" he complained, "we do not have these little tailed animals in Sola Khumbu and if we did, they could not become what frogs look like; frogs have legs and they can jump. Sahb, these tailed things are more like fish." Ah! If I could have only given him a lecture on why they looked like fish and how embryos fit certain stages in the evolution of the species. Frogs and all amphibians, reptiles and mammals evolved from fishes and tadpoles owe their fish-like form to their ancestors. Even human embryos acquire gill-like structures, fin-like arms and legs and a heart that could be a fish heart along with many other fish-like attributes that attest to our origins. But human embryos don't swim around like tadpoles.

Although these Sherpas recognized the fish-like quality of tadpoles they seemed to have no knowledge that they grew into frogs. This seems to emphasize the miraculous sort of metamorphosis that occurs when a tadpole emerges from water and replaces its gills with lungs; it changes its diet from organic debris to insects and similarly completely alters its digestive tract. It grows legs, changes its eyes, changes its skin, loses its tail and presumably reconstructs its whole outlook on life to become a totally different thing. It is all so incredible because what it does it does out in the open where we can see it. Other embryos of vertebrates do similar things but they are usually hidden inside an egg shell or in a uterus. It is all so remarkable and yet most school children in this country take it for granted. Real miracles are seldom recognized.

After collecting a tadpole and not finding any adults, I began to wonder what my prodding taxonomists would say. Is a tadpole a frog? Zoogeographically it indicates the presence of a species but what species? Can scutiger species be identified from the tadpoles? No tadpole of a Himalayan scutiger had ever been collected before. I realized whether or not tadpoles are frogs that it behooved me to find a real frog to avoid the caustic derisions of the taxonomists. So my eyes were ever alert but the weeks went by and now as I was leading a group of about 100 Nepalese porters over the passes from Kathmandu to the Mt. Everest area it was far into November and with the coming winter my chances of finding an adult scutiger began to dim.

And then it happened. Between the towns of Those and Junbesi there is a 12,000' pass and as I jumped over a small stream I had to nearly stop in mid-air. There was a movement, a subtle, inconspicuous movement, something that would surely have been overlooked by someone less primed than I was. Something moved under a floating leaf. I had seen a few millimeters of a wagging tail sticking out from under a leaf, a tadpole's tail.

I immediately grabbed my insect net and started making those sounds of excitement that are so necessary on such occasions. Pemba Norbu responded to my noises with bewilderment. I leaped down to the stream to where some ponds had formed and started probing with my insect net and I found them. At first there was one and then another and finally I had a dozen or so. Not only were there tadpoles, there were two sizes of tadpoles, little ones and big ones. It fit! These cold-weather frogs had tadpoles of different sizes because it took them two years to complete their larval life. The larger tadpoles must have been two years old. But most of all there was in my mind the obvious message, there must be some adults around here somewhere. From my last frustrated effort to find frogs I decided that I would stay by that stream and hunt and, if necessary, camp right there for the night until I found those elusive creatures.

I started dismantling the forest floor looking for their hiding places. I dug here and pushed there and scraped in another place and nothing in the way of frogs showed themselves. Finally I started chopping at old and soft logs that lay beside the stream and, as my ice axe went in and I tore away the old wood, I finally pulled away some spongy wood and there it was, a lonely frog deep in the heart of log. It must have crawled in through some crack. I looked at it. It was a scutiger! At last!

I could not risk placing it in a plastic bag to hope to see what it did when it was alive and so, in the tradition of taxonomy, it went into a bottle. Ecology and behavior have to await the prime function of biology, taxonomy and the identification of the species. And then I started in again. There should be some more and, perhaps, a male, for the first specimen was a female. Now my desperate activity increased. Pemba Norbu seeing the frog and perhaps wondering in some part of his mind that, after all, I might actually be correct in the asinine assumption that tadpoles were young frogs, now started to follow me in my project of dismembering the forest floor. Neither of us found anything.

By now the porters were coming down the path in groups and they saw us frantically digging away the land. They asked what I was doing and Pemba Norbu told them what he should have told them. "The Sahb," he said "is searching for frogs." It would be hard to understand the look of vacant emotion on their faces when this answer came to them. I asked if any of them would be interested in helping us but, to a man, they shook their heads and went off down the path. Time and again I gently offered the opportunity to catch a frog and each time they seemed to ignore me. With one passing group of porters I even proffered the possibility of a whole rupee to the man who could find me a frog.

When this was continually refused I realized that there was more to their seeming innocence and refusal to participate than I had imagined. So I asked Pemba Norbu for an opinion about why the porters seemed so obvious in their avoidance. Pemba Norbu at first gave a small chuckle and then started to laugh. He finally sobered sufficiently to say something. "You see

Sahb," he giggled, "among these people of Nepal they know of only one sort of person who collects frogs. He is a sort of strange man, a sort of doctor, and he uses frogs in a strange way." "What way?" "Sahb, these men of strange reputation collect frogs for one purpose. It is said among these people that frogs stimulate men who have trouble sleeping with women. Frogs stimulate sexual desire and people who collect frogs for the doctor are doing so with some risk to their reputations for being strong and virile men." I went on digging for scutigers. They were more important than my dignity. And then, in the heart of another old log, there was a male which, like the female, was all cold and secreted away for its long winter hibernation. This one I did put in a plastic bag to see if it would make sounds or do anything that may give me some insight into its life style. Eventually it did end up in a bottle.

This tale continues now after several months when I had returned to the United States, and at the California Academy of Sciences, I strode in with my precious specimens and handed them to Alan Leviton who had goaded me for so many years. I said something simple like "Here are your blessed scutigers," just to see if his sober demeanor could break into something more than a lifted eyebrow. He did actually smile and make some enthusiastic comment that may have reached the excitement of a phrase such as "I don't believe it." He did actually give up what he was doing with some snakes and reach for some books and then poured out the specimens into a glass bowl. With his fingers probing inside the mouth of a frog, testing its arrangement of teeth, I excused myself for I had to go over to the Entomology Department and talk about several thousand insects that I had delivered earlier. While I was with the insect people I received a phone call and it was Alan in one of his more delightful moods. "Swan," he was shouting, "these things are not scutigers, they're something else! Get back down here!"

I went running. Oh! Not again! What could they be? I knew they were pelobatids and what other pelobatids are cold weather, high altitude species? I was wondering about all this when I got back to the Department of Herpetology and found Leviton with all sorts of books and papers around his desk and the two frogs hovering under a dissecting microscope. "They must be scutigers," I insisted.

"Maybe you're right," he said,"I have found that original description of *Scutiger sikkimensis* and this specimen of yours seems to fit; it seems that you actually do have the same species. But that means that all those Chinese frogs cannot be scutiger frogs. They must be something else."

It was a relief to hear this speculation. I knew I had collected the second specimens of *Scutiger sikkimensis*, the first to be seen in the USA, and with them the only tadpoles of the species. Alan Leviton and George Myers then went on to publish a paper that revised all the Chinese specimens and invented some new genera for them to sit in. The corrected taxonomy opened some new doors for my zoogeographical conjectures. It would appear that these miscellaneous pelobatid frogs that rim the Tibetan Plateau, together with those few similar frogs that still survive in the ponds of Tibet, are remnants of an ancient population of frogs that were once widespread when the area was lower and warmer and wetter. In the dry, new, harsh world of the elevated Plateau of Tibet they have been virtually eliminated and survive in a few aquatic habitats. Others are still found on isolated ranges and high passes where their populations have been cut from contact with each other and they have gone their own evolutionary ways and formed different isolated species and genera. They leave, in their disjunct distribution, the message, written in the obscure language of zoogeography, that the land has changed underneath them and the great mountains have destroyed their continuity. They have adapted as best they can. They are relics of a distant time when the world was different.

Leeches and Lice

There are few creatures that have such a squirming effect on the psyche as these connivers after our blood. Tapeworms, flukes and similar parasites do their dirty work out of sight. Their influence upon our minds seems less apprehensive although their actual effect upon our wellbeing is much greater. Leeches and lice are right out there on the skin where we can watch their avaricious behavior. The sheer shock and anguish of some fastidious novice who first sees the brownish blob of a blood-filled leech hanging from his or her thigh is an exhibit of some primordial human dread for these animals. There are people who deal with ordinary creatures with aplomb, even snakes and cockroaches, but who tremble with fright at a little leech. It is the way in which it works its surreptitious way towards its goal, its slimy inching way, when all the time you think you are above such an invasion of your privacy. It is the same with lice which are less obvious but when discovered, send waves of chills around the body and subtly alter one's outlook about self security. It is hard to tell which is worse, leech or louse.

Leeches are worms but of quite a different group from earthworms. They belong to the Class Hirudinea of the Phylum Annelida and they are equipped with suckers on each end. The front sucker contains the mouth

118

where there are usually three chitinous tooth-like structures that slice into skin and leave a tiny three-rayed mark. They secrete an anticoagulant, hirudin, that resembles the standard heparin derived from animal livers that is used in medicine to prevent the clotting of blood. The various families of leeches can be found in the sea, in freshwater and on land with a few that burrow around in the mud of swamps. Most of them suck blood from vertebrates, mostly fish for the aquatic species of leeches, but anything in the water may be fair game—turtles, frogs and even crocodiles. Some live their lives on fish and avoid having to go searching for a meal, reproducing and raising families in one spot so that they leave patterned sucker-marks on the skin. The famous medicinal leech that has been used throughout history for blood-letting under the spurious notion that some people have too much blood is an aquatic leech and swims by undulations after its normal fish prey. It is still used sometimes in medicine where blood must be removed and there is no easier way to do it. Some aquatic leeches have the nasty habit of lodging in the throat after having been in the drinking water to hang there around the tonsils or even near the larynx and stay there sucking blood for long periods. This was an annoyance to the troops of World War I in the Near East. Leeches that wallow around in mud, such as the giant *Macrobdella valdiviana* of South America, are reported to grow two and one-half feet long. Thankfully, they disdain blood meals since snails and small creatures are their usual prey.

It is the leech of land that attracts my comments for these things (which may stretch out to be only two inches long) are the prime villains. They range over much of Asia and Australasia where there is a moist enough climate, from Japan to northern Australia. Some are also found

Example of common leech.

in South America. I have encountered them in New Guinea and, strangely, Madagascar (not listed as part of the Malagasche fauna), and what I have seen of them in these far spots leaves me convinced that the Himalayan species are a brand apart in terms of their sheer rapacious intent. In the Himalaya they love the wet, brown leaves of the forest floor where they hide in camouflaged patience for the arrival of some juicy animal. There could be several species. A few live at fairly low altitudes below 3,000 feet, but most thrive in the rain-soaked forests and fields chiefly between about 5,000 and

8,000 feet, and as high as about 12,000 feet. They all come with the distinctively apt genus designation, *Haemadipsa*, which is Greek for "blood drinker."

Their behavior is wonderful. They lie in wait in dampish places during the Monsoon and from these cloisters they feel vibrations in the earth made by an approaching animal. They stretch out their front ends and wave the uppermost sucker back and forth. If anything gets near enough they stick on with a gluey persistence that is phenomenal. For instance, if you try to knock them off with a simple flick of the finger, they end up stuck to the flicking finger. That it is the vibrations in the ground that alerts them can be easily demonstrated. In a place where leeches abound, a stamp of the foot will reveal a circle of about eight feet in diameter where dozens of these little stick-like things are waving their suckers high. If you stamp harder, the circle of movement widens.

They have some sense of sight for leeches are equipped with ten tiny eyes behind their front sucker. I believe they have some sense of direction or some ability to sense a body, perhaps by heat or odor, a few feet away. If leeches are removed and thrown some distance away, they will wave around in frustration for a few seconds and then start their head-to-toe "leeching" back toward their potential food supply. I have tested leeches that seemed to sense my presence about ten feet away. It would seem, therefore, that if you were walking, you must nearly step on the animals for them to catch you, but if you sit or stand for a minute or two, they will inch their way toward you from some distance. They are wonderfully quiet, deliberate and sneaky and when they get to your skin, they can cut their way in without your feeling a thing. If they were not so damn obnoxious they would be admirable.

Since I grew up with these blood-suckers of the forest, I do not cringe at their presence like some newcomers to their habits. However, that they are obnoxious remains one of my oldest recollections, but fear and resentment have never really entered the picture. They were just part of the environment. If you hiked in the hills, they were expected and quite normal. In those days of youth my friends and I, as we climbed around the mountains of Sikkim and the Darjeeling District, wore the standard khaki shorts with knee-high black stockings, a garb designed to offer leeches their least resistance. After a long day of hiking and after a fire had been started at our camping site, one of the first rituals we had was to start pulling them off from our bodies, from head to toe, and counting them to see who could set a record. I recall something like 125 on my person. I don't think this number included the many little red holes with a stream of blood coursing down from it where a leech had dropped off before it was collected. But what followed next could approximate our disdain for these little things. Perhaps, it was just schoolboy boisterousness for we would take a small can and heat it in the fire so that it had just the right temperature to fry these little blood-filled, sneaky things. Sometimes they would make a sounding pop when we threw them in and we would all luxuriate in success. And always wafting from the smoking can there was the odor of cooking flesh, human blood, like some ancient cannibal rite. Leeches do not evoke much sympathy. They do reach down and grab at our most callous and malevolent natures.

In the morning there was another sort of ritual. As we got dressed we found that our black stockings, that had filled with blood the previous day, were now as stiff as boards from all the coagulated blood. In trying to flex the stockings and rub them soft again, flaked and dried blood, like a mighty fall of reddish dandruff, descended in a cloud to the floor. It never occurred to us that losing blood is not recommended.

As an adult I have become more sanguine about allowing leeches on my body. My approach has been to afford them as little hope to gain access to my blood as possible but knowing full well that, since they can insert themselves through the lacing eyelets of boots, they could probably defeat any mechanical barriers I could present to them. I therefore contrived to put drawstrings around the cuffs of my trousers that would tighten around my boots. This, I thought, should have deterred some of them and reduced my total blood loss. Alas! The results went far beyond my expectations. Leeches scoffed at such simplicity. They stretched themselves into threads and worked their way under the tie at the ankle as if it never existed and quietly and eagerly explored the blood pastures of my thighs. Here they would feed and gorge themselves and swell into succulent-looking round balls, tense blood-filled spheres, and after their bloating gluttony they would release themselves. But now their fat little bodies could not find a way out. They were too plump to squeeze back through the ankle tie and they accumulated at the bottom of my trousers. When the day's march was over and I sat down to untie my ankle strings there was a great surprise. Dozens of round and tumid leeches poured out and rolled like marbles across the floor.

The Sherpas had experience with these invidious creatures and it became evident that their association had engendered a deep antagonism that bordered on sheer hatred. Various and imaginative ways had been devised to murder the animals. The round ball of a helpless and satiated leech attracted some heinous motivations. The villain leech having done its dirty and quiet work was now ready for the Sherpa's vengeful mayhem. I watched an otherwise gentle Sherpa searching for rocks that were small enough to handle, and flat on one surface. He would take minutes to find just what he wanted. He would then take a particularly bloated leech, a leech so distended that it had stimulated this madness, and put the leech on the flat rock. He would put the other flat rock on top of it and then would start to roll the leech between the stones. The rolling motion increased and the pressure between the stones also increased. There was some facial evidence that the man was straining and yet the leech held. And now as he passed around showing his technique, a small crowd gathered to egg him on. The exertion of the executing Sherpa now was clear. It seemed that at any second the end would come. But the stones kept going round and round. How could a leech stand such pressure and trauma? What incredibly tough skin it must have? Finally, what the crowd was waiting for happened. There was a resounding squish and a splash of blood and a mighty squash. Red color exploded from between the stones and splattered the onlookers and there was a great shout for a job well done that must have been mixed with a sense of relief from the tension. And then someone found another leech he had favored for its round and juicy appearance and asked for an encore. It was primitive and overtly exuding revenge. It seemed to reach into far, unsampled corners of human behavior. There was also sheer and unadulterated glee. And these men were Buddhists who usually have a very benign attitude toward other life. As I have said, leeches don't promote our better attributes.

Another such exhibit of retribution directed toward the leech came one evening when we were all waiting for the cooks to finish their preparations. I saw a Sherpa sitting near a lantern working diligently with something in his fingers. Soon another Sherpa looked at what he was doing and gave out a sound of approval and still another Sherpa came over and added his commendation. This interested me so I went over to see what was happening. And now I witnessed a sort of ultimate in malevolent revenge. This man had impaled a leech through its length with a long sliver of bamboo. Using his fingernails, and another sharp sliver of bamboo as dissecting tools, he had cut through the skin of the animal around its front sucker and, with remarkable precision, had rolled back the skin turning it inside out. Thus he had revealed beneath the skin the pocketed digestive tract in which the animal's meal of blood was distributed in the array of segmental caeca that are like packets along the digestive tube. It was a splendid dissection worthy of a fine zoology laboratory. He finally finished his work and, as if it were some artistic masterpiece, he started around camp exhibiting his skill of refined vengeance.

The enormous abundance of leeches in the Himalaya poses something of an enigma. After all it is rather precarious to have to just wait for something to come by that has blood in it. Furthermore, after a meal, the leech may have to drop off in some rather hostile environment where eggs or young leeches may not prosper. Leeches are not renowned for laying large quantities of eggs for, at least with aquatic forms, the few eggs are laid into a cocoon of sorts that the mother leech leaves behind unattended. The young leeches, when they hatch, survive for a time by eating the nutrients of the cocoon and they have to be big enough when they leave the cocoon to fend for themselves. This is not the way to produce great quantities of offspring. Counteracting this is the fact that a single blood meal may serve the leech for a year or more. The blood meal remains liquid owing to the anticoagulant hirudin and is seemingly unaltered for months within the leech's body. Another contributor to success in the random world of the leech is that it is hermaphroditic, that is, each leech has both ovaries and testes. Mating, however, requires two leeches who each fertilize the other. They can all become mothers.

Within the altitudinal range of the Himalayan leeches there are relatively few likely wild mammals that could serve as prey. Barking deer (muntjacs), monkeys, lesser pandas, various weasel-like mustelids, civets and so forth are not all that common. I have not seen monkeys or deer covered with leeches, at least not in the way cattle can be festooned with them. I rather believe that man and his herds are responsible for the blossoming population of leeches. One might assume that prior to the arrival of people, leeches had to survive on a limited offering of mammals and their numbers exploded with the beginnings of deforestation that accompanied grazing land. Adding to this hypothesis is the apparent absence of any predator or parasite of the leeches. Crows and magpies who seem to eat anything avoid them and I suppose they have learned that such an adhering thing is very hard to dislodge and could even stick to a beak if it tried to be swallowed. And trying to peck them to death and break their tough surfaces, as the episode of the rolling leeches implies, would be difficult. People of the far eastern Himalaya, the Abors, Akas, Daflas and so forth, who eat almost any sort of insect larvae and miscellaneous crumbs of the jungle, do not touch the leech as an item of diet.

In search of possible parasites or diseases of leeches, I have carried these things in plastic containers, feeding them on my own precious blood, and waited for some fly or worm to come out or some spot of fungus or whatever sign to show itself as a nemesis to the leech. Nothing happened.

Their present numbers call out for some moderator of their abundance and, in its absence, I would assume that the population surge has been so recent that no such appropriate predator has evolved into this niche. Large populations of living things are seldom without the presence of some avid creatures that like to eat them. Whenever I run into some historical problem concerning the Himalaya I look to Sir Joseph Hooker's wonderful "Himalayan Journal," to see what he might have experienced during his two-year botanical exploration of Sikkim and the Darjeeling area in 1850 and 1851. That was a time when he describes the great forests around Darjeeling where now there are miles and miles of tea estates. But people had moved into that region long before this, chiefly from Nepal, and agriculture was widespread. Hooker's attitude towards leeches can be judged from the following quote: "Leeches swarmed in incredible profusion in the streams and damp grass, and among the bushes: they got into my hair, hung to my eyelids, and crawled up my legs and down my back. I repeatedly took upwards of a hundred from my legs, where the small ones used to collect in clusters on the instep: the sores which they produced were not healed for five months afterwards, and I retain the scars to the present day." So it seems that leeches were as abundant as ever 140 years ago. (It is clear that some people get infections from leech bites and some do not. I never had any sort of lingering inflammation and no leech bite ever induced me to scratch at it.)

It would seem that whatever checks the population of leeches can center on the vicissitudes of weather and the chancy nature of their lives wherein they must be just in the right place to catch a passing animal. Leeches are found only during the Monsoon from between June and September and so leeches must climb down into moister levels of the soil using their intruding ways.

Periodically, I have collected the leeches from a day's march and preserved them in alcohol. Here they shrivel into shortened hard brown things that offer little resemblance to their original mobile and slimy selves. I have measured these shrunken bodies and they reveal a gradient in size that suggested three minor plateaus or three groupings in their sizes. Perhaps this indicates three stages of growth and perhaps three Monsoon seasons and a leech's lifetime. Curiously, the smallest leeches were less than a centimeter long and perhaps a whole centimeter in life. Nevertheless this is so small that one wonders how anything smaller could chew its way through mammalian skin. But, a centimeter seems too large for a baby leech emerging from a small cocoon. There appears to be a hiatus between cocoon emergence and blood feeding and one wonders what little leeches do for a living during this time. Perhaps, like their distant relatives who squirm around in the muddy soil eating snails and miscellany, the young leeches also spend time groveling among the dead leaves and soil eating insects and whatever they can catch with their front suckers.

Someone has to go off there in the Himalaya and devote some real observations and experiments on these strange animals. There are so many gaps in our knowledge about them. With their abundance and their obvious detriment to cattle where blood pours down a cow's legs over swollen masses of leeches, it would seem that on economic grounds alone much more should be known about their life histories. They do not seem to transmit any diseases, an assumption that arises from the absence of chronic health complaints. Aquatic leeches living in flooded rice fields were once thought to transmit rinderpest, a virus disease of cattle in China and other parts of Asia, but I do not see those accusations nowadays. They must surely have some potential for transmitting diseases, but it should be realized that the many diseases transmitted by insects and other arthropods generally involve a blood sucking apparatus where the parasite injects its saliva or some such fluid that facilitates its sucking of blood. It is in this fluid contribution of the parasite that things like malarial parasites are passed on to the host from the mosquito's salivary glands. Leeches are clean in this way. They produce an anticoagulant, hirudin, but this only affects the emerging blood and keeps the blood within the leech from clotting and making the leech stiff and immobile. Leeches don't really inject anything into our bodies and I suppose that is something good about them. If they were transmitters of some strange disease affecting humanity, there would be leechicides selling for high prices and spraying devices and airplane doses of powders falling from the sky. And still more of the forests would see their wildlife disappear. Leeches could be worse.

It is now time for sucking lice. Lice are common and millions upon millions of people harbor them along with an entourage of other little beasties that favor human skin. This remark draws forth a small digression for did you know that you and I (I know I do) have little mites that live in the oil glands of our noses? When you squeeze your nose, there are tiny blobs of a whitish, fatty secrection that emerge from pores. Here (if you dissolve the fatty stuff in something like benzene, the microscope will reveal their little bodies) you can find these little fellows who usually don't do any harm. What is even more surprising is the way these creatures may be passed on from generation to generation. Look at a mother or father with a little child. Sooner or later they will rub their noses against an infant's little nose in a sign of affection. It is through human parental love that these things have found a way to spread and reproduce, an overlooked feature in the annals of parasitology.

I suppose all mammals carry lice except for whales and porpoises and such things that do not have hair. The lice of seals, sea lions and walruses live and thrive in the tiny airspace between the sleek, waterproof hair and the skin. For months on end when these animals are out at sea, the lice are there breathing in their little layer of air and sucking blood. Their only chance to go from seal to seal is when the hosts emerge onto land and seals and their kin dry off a little and get near enough to each other for lice to find other members of their population. The one hairy mammal that seldom gets out of water is the sea otter which grooms itself of all the marine organisms that might attach themselves but, as an exception among haired mammals, I don't think it has lice and not because there is no air space under its fur but because there would be no opportunity for lice to spread from one animal to another. These sea-going lice belong to their own special family, the Echinophthiriidae, a tongue twister that means, simply, "spiny lice."

There are things called biting lice that live primarily on birds (and a few mammals) that do not suck blood and eat pieces of skin and so forth. These biting lice belong to the Order Mallophaga and are easily separated from the sucking lice of the Order Anoplura. At least that was the case before my professor at Stanford, the late Gordon Ferris, discovered the elephant louse, *Haematomyzus elephantis*, that lives only on the Indian elephant (in little creases and grooves where the skin is thinner). This creature is half way between the biting and sucking lice and unites the two groups suggesting that biting lice have slowly evolved into sucking lice. Some entomologists want to unite the two orders and the elephant louse and lump them into one Order. I prefer the easier route of relegating the elephant louse to the biting lice for it has not acquired the distinct and remarkable stylets of the Anoplura that puncture the skin and draw blood. The ordinary sucking louse has evolved a unique method of acquiring its blood meal and this fact pertains to the tale I wish to tell about Tibetan lice, the Himalayan variety.

But first there must be some more scholarly explanations. Lice are so common. Why should I spend all this time with lice? A full appreciation of an event requires some background knowledge. One person looking down from an airplane at the Mediterranean may spot a small brown island, a brown spot in the blue. Another who has heard about Santorini or Thera, a volcanic caldera that was once a center for Minoan culture (and from which the Minoans escaped the volcano to join the Mycenians and begin the

126

dominance of Greece) would look down and exclaim "There is the origin of Western Civilization!" The major function of education and knowledge is to change brown spots into gems. And so it is with lice. To one person they are a pest and a threat; to another who has studied them they are diamonds of evolution and behavior.

Human lice, which are not unlike the lice of apes, come in two forms, body lice and head lice. There are those who would call them separate sub-species of *Pediculus humanus*. There are more biologists, including myself, who would make them separate species, *Pediculus capitis* for the head lice and *Pediculus corporis* for body lice. There is also the pubic louse, *Phthirius pubis*, a denizen of pubic hair, that is one more of the dozens of venereal attributes of mankind. It has nothing to do with this present deliberation and it does not transmit any diseases worth noting. It is merely an indicator of who was a recent bedfellow. It is the head and body lice as separate species that deserve more comment.

Lice of all mammals ostensibly live their entire lives on the host, unlike things such as fleas that have to grow up as larvae in dusty areas where they feed on organic debris. Newly hatched lice have to go out and feed on blood like the adults. Different species of lice are found on all animals that harbor them and so they are stuck to one kind of host. It would seem that somewhere around 200 million years ago with the first mammals, some original louse form speciated just as its host speciated and as mammals evolved into their diverse forms, so did the lice. Today this history can be inferred from the fact that related mammal species carry related lice. At any rate, human lice have lived with mankind since the inception of the genus *Homo*. They are intrinsic to our lives and history. They are almost part of us.

I have noted that all lice live their entire lives on one host species laying their eggs that are glued to hair. This is not quite right. The one exception among all the lice is the human body louse. It does get off the body of its host periodically because it must find seams and crevices in the host's clothing and that is where it lays its glued eggs. Now think about that. This louse has evolved into a new species that is totally separate in behavior and location from the head louse and it has done so since humanity has worn clothing. That could not be too far in the past. What else has speciated so recently? I think of some species of fish in Lake Lanao in the Philippines that could match this but I feel sure that the body louse is our most recent faunal acquisition. On these grounds it is more than just a common pest.

This prediliction for clothing implies that it is people who wear clothes who have body lice. Hence, people of the warmer climates, the tropics, favor head lice, and body lice are found chiefly among northerners (the chief exception to this are the Arabs who wear robes and such even in hot weather). It is those who wear the most clothing, such as Europeans in winter, that have the most body lice. This was truer throughout history when baths were less frequent and central heating was scarce. There is a story about the Archbishop of Canterbury, Thomas Beckett, who lived in a cold, unheated cathedral and was murdered by King Henry's henchmen. The body lay on the chapel floor for long hours. Armies of lice from his many layers of clothes, feeling their host's temperature decrease, started to leave the corpse and spread out in an ever-widening circle of crawling multitudes in search of warmer environs.

Head lice are transmitted from person to person by direct contact between heads, in one way or another. Body lice get carried from person to person chiefly by the exchange of clothing. When people start changing clothes or picking up stray trousers and coats, the body lice are at their best. It is during times of crisis and starvation when people die and their clothing is acquired by others, especially when it is cold, that body lice have an opportunity to spread around human population. It is at times like this that an individual carrying the rickettsial organism that causes typhus, and does not become ill with the parasite, gives the lice to some susceptible person. With infected lice on the loose the disease of typhus fulminates among refugee populations and kills them in huge numbers. Far more people died of typhus after World War I than were killed by guns. Napoleon's military success depended on his meticulous health care of soldiers. (An example being his acceptance of the English physician Edward Jenner's discovery of a small pox vaccine that made little headway in England but which Napoleon forced on all French soldiers and averted a major scourge in France.) He, nevertheless, failed miserably in the Russian Campaign. This was not so much from the cold, as everyone seems to think, but much more from the terrible wave of typhus that swept through his armies as they tried to acquire warm clothing from dead soldiers. And so it was with Gustavus Adolphus of Sweden, when he was to fight the Prussians for the rule of Europe and called off the war with Prussian agreement, because both armies were sick and dying of typhus. Lice may have controlled human history more than kings and queens and politicians and generals combined. If you don't believe this you should read that classic by Hans Zinsser, *Rat's Lice and History*.

Let us get back to those wonderful mouthparts of lice. All other insects with sucking mouthparts, true bugs, aphids, moths and butterflies and so forth, together with all insects whose mouthparts penetrate skin such as mosquitoes, assassin bugs and the like, have some sort of tube inside the proboscis. They can bore their way into the skin, secrete through their tube some sort of blood conditioning saliva or anticoagulant and then suck up the blood through the tube into their crop. Not so lice. Lice have a special little sac beneath their crop where a pair of stylets are held. Their mouthparts do not protrude as with other insects. They also have tiny teeth on the inside of their mouths which can be everted so that these tiny teeth grab the skin and hold the louse head to the skin. Nothing obvious is injected.

The pair of stylets working back and forth quietly penetrate the skin and blood starts to ooze out. With its mouth fixed to the skin and blood oozing out, the pumping pharynx sucks up the oozing blood. It seems primitive compared to mosquitoes. Without any injections of saliva there should be no immediate sense of itching (that may come later), but how is it that the rickettsial parasite gets into the blood? Apparently by merely infecting the wounded skin and perhaps by rubbing or some later scratching that allows infection from the feces. It is not a refined method and hardly a good step beyond the techniques of their biting lice ancestors. It would appear that the ability to carry the typhus organism is only a recent and accidental acquisition of lice. Where did they pick up this odd method of transmission for rickettsial bacteria? With few exceptions, rickettsiae are transmitted by ticks and mites to cause such things as Rocky Mountain Spotted Fever and Tsutsugamushi fever (scrub typhus). How did lice find rickettsiae or rickettsiae find them? Adding to the concept of newness for this disease (besides the fact that typhus is virulent which is characteristic of a newer disease) is the observation that lice themselves often get sick and die from the rickettsiae. Humans, it seems, by having rickettsial infections, pass them on to the louse. It seems like a dirty trick on the louse.

All this has been preamble. I should say that I acquired lice every so often as a child in Darjeeling playing with the local Sherpa and Nepalese kids. My mother would vent her exasperation on me by bathing my head in some stuff called "pheneel" which I gather from its name must have been some concoction of phenol, carbolic acid. This stuff hurt and just smelling it was enough to persuade a youngster that getting lice was no laughing matter. (I am reminded here of the wigs worn by those such as George Washington. These wigs covered shaved heads. Head lice without hair are at a disadvantage.) But those were head lice which can still be found spreading through children's heads in some of the finest schools of the U.S.A. Body lice have a more sinister reputation and a greater aura of uncleanliness.

Now we can come to Himalayan body lice. The ground of appreciation has been prepared. It happened like this. I was acting as a sort of coolie carrying a load up to a camp on Makalu at about 18,500 feet. Here there were a few tents erected for passing climbers or the Sherpas who carried the heavy loads. I had intended to return to Base Camp so I had not brought anything for a night stay but the weather changed very rapidly with a howling gale and wind-driven snow. I decided I would have to spend the night in one of the tents and hoped the next day would be better. Within the tent there was, fortunately, a sleeping bag, a necessity for survival. However, the sleeping bag just lay there accepting all comers including transient Sherpas. There was no sign on it stating who its last occupants may have been. I crawled in and let the howling wind outside do its utmost.

I have had some experience in tents blown around by gales. Once, in a hurricane while testing an Army mountain tent, I slipped out for a moment and immediately the wind got under the tent and flattened it in a second. My body held the bottom down and without this weight, the tent was defenseless. I learned that leaving a tent in the wind could promote disaster. Now the wind was howling again and the tent walls were flapping with explosion-like sounds and I wasn't about to leave my snug place in the warm sleeping bag. But my warm security was challenged from an angle I had not anticipated. As I lay there in my communal sleeping bag, I realized I was not alone under its sheltering insulation. Without looking I could feel the surreptitious explorations of something along the sensitive skin of my belly. Without looking I realized that I was experiencing another attribute of Sherpa life. Some Sherpas are more populated than others with parasitic species. It was not difficult to realize that I had as guests in the sleeping bag that old and wonderful species *Pediculus corporis*, the body louse. Under these circumstances there is a sudden and powerful motivation to get out and away. The wild wind reminded me that alternatives to staying and meeting my guests were definitely limited. I would have to greet them and perhaps show them around.

It was in fact a biologist's enigma. My cultural aversions were challenged by my biological curiosity. At times like these old visual diagrams of longitudinal sections through a louse's head are drawn out of distant file cabinets in the brain. I have spent nights watching for any perverse behaviors of hyenas. I have followed lions around for days watching to see how they stalk their prey. Such things get seen on television and, therefore, must be worthy observations. What about an encounter between man and a sucking parasite? One could be conditioned to believe this event was a near miracle

130

of evolution. Furthermore these things had come to me, not I to them. They deserved some observation. No one that I know, and perhaps not even Hans Zinsser himself, had ever had such an opportunity to see these little suckers perform their delicate task of invading the skin.. The biologist's part of me won.

I took my flashlight and a lens down inside my sack and explored. Sure enough, there they were, at least four of them. I twisted to get a better look, a more intimate view, a close up as they say in photography, but it is hard to see something closely that does its work in the middle of your belly. My view now was of something that was quite colorful and oddly beautiful. This Tibetan variety of the species was large and gorgeous as far as lice go having a bright yellowish hue with brown spots scattered around. They were quite ornamental compared to the dried or pickled lice that show up in laboratories. They had not had a recent meal for they were flat and had none of the plumpness that comes with ingested blood. They seemed to be adults which left me wondering about where all the babies were. They were obviously hungry and in some obscure lousy emotion were thanking their fates that I had arrived and that I would satisfy their primary desire for food, blood food.

I watched the dextrous way they could move between and on my body hairs using their claws which, like tiny chelicerae, the claws of lobsters, grabbed and released the clasped hair with a coordination and speed that was phenomenal and admirable. Each one of their six legs is equipped with these chelicerate claws and tarsi and, judging from the locomotion of insects as a whole, three legs grasped three hairs and released them for the other three legs to take their three hairs in turn. Ballerinas who have only four limbs to worry about would be jealous. It was obvious that lice have had a long evolutionary time to practice this sort of work.

I watched these much maligned animals as they explored and then I noticed that one of them had decided on a nutritious spot about half way between my navel and my pubic symphysis. Now real courage would be required. Could I sit and watch that thing suck my blood? Certain little tinglings here and there on my back were saying "No! No! It is too much to ask of a biologist! Think of typhus! Think of the itching! Think of your own sweet mother who warned you about lice. What would she say?" But there was still a persistent voice like that which once Samuel heard that kept telling me of opportunity. I knew of no likelihood of typhus. I doubted if lice bites itch to any degree at least not until massive lice infections take over. I doubted that I could feel a thing for the vision of those stylets without sucking tubes made that unlikely. Lice, I thought, were less than mosquitoes in their injury. I tried to persuade my reticent mind that it was all a bafflement derived from the squeamish nature of these strange animals. Furthermore, I knew of no entomologist, biologist, parasitologist or what not who had ever watched a louse feeding. Furthermore, still, if you haven't lived as a professor, you might not realize what you can do to get a good story. The biologist part of my mind won.

I watched this most avid louse with flashlight in my mouth or left hand and with lens in the right hand and I saw its pointed head going up and down as if to test my reaction. Then that snout adhered. I couldn't see how the eversible teeth grabbed my skin, but when they did I couldn't feel a thing.

The fact that lice can do all sorts of things to your skin and you can't feel it requires some speculation. Consider how a tiny ant crawling almost anywhere on your body evokes a sensation. The quanta of energy its tiny legs impart upon the skin must be at a near minimum. What a remarkable sensitivity we have. And yet a louse can insert its stylets through the epidermis with a total absence of feeling. Does it find a spot where it knows there are no sense organs? A mosquito may do the same but then this silly animal inserts some saliva that quickly tells us of the mosquito's presence and we try to swat it. Why should a sucking insect be so foolish. Surely they could evolve some saliva that would not induce the great probability of death. But look at it in another way. Perhaps it is we who have evolved defenses to the insect and have elaborated a most interesting array of delicate sense organs that can respond to the presence of things on our skins for if we were not so equipped, all sorts of things would eat us up. Mosquitoes survive even with their seemingly maladapted behavior through their sheer numbers or by attacking us when we are asleep and when our sensitive network is in abeyance.

It is my contention that animals have been largely designed by insects and many insects have been designed by the mammals they hunt. Few mammals are unable to discourage flies. Horses are so shaped that they can bring their heads around to about where their tails can reach in swiping at flies and on their flanks they have some very special platysmal muscles in their skin which can shake off flies. Their most vulnerable spot is on their backs where head movements and tail flicks are least effective and it is on their backs that bot flies and such things lay their eggs. A horse could not be much longer in the body without some severe insect infestations. The small Thompson's gazelle of East Africa wags its tail over its anal area incessantly scaring away flies, and I have seen these animals late at night when they were presumably asleep still wagging their tails as if they were keeping off flies. It is a wonder why flies haven't evolved to pay no attention to tail waving. And look how flies have responded. Their nerve circuits between eyes, brain and wings are just fast enough to defeat the human hand or an animal's tail aimed at them. Horse flies that are slower to react and which hurt when they bite are designed with a collapsible body so when they are flattened by a horse's tail they remain uninjured and stay persistent. Lice, like leeches, have devised a way of intruding into our skins with such a delicate apparatus that it defies our finest nerve response. All of which is a most admirable exhibit of long association and the wonders of evolution.

To get back to that one avid louse, it was several seconds before I noticed a dark cast appearing over its abdomen. It was getting blood; the stylets had penetrated the epidermis to the blood capillaries of the dermis and I had still not felt anything except perhaps some twingy waves across my back. Slowly its abdomen started to inflate with a purplish-looking substance, my blood. It took its time; I tried to be patient. Actually I tried to wait until it had finished its meal but by now the other three were doing their bobbing act and finding a hold on my skin. Could I wait to have all four of them working at once? No! It was now time for another aspect of a biologist's personality, the desire to collect. I gently rolled over to where my clothes were stuffed into my ever present insect net and I retrieved a vial of alcohol. Gently I picked them up, one at a time and let them drop unceremoniously into oblivion. The wind kept howling. I wondered if there were more where these came from. These thoughts merged into sleep. But now those four were preserved for posterity, for some future pediculologist, to examine and compare. They are honored specimens, the only Tibetan lice the California Academy of Sciences has. I have gone over there in recent years to see them and apologize for my treatment. Most people would not care so much for lice in a bottle, but I appreciate the fact that they have taught me lessons, one of which is that even the most abhorrent things can be fascinating.

Pheasants and Philosophy

One April morning, I was comfortably disposed in the chair that is generally accepted as my personal property. The TV is not too far away. I looked out at the big aviary beyond the line of windows and saw what was beyond belief. It was a lesson of reality that exemplified the fact that nothing in color on the television screen, no images that purport to demonstrate reality, nothing in our technological world of photography and illusions can match actuality. We seem to live in a world where events recorded by camera are the real thing. We fill our brains with the idea that we have witnessed some spectacular event or beautiful scene as if we had actually seen it. That they are mere phantoms and suggestions of truth escapes us. What I did see, in reality, was a male tragopan displaying to its mate.

I have seen movies of this but had never seen the real thing before. The difference is what prompts my comments about the illusory quantity that comes with pictures. For one thing, there is a long anticipation for the event and it has a quantity of one's own personal intent. One is aware of history, of past experiences and efforts. To see something come and go on a screen at the editor's discretion is not reality. It is the filtered feelings of another individual who has to sense timing and the demands of production. But even an

134

unedited hour of tragopan movies is nothing like that short series of displays. It happens so suddenly. This burst of color is like magic. One is prepared by the movies to see some glory but the screen does not portray the waiting before the explosion. One may be awed by the peacock's tail that must surely be one of the finest displays of the animal kingdom. The wonderful spread of the Argus pheasant, or the persistent droop of the white cape on the gloriously colored Lady Amherst pheasant is quite a show as it presents itself to the female. But the suddenness and surprise of a tragopan pheasant and its unbelievable appearance as if from nowhere, in my mind, takes the gold medal for the spectacular.

The female tragopan is a drab brown as are all female pheasants (except for some eared pheasants of Tibet). They nest on the ground and their brownish coloration matches the earth or brown grass where they incubate their eggs. The males are the pretty ones and their main function is to woo the female with as much lustrous grandeur as they can command. Most pheasant males do their impressions with feathers and an outright selection from the rainbow that defies human logic. Look at those small slivers of yellow against an iridescent blue or the touches of red tipping a pale green feather. They seem so unnecessary, so extravagant, so superfluous. But they all seem to add up to what could impress the female and that is where it counts. The male tragopan is awash with colored feathers, mostly red with whitish eyespots along the wings and breast. The red head is masked with black except for a large blue patch of skin that surrounds the eye. It is as radiant as any other pheasant in its normal garb. But what is unbelievable is that when male hormones pull the trigger, it spreads its wings and bends far over toward the female in an effort to show his interest and then he stands erect, much higher than one might suppose him capable of doing and then it happens. From some totally hidden recess along the base of the neck there suddenly emerges a featherless wattle or lappet or, simply, a bib that spreads out over his chest, a flattened air sac of sorts that appears for a few seconds and then is retracted quickly only to appear again in wonder. This bib that extends far down its breast for, perhaps, six or seven inches has unbelievable blue shades and mottlings on it with dashes of brilliant red in columns along the sides. But wait! That isn't all. From the sides of its head, just above its eyes and the blue patch that surrounds them, two horn-like protrusions, once more they are air sacs of some sort, shoot out fully two inches. They are light blue in color and they come out where there is no evident place for them to emerge and they retract again as if to disappear under the head feathers. While all this is going on, the bird raises and lowers its wings in a slow cadence.

It is all so unbelievable. But while I am entranced, the dull female simply walks away as if to be unimpressed. Other females I have known can do this sort of thing very well.

There are some five species of the genus *Tragopan* that range from western China, along the Himalaya and westward into Kashmir. They are exclusively mountain birds of higher altitudes. The one in my aviary is *Tragopan temmincki* that is common to west China and the far eastern Himalaya. T. satyra, which has a little more red on its breast, is the tragopan of Nepal and Sikkim where I have seen the bird high among the rhododendron forests. This distribution leading out of western China, along a high altitude belt of the Himalaya, is duplicated by a group of pheasants that include the blood pheasants (*Ithaginis cruentus* with 13 subspecies), the koklass pheasants (*Pucrasia macrolopha* with 10 subspecies), the monal (pronounced "mon-ahl") pheasants (*Lophophorus* with 3 species). And the cheer pheasant (*Catreaus wallichi*) that is found only in the Himalaya but is related to west Chinese species. This peculiar band of resemblance between high altitude birds of the Himalaya and China exemplifies a zoogeographical entity that Alfred Russel Wallace, who could be called the father of zoogeography, called the Manchurian subregion of the Palearctic Region. It is a band of life that also includes the genus *Rhododendron* and rhododendrons and these pheasants are closely associated.

Now look at some other pheasants of the genus *Lophura*, the kalij pheasant and its relatives and the genus *Polyplectron*, the peacock pheasants. These genera are spread over southeastern Asia, Viet Nam, Thailand, Burma, Malasia and out into some islands of Indonesia and then they move out along the Himalaya but at lower altitudes below the range of the Manchurian species. These birds exemplify the Indo-Chinese fauna of the Oriental Region of Wallace.

Alfred Russel Wallace, after some years exploring the Amazon Basin, was returning back to England from Brazil when his ship caught fire and all his thousands of specimens were destroyed (some had been sent back separately) and he himself was lucky to be rescued after days in a life boat. Undaunted, he raised enough money to go off to the East Indies where he stayed for several years and while experiencing a bout of malarial fever, his many thoughts and observations congealed on an explanation for the variety and resemblances of the plants and animals he studied. He wrote up this thesis and sent it to Charles Darwin who immediately recognized Wallace's explanation as the same one as he had been pondering for many years, the theory of natural selection, that could explain how evolution occurred. So,

136

eventually, Darwin published his *On the Origin of Species* in 1859 and gave credit to Wallace as the co-founder of this idea that has dramatically altered the view we have about the world around us. Most of us today do not refer to natural selection as a Darwin-Wallace explanation of evolution, and it seems that poor Wallace (incidentally at his own insistence) lost out on this touch with immortality. However, it should be noted that the chief inspirations for an explanation of evolution arose in the zoogeographic arena with Darwin's analysis of the finches on the various islands of the Galapagos and Wallace's wonderings about how the butterflies on the various islands of the East Indies differed.

Eventually, back in England, Wallace had to make a living for he was not privately endowed with a bank account like Darwin had and so he started to write books, a host of books. One of these was a two-volume analysis of the distribution of the animals of the world. This had been attempted before, especially with birds of the world. One of these attempts was made by William Sclater in 1857 at a time when bird collections in museums had grown sufficiently so that such an attempt was possible. Sclater divided up the earth into great divisions, South America, Australia and so forth and then had the bad luck to call these big categories "Creations." Since this was only two years before Darwin's *On the Origin of Species* and the concept of evolution, Sclater's bold effort was soon forgotten. It is strange how a conceptual change can so alter our view. The botanist Linnaeus, whose terminology of 1758 we still use and was so significant in the categorization of plants and animals, must have seen how species vary and how related groups occupy related lands. And yet Linnaeus's main intent in his vast efforts to analyze the varieties of life in their many localities was essentially an effort to understand what might have been in the Creator's mind when he created all these things in different places. It was a display of religiosity, an effort to perceive the intents of God. One of the great contributions of Darwin and Wallace was to free all of us from miraculous explanations and look with greater emphasis upon natural processes that can be understood by the human mind and verified by experiment.

Wallace's *The Geographical Distribution of Animals*, that was published in 1876, divided the world up into six major Regions, the Nearctic (North America down onto the Mexican Plateau), Neotropical (Southern Mexico, Central America, the Caribbean and South America), Palearctic (Europe, northern Africa, Siberia, west, central and eastern Asia including Japan), Oriental (south Asia and the East Indies as far as "Wallace's Line" that separates the islands of Bali and Lombok), Australian (from "Wallace's

Line" through Australia, New Zealand and Polynesia) and Ethiopian (Africa south of the Sahara and Madagascar). Various efforts to alter this arrangement have been made but it has stayed on as a core arrangement, and peculiarities and exceptions can best be noted if there is some basic order that stands out for comparison. Each of these major Regions has some subregions and it is the subregions of the Palearctic and Oriental Regions that become involved in Himalayan zoogeography.

The Palearctic has four subregions, namely, the Mediterranean that surrounds the Mediterranean Sea and extends eastward into the drylands of western Asia until it reaches the wetter zones of the Oriental Region in western India. It may extend, in part, far into the dry Plateau of Tibet where there is a strange mix in the fauna that derives from the fairly recent changes of climate that Tibet has experienced. The lizards of Tibet and the wild ass or kiang have obviously expanded onto the dry Plateau from the Caspian area of the dry Mediterranean. On the other hand, an older fauna that once thrived on a more pluvial land before the lifting of the Himalaya still remains on the Plateau in aquatic situations. These are species that resemble Chinese or Manchurian fauna and are exemplified by the scutiger frogs and a water snake, the only snake on the Plateau, *Thermophis (Natrix) baileyii*, that survives in warm springs.

Next among the subregions of the Palearctic is the Siberian, that can barely be separated from the European (west of the Urals) that encompasses the northern part of Asia and extends southward across Tibet (where the Mediterranean or Manchurian is not obvious) to the Himalaya. Then there is the Manchurian subregion already referred to that stretches from Japan across China and into a high altitude band along the Himalaya that may actually touch a far extension of the Mediterranean.

It is curious that some Chinese biologists object to this old classification. They seem intent on thinking there is no more Manchuria, the Manchukuo of the Japanese invaders. Such division should be Chinese or perhaps Sino-Japanese to avoid the political implications associated with Manchuria. My response generally reverts to the stability of historical association and not to current political sensitivities. Must I rename all the species designations that show a "manchuricum" designation? I feel the same way about the Chinese insistence upon using Qomolungma, derived from Chumolungma, an obscure reference among Tibetans to the great snows among which Mt. Everest arises. The fact that the highest mountain on earth was named after a British surveyor seems to grind at nationalistic pride. I myself have a great admiration for the Great Trigonometrical Survey of India and Sir George Everest who started it, the best survey of its time (that was so accurate that much of geology and geography benefited) that originally named Mt. Everest. To casually drop this historical and honored name for some nationalistic fancy does not fit my philosophy. Incidentally, Qomolungma is derived from the new Pinyin spelling of China (Qina) that is to me an abomination and requires relearning all the place names of Tibet that I have venerated since my youth. Its unreasonable pronunciation ("Q" is pronounced "Ch or Ts" for instance) is so assinine that I must steal an example from Galen Rowell's fine book *Mountains of the Middle Kingdom* to point out that "George Washington" in Pinyin is "Zhorz Huaxington."

The Oriental Region has four subregions. The Ceylonese that includes Ceylon and the western portion of the Indian Peninsula; the Indian, the rest of India; the Indo-Chinese which includes southern China, much of southeast Asia and a lower altitude band along the Himalaya and lastly, the Indo-Malayan subregion that commences along the Malay Peninsula and extends to "Wallace's Line."

Thus it is that a crossing of the Himalaya from north to south begins in the Siberian subregion where some plants and animals relate to far off places like Kamchatka and Spitzbergen and then the Manchurian subregion where some animals and plants connect with China and even Japan. Now a crossing is made between two major Regions, the Palearctic and Oriental into the Indo-Chinese subregion and finally, in the river valleys that connect with India, the Indian subregion. In terms of pheasants and related species, there is in Tibet and the highest Himalaya the Siberian snowcock (*Tetraogallus*) with several species in Central Asia. Next there is the monal and the tragopans of the Manchurian subregion followed by the Indochinese kalij pheasant and finally, on the lower slopes, the jungle fowl, *Gallus gallus murghi* ("murghi" means "chicken" in Hindi), the progenitor of poultry, of the Indian subregion.

There is no place on earth where in such a short distance four subregions are encountered and are, furthermore, all separated by altitude. The only comparable locality is along the eastern side of Mexico where one can descend from the slopes of Citlaltepetl (Pico de Orizaba) from the Rocky Mountain subregion of the Nearctic Region into the Mexican subregion of the Neotropical Region. One can pass from ecological zones starting with the Aeolian Biome and snow, down through alpine tundra, conifer forest, and temperate deciduous forest (where corn fields now reign as in Ohio). One can continue through the subtropical forests resembling Louisiana into tropical rainforest, where lianas cover the trees, parrots scream and iridescent Morpho butterflies announce the presence of the Neotropical biota of Vera Cruz. With this knowledge in mind, an observant traveler can place biological observations into sensible categories. It is possible to identify what conforms and understand localities. One can recognize exceptions, because of the proximity of the abutting subregions, that go beyond their designated ranges.

I have used pheasants to illustrate Wallace's zoogeography. The same holds true for the whole gamut of plants and animals. Certain species become indicator species such as that magnificent yellow and black bird-wing butterfly, *Troides helena* (some taxonomist got carried away with the legend of Troy so that this genus now has species such as *agamemnon*, *achilles* and *hector*). The Himalaya harbors Helen of Troy who started all that trouble of ancient times. *T. helena* tells of its heritage across the Indo-Chinese subregion and far into the Indo-Malayan subregion where it graces the distant islands of the East Indies and was one of Wallace's (as well as my own) favorite animals.

Now let us get back to pheasants. It is significant that there are no pheasants that are widespread on the Tibetan Plateau, although one of the eared pheasants *Crossoptilon crossoptilon harmani* reaches out along the Tsangpo River where altitudes are in the vicinity of 11,000 feet. It is notable that this sub-species was first discovered in 1880 when an ornithologist visited Lieutenant Harman, a surveyor of the Great Trigonometrical Survey of India stationed in Darjeeling. On the surveyor's office wall there was a ragged skin of a pheasant that the surveyor had received from one of the trained Indian survey men who had risked their lives by exploring Tibet. The man was probably Nem Sing who was commissioned by Harman to find out if the Tsangpo of Tibet was actually the Brahmaputra River of India. Nem Sing was to put some marked logs into the Tsangpo and Liutenant Harman was to wait and see if they appeared in the Brahmaputra in Assam. Unfortunately, on this dangerous invasion of secluded Tibet, Nem Sing was apprehended, sold into slavery, had to escape several times but nevertheless went on and on down the Tsangpo and did as he had been told. This all took so much time that Lt. Harman gave up and left for England on leave. Nem Sing finally returned and no one knew of his enterprise until Lt. Harman finally returned from England. Someone finally went out and eventually found one of the marked logs stuck in the mud and proved that the Tsangpo was, in fact, the Brahmaputra. Just how Nem Sing managed to get a pheasant skin back to Harman is unrecorded. The vicissitudes of these several early explorers of Tibet would make a remarkable movie.

140

As I have indicated, with the rising up of Tibet about 5 million years ago, and with the last great uplift of the Himalaya in the last million years or so, the environment of Tibet changed drastically and most of the original flora and fauna were eliminated, with some remarkable exceptions such as the aquatic scutigers and the water snake of hot springs. However, some of these original animals and plants may have obtained a refuge on the south face of the Himalaya where wetness remained such as the discontinuous populations of Himalayan scutiger frogs. With this possibility of the Himalaya as a refuge, perhaps some previously widely distributed pheasants of an earlier Tibet remain today along an altitudinal band in the Himalaya. On the other hand, it could be that, with the elevation of the Himalaya, some Chinese pheasants expanded westward across the length of the Himalaya following ecologically compatible altitudinal environments.

Which of these processes now accounts for the distribution of Himalayan pheasants? I don't know. Birds can expand very rapidly across mountain territory and so it is understandable that one species can extend the length of the Himalaya, such as the monal pheasant *Lophophorus impeyanus*. There are three species of tragopans in the Himalaya with a gap between *T. satyrus* and *T. temmincki* and an even wider gap between the western Himalayan koklass pheasant and its near relatives in west China. These are only clues that may suggest that both processes have been working. Both processes seem to have been involved in the distribution of the amphibians and reptiles that are not as rapid in their dispersal as birds.

Here are more observations. The monal pheasant of Nepal, and much of the Himalaya, lives at the highest altitudes and can wander over the tundra grasslands above timberline. The male is the most gorgeous of the pheasants being sheathed with iridescent blue feathers over most of its body. In addition it has a crest of elongated feathers much like that on a peacock. It is impressive enough to have gained acceptance as the national bird of Nepal and appears frequently on Nepalese stamps. Butterflies with iridescent wings are called monals in its honor.

Back in 1954, Bill Dunmire had been making a collection of birds for the University of California and one of his specimens was a monal pheasant. We, the expedition members, ate what was left of it after Bill had stuffed the skin. Inside the crop of this bird was a large packet of rhododendron flowers. The individual flowers, still bright red, were so arranged in the crop that they lay like a pack of cards where each flower perfectly coincided with the others. There was an amazing order as if some careful hand had layered them without any deviation and then had pressed them into a compact, stratified solid. The packet of blossoms was over an inch thick and there must have been about 40 flowers so perfectly lined up. It seemed to indicate that the bird plucked the flowers in a precise way and swallowed each with an amazing uniform regularity. I had never heard that monal pheasants ate rhododendron flowers. No such food is offered to them in aviaries where they are bred in the USA, and none of my friends who culture these birds had known of this particular diet. Some aviculturists think that rhododendron flowers are poisonous. This close association between monals and rhododendrons exemplifies the Manchurian relationship of both the plant and the animal.

Once at about 14,000 feet, I came into camp to find that my stalwart Sherpa, Pemba Norbu, had trapped a monal. It was already stewing for a curry dinner that night. From all the glorious feathers scattered around, I knew what I would be eating. Pheasant makes delicious curry and I was not about to reprimand my faithful Sherpa for his ecological excess. Sherpas have trapped these animals frequently but their inroads on the population could be minor. But as human populations increase and people from farther away who lack food come in to share the Sherpa's normal hunting grounds, one can see the stresses of the future. Add to this the rising population of guns and the ease with which guns can be used as opposed to the ancient method of trapping, and the destiny of pheasants becomes threatened. Since those times of pheasant consumption, the Nepalese Government has tried to institute a National Park around the Mt. Everest area with an education program that includes the elimination of pheasants from the Sherpa diet. I hope it works.

To continue tales of pheasants, I am reminded of a time on a minor trip at lower elevations, but still in the zone of rhododendrons, when I witnessed a technique for trapping pheasants, in this case, the magnificent tragopans. The Satyr Tragopan (*Tragopan satyra*) is a bird of gorgeous red and blue that gives the animal extraordinary splendor as I have described. The Sherpas find openings of sorts in the dense growths of rhododendron shrubs, small glades in an otherwise continuous extent of bushes and trees. Here they place nooses made of strips of bamboo in likely places around the edges of this opening. Now they go nearby and hide and wait for a pair of tragopans to fly in, for these glades are the favorite feeding places of the birds. When everything is just right, the Sherpas emerge from their hiding places and shout and yell. The birds, under these circumstances, do not fly out of the glade but run for cover among the thick brush. And so, sometimes the loops snare them. If they are lucky, the Sherpas may lasso more than one bird.

This was the case one day and that evening, a rainy night with several of us huddling under a tarpaulin, the Sherpas cooked and curried a tragopan. They took the bird with all its incredible plumage and tore off those magnificent feathers which they discarded for it seems that even though Sherpas use just about everything from their animal food, they have no immediate use for feathers. Now the whole animal was simply chopped up with a minimal of intestinal cleaning and they did some of this only when I inquired whether those parts were actually going into the pot. Later, with the barest of light from the smoky fire, we sat down to have our feast. My plate was heaped with an enormous quantity of rice and for those who have never witnessed a Sherpa heaping of this sort, it is always a great surprise. Now all this was topped with curried tragopan. On the summit of my pile was the pièce de resistance that had been placed there in a prominent position by the Sherpa cook. This piece was partially covered with soupy curry so I could not immediately see what it was. I picked it up with my fingers and blew off the obscuring sauce. And there it was. Looking up at me was the eye of the tragopan. I was holding the beak. This is what I was being honored with, the head. It is supposed to be crushed in the mouth so that the juicy brains can best be savored. My hesitation brought on demonstrations from my associates. They went through motions of crunching their teeth down hard and rolling their eyes as if they were making some pantomime in that game of charades. So I practiced a few exaggerated chews and that met their approval but now it was time for the real thing and they were waiting for my effort. Should I or shouldn't I? In that dim light in the rain in that far off hidden place with wild Tibetan eyes peering at me so that they showed the red glimmer of the fire, I had to. I could not act too civilized and so I crushed the skull like a Sherpa.

It wasn't really all that bad but at times like these the relish of flavor takes wings in the face of anguish. It becomes merely something in the mouth that must be manipulated and separated from the bones and swallowed. Brains have little taste to me but I see them in my mind, the neurons, the neuroglia, the tracts and the inflated corpus striatum of a bird. It is strange how food uncovers our deepest and most unreasoning biases and taste incorporates our most irrational prejudices. Perhaps we build these bulwarks that limit our diet and constrain us to narrow viewpoints because, once the mouth has been passed there is the long and unavailable digestive tract that follows. We can do little to assuage that delicate mucous membrane that can so easily erupt into painful peristaltic contractions. Taste, the opinion of food, its visualization all combine effectively with our past and culture to censor what we eat. Crushing the skulls of birds for their nutritive brains is not a matter of logic—it is sheer emotion.

Today, as an aviculturist, with tropical birds flying through wire tubes that range around my beautiful acre in the hills above Redwood City, and where various large aviaries hold some marvelous birds, I have raised tragopans. They are rare and precious. If one is lucky enough to find them, a pair would cost close to $2,000. At the time when I ate one of them they were more or less unavailable in the USA and that bird I sampled on my dish could have brought a price in San Francisco of, perhaps, several thousand dollars. But that was then. Now they demonstrate their hormonal excesses outside my living room windows. And what a difference it is to eat an unspecified bird out of the wilderness and to contemplate the demise of my cock tragopan that comes to me when I call and eats lettuce and seed and dog food from my hand, or to consider that drab female who persistently avoids the male and insists that I have to wait another year to see if there may be eggs, to think of it as potential food. There are things one can learn from captive birds that would be impossible out on the hillsides. I never saw a tragopan display in the wild but now I know what goes on far up the rhododendron covered slopes of the Himalaya and I wonder how they perform their miracle of color when there is no one to see them. I also look into the eye of my tragopan and remember.

A Sampling of Sherpas

Sherpas are Tibetans who moved to Nepal several hundred years ago. Sherpa ("Sher" - East; "pa" - people) refers to their origins in eastern Tibet. They are nominally Buddhists and their culture seems to identify with the Monastery at Thangboche just south of Mt. Everest where their central villages include Namche Bazar, Kunde and Kumjung which, in turn, lie within the part of Nepal called Sola Khumbu. They are a mountain people and their involvement in Himalayan mountaineering stems from the fact that many of them migrated to Darjeeling where most of the early Himalayan expeditions began. The earliest Mount Everest Expeditions did not really differentiate between Tibetan porters, whom they also hired in Darjeeling, and the Sherpas who joined in as part of the porter gangs that carried the loads across Tibet. Tibetans and Sherpas lived together in the section of Darjeeling known as "Bhutia Busti" or "Tibetan Houses." When Nepal became open to western travelers in the late 1940s and early 1950s, the Sherpas became identified with their homeland south of Mt. Everest and were distinguished from their Tibetan brethren. It was Tensing Norkay of Everest fame and his associate Ang Tharkay, who had both been residents of Darjeeling and who accompanied Eric Shipton and H.W.Tilman on their adventures around Nanda Devi,

145

the first Sherpas to emphasize the uniqueness of their homeland in Sola Khumbu. This identity was heralded by the books authored by Shipton and Tilman and thus the Sherpas became associated with mountain climbing. This is an assessment of the origin of their notoriety.

Normally, expeditions to the high peaks, involving many porters, hire lowland Nepalese to carry loads from Kathmandu, or other towns, up to the vicinity of a base camp. Sherpas are then engaged for the high country and the necessary traveling on ice and snow. On our expedition of 1954 we broke with this tradition, and under the leadership of the illustrious Ang Tharkay, Sherpas came down to the Plains to carry loads all the way. This appeared to be good for Sherpa economy. However, it involved Sherpas in lowland travel and, perhaps, they were not entirely used to this environment. One episode may express what I mean.

It was early in the expedition. We had left Dharan and passed Dhankuta and had crossed a tributary of the the Arun River and up a ridge beside this great valley that can be accurately described as the greatest valley on earth. After all, it lies below Makalu on one side which is 27,850 feet and there are some stupendous peaks on the other side while the valley floor between these monsters is a mere 4,000 feet. Such a cleft in the earth is my definition of stupendous. And here, up on a ridge at about 7,000 feet, I shall begin a tale.

Ten sahbs, 150 Sherpas and some 50 Nepalese porters had all poured into an opening in the forest at the end of a long march. Everyone had acquired a choice spot for the night. The Sherpas and the Nepali porters had their groups scattered around and the fires were lit and cooking well along. All was at ease. I noticed, however, while I was off on a brief collecting hike, that there were clouds rolling far to the south and as it darkened, I saw a single flash of lightning. I thought that those ominous things could be headed our way and so I moved my sleeping bag to where I could erect a tarpaulin over my little piece of earth. I went into my bed quite cozy and the stars showed no signs of losing their rule of the sky. I did notice that few, if any, of the multitude around me bothered to make a shelter. I fell asleep.

Much later, in full darkness, I was awakened by a loud clap of thunder and the rain clattered in a surging downpour on my tarpaulin. Shouts and pandemonium reigned all around me. There was much shuffling around for ponchos and anything that might deflect rain. And then I was overwhelmed. Five or six bodies rushed under my canvas and squeezed over my supine postured body. I could tell they were Sherpas, if not from their grunts and epithets then from their normal Sherpa fragrance. It was all so sudden that my sleepy wits were not working quite as well as they should have been. These new bodies now positioned themselves in one way or another under my slight shelter and I was more or less at the bottom of the heap. Some shoes were near my head, part of a torso straddled my lower legs and a head seemingly found my abdomen as a comfortable pillow. There was, of course, a touch of inconvenience in all this but I could not disapprove. The emergency was clear. Furthermore, such a usurpation of my territory would not occur if the Sherpas had any inkling of a notion that I was not their equal and that, by definition, we were friends and should offer our comforts to others. These are not a servile people. They work for you, they help you, they serve you and they would give their lives for you, but they are not servants. And so I tolerated this intrusion and considered it, in my bemused philosophy, to be a ludicrous necessity, something that in the course of time might even appear rather jolly. It was also an overt demonstration of democratic principles.

I dozed periodically during the night to be awakened only when something shoved against my face or some elbow found its mark on my ribs. Light began to show in the east and as dawn touched our wet scene, I could make out the general position of the bodies strewn around and over me. Finally a disheveled head emerged from the piles of rags and called to another mass on the ground while a hand poked another form. Several heads rose around me and only now I realized what had happened. I cannot remember having any clue enter my mind during the night that could have attenuated my surprise. My night guests, the bodies that had swarmed me were all Sherpanis, that is, the female of the species. I had spent the night with six ladies!

After this affair, we took the long path down to Num and the sun came out and we dried out. Num, which shows on some maps, is not a town; it is the location of a bridge that crosses the Arun and where people from miles around must congregate to get across this barrier. The bridge is spectacular, something of vines and bamboos that stretches in an arc fully 200 feet long and ominously high above the water. I have contemplated writing a whole chapter entitled "Bridges I Have Known," but I shall scatter my references about these mysteriously engineered contrivances as they appear among other tales. Nepalese bridges come in all stages in the evolution of technology, reflecting the knowledge about construction of all societies dating back to the stone ages. Some that look secure are in reality the worst traps, for you may not be alert when you see some trappings of modern devices. Some of these bridges come complete with huge iron chain links that seem to make claim to the edge of our century, but they should be viewed with suspicion for they are probably home forged. Look carefully at those monstrous links that may weigh ten pounds each. Some may be cracked and others so parted that only a slight curve in the once oval link holds the adjacent links together.

The cantilevered varieties of bridges seem ingenious. Long tree trunks are arranged over some rock so that a long end protrudes over the stream and the short end is held down by weights of amassed boulders. Pairs of such projecting trees from each side of the river do not meet in the middle. There may be 20 or 30 feet or even more between their outstretched ends. But this hiatus is bridged with poles and bamboo straps hanging from these poles that can be arranged to support smaller poles and sticks which become the walkway. The dread of these contrivances that seem to defy natural laws is that the weight of the center span can, by acting through the enormous levers of the tree trunks, lift and destroy the piles of boulders that weigh the trees on either end. These crucial items of ballast sometimes roll and move just when you are in the center of the contraption.

It is, thus, prudent to walk gently in the middle portion which is, of course, impossible. The rolling sticks of the walkway, and the common gaps in the footing where the river can be seen vividly roaring down below, do not promote an even and discrete pace. And if you do start across, be sure that you first arrange your load-carrying Sherpas to cross one at a time. They seem to trust these delicate wonders as if they were made of reinforced concrete. And do not leave some Sherpa behind you. He may notice your slow and deliberate step and consider that you may need help and come and join you. This altruism can threaten disaster in your mind, for the weight of two of you and the increased shifting of the ballast rocks is not reassuring. But what I say here applies chiefly to the newcomer, the uninitiated to these prodigies of nature and man. After a few hundred crossings and few episodes of actual collapse an inurement supervenes, a sort of resignation, but nothing quite like the indifference shown by the average Sherpa. That is, unless an actual disaster is threatened. Then, there can be an outbreak of all sorts of chanting, gesturing and exaggerated hysteria. Danger, it seems, comes only with complete surprise. Anticipation of danger may just breed cowardice.

To get back to that monstrosity that hung over the Arun. We camped and spent the night before we crossed. The next day, early in the morning, we found that some shepherds had brought at least 200 sheep to the edge of the river. It would seem that if people would have difficulty crossing the bridge on rolling sticks, that lie in hoops of stripped bamboo strung from giant woven bamboo and vine ropes that swung across the river, what would sheep do? I envisaged a mass of wooly bodies falling into the water. But that was not to be. The inventive shepherds laid down mats of woven bamboo and tied them high on the sides of the bridge so that there was a continuous U-shaped passage across and they led their flock over to the other side without losing a single animal. As quickly as they removed their mats we were ready to cross, all two hundred of us carrying our precious supplies.

We had to carefully control the crossing with no more than about three people on the bridge at one time. During my own crossing I noticed a strange but perfectly natural physical phenomenon. The bridge, like a violin string, had harmonics, that is, certain positions on its length coincided with the bridge's natural vibration periods. When standing on one of these nodes, a slight motion of the body set up waves along the length of the bridge, and, when another individual reached such a place, the waves would set you moving and increase the sense of peril that you already had to some considerable quantity. One may envisage this phenomenon occurring on a violin string but what the violinist does not appreciate and which some physics texts tend to overlook is that, in contrast to the string, the cord which you are actually on (rather than theorizing about) has up and down movements, side to side motions, and twisting actions, the last of which is casually referred to as torque, or rotation tendency around an axis.

According to my brief readings on this subject, there are empathetic vibrations with harmonics that occur in all three dimensions of this movement, and all the nodes for each of these harmonics do not arrive in the same place. Thus, this V-shaped passage of two long fibrous ropes of different lengths stretched across the river, tied loosely together, and supported by a treadway of poles lying on strips of bamboo hanging from the ropes, was not some theoretical violin string.

At one place the bridge's vertical momentum was augmented, then in another it swayed and in places the worst happened — the slight torque became a terrifying roll. The best thing to do was to travel as rapidly as possible so that if you passed a more violent spot quickly you would not add to the complex movements of the whole structure. It was important not to be on the bridge when some terrified individual stuck to one spot and, just by responding to the movements upon his body, set the whole thing to rock and roll even worse.

We all got across without incident but as I neared the far shore, there on the bank, hanging limply down the slope, like the dead and withered bones of a giant serpent, was the remains of a previous bridge, an insidious reminder of the pitfalls of homemade engineering. I was told that its demise came some weeks earlier when a wedding party of celebrants carried their test of the bridge's strength too far. I was told that some of the unfortunates were still unaccounted for.

From Num we climbed up forested paths, up into groves of oaks and laurels with patches of color from the pink and white blossoms of magnolias and then, a little higher, hillsides of rhododendrons and fir. This was unspoiled country unscathed by axes and human intrusion. Eventually we encountered snow. We kept climbing thinking that the disappearing path would go somewhere but it left us in the trackless snow and we were lost. We camped in a glade. The whole expedition of 200 or more relatively sane people were completely lost and not even a local shepherd could help us with directions in the deep snow. These mountain men were too wise to go this way in March. Our lowland Nepalese porters were not dressed for this weather and we understood their eagerness to return. We piled up their 50 loads and decided that some of us would have to return to carry them on to base camp.

The weather remained overcast and sullen. We thought we might be above the great gorge of the Barum River that led down from the glaciers of Makalu but we couldn't see down into it or any distance in any direction. We were the first outsiders into this part of the world and we had no previous intelligence about the route into the Barun Valley. Our maps were crude and ambiguous for this area. It was now time for our eager mountaineers, accompanied by Sherpas, to win their spurs—they would have to go off in three directions to see if there was a way out.

Bill Long and Willi Unsoeld set off up the ridge to see if that would lead us out of our trap. Bruce Meyer and Fritz Lippmann tried to traverse the steep slope of the gorge and Al Steck and Bill Dunmire decided to go straight down the near precipice to the bottom of the gorge to see if there was a route along the bottom. Dick Houston, Will Siri, Nello Pace and I held the lost fort.

The first two teams returned after many hours and reported near impossibilities for a route that would have to allow 150 Sherpa porters a passage. Later, the last team dragged themselves up from the bottom of the gorge and reported a dim hope. The bottom of the valley, where the river should normally be a formidable barrier, was now completely covered with snow that had avalanched from the steep sides of the gorge. We could walk on this mass of snow and ice that completely covered the river. The problem might be that additional avalanches might come just when we didn't want them. Our messengers also reported that they had gone far enough up the valley to note that at one place the gorge closed to almost a cleft and here the hard cover of snow over the river ceased and the roaring river emerged. It shot out from under the snow beyond the cleft, churned and foamed and roared for a spell, then squeezed its fury back under the mantle of snow. This perilous section could, they thought, be crossed if we could construct some small bridges of bamboo upon the overhanging cliff and place some fixed ropes along a route they had examined from a distance. The route, they pointed out after some worried inquiries, did indeed overhang that nasty strip of wild river and, yes, anything that might fall would be immediately carried away in the gray and spuming water and be lost forever under the snow covering.

But this route was all we had and we knew nothing of the vicissitudes that might greet us on the far side of that threatening cleft. The next morning we set out almost straight down the wall of the gorge. It was difficult going and I wondered how Bill and Al had managed to get back to our camp the day before. We finally emerged onto the valley bottom and I found that Al Steck had lived up to his reputation for "understatement." I found, also, that if you were not careful and did not remember you were walking over piled snow that held a violent river beneath its unpredictable surface, you could find a quick way to disappear from the earth by falling through an innocent hole. And some of these holes were made by rocks that had fallen from far above on the wall of the gorge.

And then came the view of the cleft with that monstrous precipice that overhung the grayish green torrent of foam and spray. My first thought suggested that someone was crazy to think that one person, much less 150 people, could make the passage. But I underestimated the lineage of climbers who could scale Yosemite's walls and who seemed to thrive on exposed routes. And I should never have underestimated the agility and perseverance of Sherpas, even heavily loaded Sherpas. Very shortly, small sections of impossibility were being bridged by strands of bamboo wrapped together and tied by ingenious means to the rock wall. Then came a series of pitons driven into cracks that would hold a fixed rope and then, perilously, climbers went out and shored up or added rope to parts of this incredible route until, in places, it looked as if giant spiders with their webs had taken over. The Americans and our experienced climbing Sherpas now positioned themselves along the way. I was assigned my spot. And so all was ready and we could all help the Sherpas with their loads as they traversed the worst parts of this absurd journey. Slowly the procession of laden porters inched their way across. It seemed to work.

Then there was a cry just ahead of where I was holding to the cliff. There were frantic voices. It was obvious that some disaster had occurred. Carefully I slipped the rope that bound me to the rock and moved ahead and peered around the buttress that obscured my view. The scene was unbelievable. There was a Sherpa some feet below the route hanging in desperation from some twigs of bamboo. His feet dangled over the abyss and all I could see below him was that frothing gray storm of the river. He was in terror. And now I witnessed the impossible. A Sherpa held the hand of his neighbor and on that narrow ledge, he somehow gathered the support of others on his arm and a leg and, with the epitome of courage, he let his body swing over the edge, farther and farther, until he touched and then grasped the fallen man's wrist. How they all managed to pull and heave and thrust that man back up onto the route is beyond my belief and my ability to describe. But my doubts that it was all impossible once again faced an underestimation of Sherpa ingenuity and resourcefulness. The poor man slowly regained some composure and was soon helped along the way to safety. However, he had lost his load. It had hurtled into the river and was instantly swallowed into the fury of the maelstrom below.

The crossing took most of the day and it was getting dark when the last of the loads finally made it to the other side. We ate a big meal and enjoyed the feeling of success and then it was Ang Tharkay's turn. Ang Tharkay was our sirdar, the leader and absolute monarch of the march, the dictator of all the Sherpas and lord over all the porters. His word was law. Ang Tharkay deserved his position. As a young man he had accompanied the great pioneers of Himalayan exploration, H. W. Tilman and Eric Shipton and accompanied a young Tensing Norgay with these men. No Sherpa had acquired such a reputation as his except, recently, within the year, his friend Tensing Norgay, who had climbed Everest with Hillary. Tensing had passed him in world recognition but among Sherpas Ang Tharkay was still the exalted one. We had been among the fortunate expeditions to obtain his services and it was he who had arranged for 150 Sherpas to come all the way down to the plains to pick up our loads. In this way, Sherpas, themselves, could be paid for the long journey into the mountains. It was a first and Ang Tharkay did not want it to be the last. As I have said, it was all very good for the Sherpa economy.

Now, Ang Tharkay, in front of all the expedition, called for the man who had fallen. The confrontation was center stage. Any thought that Ang Tharkay might be gentle or even subtle or consoling was instantly dispelled. He merely pointed at the man and said the equivalent of "You!" The wretched man fell to his knees and bowed his head as if to permit it to be cut off. And it nearly was. There followed a torrent of words from the sirdar and sufficient gestures to easily indicate the power of his words. The tirade finally ended and the poor victim was devastated in tears. The main words were "You! You are a Sherpa! You lost your load! Sherpas do not lose their loads! You are no longer a member of this party! Go home!"

I wondered how this unfortunate man could go home. Where would he go from where we were? Back over the precipice? I think Ang Tharkay's compromise, involving a touch of necessary compassion, allowed the outcast to follow the expedition at some distance and to join the others when they delivered their loads to base camp and headed home over the high passes to Sola Khumbu.

Late into that night at our camp, deep within the vertical walls of the gorge, we searched through all of our loads trying to account for each one. Finally, one number failed to be scratched out. We looked at our list to see what the lost load contained and found, to our dismay, that all our base camp candy was in that box that had been swallowed by the churning river. No candy in a land where sweet things to eat are a driving craving!

During the next few days the river valley widened and soon we reached a level where the firs and rhododendrons swept down to the river banks. We were in what looked like Sherpa country and happiness reigned. That evening there was a big dance around the fire. I now quote something that I wrote at that time. "Here one of the Sherpas was married in a riotous ceremony to one of the Sherpanis. The affair was carried out in true Tibetan style with swastikas in rice, the bride being chased (not chaste) all over the place, and butter rubbed in the hair. The evening was spent in singing Tibetan songs to the accompaniment of a shuffling dance performed by the singers, including various sahibs. Tibetan dances, fortunately, have frequent pauses that are obviously designed for deep breathing at high altitudes."

The scene now changes to a time when we were about to leave the base camp at Makalu. The word had spread across the passes that we needed some porters for the journey out of the mountains. Sherpas from their home villages of Khumjung and Kunde now started to appear having traversed three passes of 20,000 feet. They now came into basecamp in straggling groups. Some had been with us before and others were new. One of the first to arrive was Dorje, a Tibetan refugee now living with the Sherpas. He was witnessing his first view of Western Civilization and even our remote and unsubstantial representation of a civilization was completely baffling to him.

He would keep looking at me and touch my things in a gentle unobtrusive way and he smiled a lot. I liked him. I therefore suggested that instead of waiting for the others and enough porters to arrive from across the passes that I would go on alone with Pemba Norbu, one of our climbing Sherpas, and Dorje who could carry my load and supplies. I needed more time for collecting and the monsoon was soon to be upon us.

The three of us set out down the valley and we searched out a new route that would take us far from that frightening route through the gorge where the Barun River spumed its gray anger. We climbed out of the Barun Valley by way of a ridge that seemed to get higher and higher and sharper and sharper. We were well on our way and more or less balancing along the summit of a knife-like crest at about 14,000 feet when it started to blow and rain. We were in a storm that came out of the valleys to the south and hit us where we were on the most southern of the high ranges, the first high obstruction to the monsoon. We had to lean against the power of the air but as we did so we were flirting with disaster and the prospect of sliding down the sharp and endless slopes that plunged down on each side of us and disappeared into the whirling white mists.

On and on we went but there seemed to be no end to either the rain or the precarious ridge. There was no likely place to camp. We tried to descend on one occasion to find a less exposed position but there was no easy way along the side of the ridge. We went on and on and soon I realized we were going beyond our capacity waiting for some broader spot that would offer a place for a camp. I became soaked through to the skin. My jacket was more appropriate for snow than this accursed, persistent, near freezing rain. I got colder and colder and now each movement that brought some cold garment against my skin set me shivering. I was trying to walk on that ragged edge of the ridge and my body started to shake with a shivering that convulsed me so much that I almost fell. I knew it was time to stop. We must make camp. I must recover heat. It must be done now! The emergency seemed only too clear when I saw Dorje, similarly soaked as I was, and Pemba Norbu both shaking in the cold. When Tibetans and Sherpas shiver, it is cold.

In the raging wind I pointed down the slope hidden in the cloud. I made Pemba Norbu understand that we had to go down and find anything that would hold our bodies. We could not stay on this whipped ridge. He agreed and we started down partly sliding on the rock and low plants and then in the mist we finally found a small flat spot. It was covered with a display of primulas waving in the wind. We set down our packs and with wet and stiff hands pulled out our tents. I could hardly move and neither could Dorje. It was Pemba Norbu who still had an iota of warmth and he recognized that he was a touch better off than we were. He was in his own misery but he automatically gave his first interest to me. "Sahb, give me your tent! Sahb, I put it! Sahb, I do it! Sahb, I get sleeping bag! Sahb, I roll it! Sahb, get in quick!"

I climbed into my tent at the limit of my endurance. My shaking was so extreme, I could not coordinate my movements. I could not loosen my boots. But finally, I had my wet things in a pile and in that cold my nakedness was a relief. At least there was not that freezing water in my clothes that sapped my heat. I tried to rub myself dry but that was only a gesture. I shook my way into my sleeping bag. It was mostly dry. I shivered until I was tired and my muscles did not seem to work. But I felt the distant edge of some accumulating heat. I sensed that, given time, I would get warmer. Life would return.

And now the rain was crashing over my tent. It was not a continuous downpour and therefore not a solid roar. No, this stuff came in waves like the spray off curling ocean swells -roar-roar-roar. I could hear the waves of rain hitting the rocks around my tent first before they struck me. I felt I was in some sort of atmospheric quirk where the air formed in undulations that carried pockets of intense rain. I thought I had witnessed the monsoon in every shape it could thrust at me but this was something new, for here I was at nearly 14,000 feet where the air is supposed to hold less moisture and where the rain should have been attenuated by its losses at lower altitudes on warmer slopes. The mighty monsoon, it seems, defies ordinary meteorology and usurps a great slice of the world's air and carries its load of water higher and higher, much higher than an ordinary gale.

I lay amazed. And then the sounds of Pemba Norbu and Dorje came to me. I could tell they had erected their tarpaulin and they were under shelter. Pemba Norbu had also saved Dorje's life. And now, was I correct? Did I hear a fire crackle between the roars of rain? Did that Sherpa go out and find some shreds of juniper? How could he start a fire in this wall of water? Incredible! I hoped that its warmth would heat up my friends for I was sure that Dorje, at least, did not have the protection of a sleeping bag.

I waited for life to return. And then my tent opened and Pemba Norbu, in the rain, was handing me a mug. "Soup!" is all he said. Oh my Lord! Soup! Hot Soup! I had waves of wonder interspersed with overwhelming surges of gratitude. Sherpa! Sherpa, you are more than life, more than mankind and more than the angels!

I started to doze off with a sense of infinite appreciation in one of those moments when all the frailties of humanity are forgotten and the quality of the lives of people takes one's mind and makes it insist that life and living is the greatest gift any universe can offer. And then, softly through the waves of rain I heard the tones of a deep chant. Pemba Norbu was sounding his reverence. I could not hear the syllables for they drummed too low but when he raised his pitch I could make out the holy "mani, mani" before the droning continued. Then Dorje added his bass and tremulous tones "Om, Om, Om, Om mani peme hum!" This was the Himalaya! I went to sleep.

Some days later, down in a warm valley, I was awakened with loud shouts. Pemba Norbu was screaming at Dorje. I hurried out to see what the problem could be for I did not relish having my companions end their argument with blows and hatred. I saw Pemba Norbu was pointing his finger at Dorje and the latter stood somewhat cowed and apologetic. "What happened?" I asked in Hindi.

Pemba Norbu turned to me with an expression of disgust on his face. "This miserable Tibetan," he said, "this untrained dog, this thief, felt hungry during the night and without asking me, without thinking of any one else, he ate our whole pound of butter." "Our whole pound of butter? You mean he just ate it?" I asked. "Yes, Sahb. The man has no feeling for others. We will have no butter for cooking, for eating, for bread, for anything!" "He likes butter plain and straight?" "Yes, Sahb, he has eaten it during the night. He should be hit on the head." What was I to do? Reprimand Dorje? Assuage Pemba Norbu? Actually, I had to leave quite rapidly and when I got out of their sight, I had to laugh. Poor Dorje, this man who had been extracted from Tibet, presumably, had been craving butter, one of the delicacies of his Plateau, and now he had given in and turned pig. My course was to let the whole thing slide but not to let Pemba Norbu think I didn't care. I include this minor episode as just a sample of the subtle decisions that always had to be made during this and other journeys in the Himalaya.

The scene now changes again to an occasion where I was taking 100 porters from Kathmandu to the base at Mt. Everest along with my Sherpa knights. We had camped at a fairly high altitude on a pass that led down to the Dudh Kosi, the river that drains the Everest area and along which our path would travel for several days. The Nepalese porters in their light clothing and sheets were huddled around the fires just after sunset and I had turned into my sleeping bag for warmth while I wrote up my notes for the day. It was then that the Sherpas started mumbling and making noises of wonder. I slipped out to see what was happening and found Old Bloody and Nu Phutar pointing up into the starlit sky. A bright spot had caught their eye, a very bright star was coursing through the heavens, slowly and evenly, but its speed among the other stars was obvious. This thing moved inexorably across the sky from near the south to near the north and it was like nothing they had ever seen before.

Pemba Norbu now began to explain to these naive nomads about the wonders of the western world. He told them that there are great machines that fly in the air, the "oorujahaz," the ships of the air, that can take people and fly them over the tops of the highest mountains. He told them that if they went to Kathmandu they could see some of these machines on the ground. I had to correct him now for this moving light in the sky was no airplane. But how was I going to explain a satellite? This extra-bright man-made satellite was the recently launched ECHO satellite. Its brightness came not only from its covering of reflective foil but also from the high altitude from which we were observing it.

My explanation went something like this. This strange light was a device that had been made by the "Amricans" and it had been shot up into the sky very high and far, so high and far that it would not fall and would keep circling the earth. All this was met with completely disbelieving faces partly, I assume, from my rather crude Hindi mixed with Nepali words that surfaced in my mind as they seemed appropriate. I therefore started the impossible sequence of logical arguments greatly emphasized by gestures that I hoped would clarify my obscure point to men who only now had heard that the world was round. How could I, in gentle conversation, high on a pass in the Himalaya and surrounded by men of the 8th or 9th century, explain about Isaac Newton? So, to put some measure of association between the satellite and their own experience, I pointed out something that they knew very well, that down in the valleys the air is thick and easy to breathe while up here and higher, the air is thin and hard to breathe. Yes, they followed that and even conceived how, on the top of Mt. Everest, the air was so thin that air must be breathed from a tank. I went on from this toward the inconceivable, that much higher than Mt. Everest there is so little air that there is really no air at all. There were now some grunts of wonder but not disbelief so apparently the idea had reached them.

Now I went on to tell them that airplanes need air to fly and that is why they have wings. They sail in the air like birds or like leaves that flutter slowly to the ground. Air is something, it is not nothing. So, with the satellite far above the air it is not flying or sailing; it is shooting so fast that it stays up and does not fall. Oh how I was reaching! Now there were some groans and indications of disbelief. A question arose as to what kind of gun could be so powerful and I did not want to get trapped in rocketry. I just described a very big gun that blew with much fire and pushed the satellite

157

faster and faster. But the question did seem to offer the possibility that they were still with me and had some understanding. The problem, I tried to explain, was getting the machine up above the earth and its air and then turning it and pushing it at great speed. Far above the earth the pull of the earth would still act upon it and it would start to fall, but as it fell the earth was not there for it to fall onto. Now I was getting some real sounds of disbelief and I realized I had gone too far.

A voice from the darkened periphery around our fire now asked, "Sahb, how is it they keep the fire going in the "Amrican's" star?" It came from one of the Nepalese porters who had gathered around to hear about what they had seen.

Ah, I thought, he had used the word "star" and there was a connotation that he had some realization that it was indeed like a star. "There is no fire," I tried to explain, "It is only the light of the sun. Have you not seen the light on the top of Mt.Everest and the high peaks long after the sun has set upon your villages? So it is with this star. It is so high, so much higher than Mt. Everest, that even now when all of us are in darkness, it still catches the sun and is made bright by it. It does not have fire."

I realized all this was getting too vague and beyond their understanding, and this clue came when they started asking each other for explanations of what I had said. It was now Old Bloody's turn. He had heard everything I said and seemed to take it all in with aplomb. He would now show his authority and acumen to some of the Nepalese porters who were willing to listen. In coarse Nepali and much arm waving and vehemence he was repeating what I had said as it had filtered through his own understanding. Finally after this impromptu lecture one of the Nepalese porters shook his head as if he understood and he spoke the crucial words that seemed to negate the need for additional questions and any further obscure answers. He simply said, "Ah! Amrican jadu!" It was a final and satisfying realization. He had said "Ah! American magic!"

This, of course, was the best explanation to fit their experience, an explanation that transcended technology and all of its complexities. Was it not true that the great teacher who brought Buddhism to Tibet sailed high in the sky and spent some time on the top of Mt.Everest meditating? Such was the magic of great thoughts. And did not the demons, if they wished, sail high in the sky and pretend to be stars? And now the "Amricans"have learned these ways that we have known about all along and they too are trying to make stars. Why not?

But if this sounds like some inference of primitiveness of the logic of ninth century hillmen, I should point out that this medieval recourse to magical explanations is not confined to distant uneducated tribesmen. Such understandings pervade our own so-called educated civilization. I noticed one time how the man next to me in an airplane that was circling in a fog waiting for a chance to land reached into his pocket and brought out a rabbit's foot that he held and rubbed gently. This is a sample of our magic and such equivalent behaviors, sometimes obvious and sometimes more obscure, that fill our lives with occult explanations. "Amrican jadu" is all around us.

A sequel to this affair with the satellite occurred a few days later. We had finally arrived at Kunde, Pemba Norbu's home village, and the great occasion was for me to meet his wife, Urkein. She turned out to be a buxom young woman, like any other of the Sherpa women, who do all the work in the fields, who cook, look after the children, and weave the clothing. She greeted me by putting a kata around my neck, one of those thin cheesecloth-like scarves. As she did so, she noted my camera in its leather case that was also hanging around my neck. She now held the leather case and fondled it and followed the stitching with her finger on this very ordinary leather item. And then she looked up at me with real wonder in her face and said "Sahb, your wife in Amrica does very, very fine sewing. It is enough to sew so regularly and straight on cloth but to sew on leather with such care and correctness is most wonderful!"

Of course, the camera case was machine sewn, a phenomenon we take so much for granted that it is seldom we notice the quality of stitching done by some unknown machine in something as common as a camera case. The woman, however, saw something she could associate with, her own efforts to sew with detail and care and with a sense of quality. And so, here on a camera case made of leather, a known material, she gave technology a compliment of understanding. Well-sewn leather would seem far more significant to her than the technological wonders of the space age. And so it is with most of us. If it were not so we would be absolutely awed by car engines, typewriters, refrigerators and airplanes. Computers, space travel, remote sensing, and the arrangement of genes on the human genome, the things that may awe us now, will also pass away into those voids of the ordinary. We can never be satisfied; ephemeral appreciation for the real is the sign of the times.

Another of the episodes with Sherpas, which could go on and on, occurred when I was leaving Kunde in the heart of Sherpa country to try the long route back to Darjeeling. Some Sherpas have taken this route but I could find none of them among the acquaintances of Pemba Norbu, a Sherpa from Kunde, who was my chief Sherpa companion on many trips through the mountains. I was assured at that time no westerner had ever made the trip and so it would be an interesting exploration. We gathered at Pemba Norbu's house and spent the night. Sherpa houses are generally two-storied affairs where the first floor harbors the animals, sheep, goats and yaks, and all the hay. A ladder leads to a second floor where the walls are lined with huge copper pots that function both for cooking and decoration. In one corner of this large room is a cooking hearth made of clay and around which social affairs take place. I slept beside the hearth in the honored place while the others rolled up in blankets in various arrangements around the room. When night fell the only light was from an open flame from a wick dipped in yak butter. In this darkened environment we sat around and talked and told tales. The Sherpas had to explain much to me and so this story telling time lasted until the wee hours.

On all of the occasions that I have spent in the homes of Sherpas, there seemed to be this ritual gathering together after sundown and the evening meal, to sit and tell stories. I am not a sociologist and I do not know much of that literature so I cannot assess the significance of what I report now. I was impressed then as I am now of the role played by adequate lighting in the lives of people. In the Sherpa post-meal darkness there are only two options for activity, story telling and coitus or both. Better lamps would radically alter Sherpa culture. If they could see during those hours of darkness, these intelligent and industrious people would surely find a wider range for their talents. It is surprising that there is very little in the way of carvings, weavings, paintings and other works of art that are available for sale in Sherpa villages. Such things may be made for themselves or for the monastery but it is a labor of necessity. There is very little craft work that arises from sheer pleasure, or hobby.

How different it is in Switzerland where the winter evenings in rural houses are so given to woodcarving and the making of intricate objects. The Swiss, it seems, make good lamps and the Sherpas do not. The resultant difference in creativity between the two cultures becomes more apparent. Furthermore, without good lights, the incentive for reading or learning to read is diminished. And so it seems that this little step in technology could have vast consequences. As it stands, however, they are remarkably good at what they do after dark.

In the morning of our departure a little ceremony took place. Urkein and another female, who had presumably spent the night among the scattered bodies on the floor, decided to honor me. Each of them took a kata, a thin scarf, and placed it around my neck and now Urkein reached far behind her hearth to a small wood cabinet and brought out a ceramic jar. Inside this jar was a messy substance that I eventually recognized as cheese, but cheese that must have defied the texts of microbiology for it was colored with greens and blues and yellows and specks of brown. It dripped a fluid that resembled a watery pus and it smelled rather cheesily gangrenous too. It was, I gathered from Urkein's gentle handling of this substance, something of value as if this moldy stuff was some sort of treasure. I got the impression that the cheese was almost an heirloom passed down by generations. Its appearance justified the suspicion.

I was first handed a small glass that had a Victorian quality about it and also seemed to be valued family property. Into this glass was poured some very special rakshi, the distilled product of various Sherpa alcoholic beverages. This too had a very penetrating odor, like raw turpentine with a touch of some other organic volatile substance that resembled a faint whiff of a barnyard. And now the intriging part began, something that could be mimicked by some fancy hotel or bar or any celebration of formality that required distinction on the menu. I stood with two katas around my neck and was handed the glass of rakshi. Urkein opened the jar of cheese and stuck in her thumb. It came out with a lump of dripping cheese that had just sufficient solidity to hold itself together and then the thumb, that was far from immaculate, rubbed the cheese onto the far rim of my glass. It stood there as if ready to crawl away and it seemed to do just that. It oozed down the side of the glass, partly outside and partly into the rakshi where it spread on the surface like an invading amoeba.

Now my hosts were gesturing for me to drink so I put the glass to my lips and then I saw the meaning of it all. The glass had just the right diameter. When I put one side of the rim to my lips and tipped the glass, the other rim, the rim infested with cheese, came right up to where they wanted it, my nose and nostrils. What an infernally sensuous device this was! All the taste of an alien rakshi with its assorted aromas were now challenged by the proximity of an overpowering attack of olfaction, the cheese, which was also about to add some gustatory wonders of its own as it fairly writhed on the surface of the rakshi. How incredibly sagacious! A drink that should bring both varied tastes as well as increasingly vivid odors.

I drank this composite concoction in little testing sips and tried to control the mimetic muscles of my face so that they would send a message of curiosity rather than distaste for, after all, they were staring at me and appraising my response. I held my poise for I saturated my mind with the prospect of selling this idea, to be sure some sort of tempered idea, to someone like Trader Vic to add to his exotica in food and drink. A drink like this needs a distinctive name that matches its ingenuity and so I still search for a suitable appelation inasmuch as I have rejected the option of "Sherpa Slime."

After this ceremony, with much waving and hugging among the assembled villagers, we started off on the long and unknown path to Darjeeling. Our first days were down the gorge of the Dudh Kosi and then we started up the long slope over the divide that separates the Dudh Kosi from the Inukhu Khola. This rise is from about 6,000 feet to over 12,000 feet and the path zigs and zags its way up in endless repetition. This accordion of a road became the stage for an interesting drama.

We had hardly started up when one of my new knights looked far up the slope and saw some tiny spots far above us. Some people were coming down. A few zigs and zags later one of the Sherpas looked up again and now, when we were a bit closer, suggested that the party coming down and who were still mere specks far away, were some Nepalese porters bringing oranges into the Sola Khumbu area. Something about their loads suggested this. Now there was some mumbling about whether we should buy oranges and for how much. Some more zig zags later, one of the Sherpas called up, a sort of wavering long "Haloo," and on the edge of hearing there came a distant answering sound. Still later, one of the Sherpas called out a word "Suntalla?" The still distant answer came quietly down the hill, "Suntalla." That confirmed our suspicions that these were men carrying oranges.

As our zig zags continued up and theirs came down, our approach was hastened. Soon we were within distance for loud shouted sentences and the inquiries and exchanges began which became more detailed and extended as the distance permitting understanding became less and less. It went something like this: Sherpa: "To Sola Khumbu?" Nepalese orange carrier: "Yes." "Namche has oranges." "Not these." "It is a long way." "We have come six days already." "Maybe we can lighten your loads."

"You must pay." "We shall pay if it is cheap enough." "You will pay what we ask."

"How much are your cheapest oranges?" "We have no cheap oranges." "How much are your oranges?"

There was now a pause before this crucial answer could be given and a couple of zig zags filled in the gap of time. Then the answer came from far above. "One rupee, thirty two." "You say thirty-two for one rupee? That is two for one anna. You are thieves!" "That is what we will get in Namche."

"Nonsense! We have just come from there. There are plenty of oranges in Namche and cheaper. You will not sell anything at that price."

We were now approaching each other and the faces of the Nepalese porters could be seen along with their full baskets of bright oranges. It was now Lhakpa Diring who did most of the talking. "We will give you one anna for four oranges." "No, we can do better in Namche." "We will save you some weight." "We can carry our loads."

And now we turned the sharp corner of a zig and found our Nepalese contestants directly in our path. Both parties now lowered their loads and started their haggling on a more personal level, the Sherpas squeezing the fruit and pointing out how it did not compare with the usual fruit of Namche while the Nepalese poured out praise for their product. Finally Lhakpa Diring offered a compromise.

"What say you to three oranges for one anna? That is forty-eight for one rupee. That is as much as we can offer. Now it is your turn." The Nepalese would not be bluffed. "We will get thirty-two for one rupee in Namche, why should we lose money on you?" "You came to sell oranges, why don't you sell them?" "We sell in Namche."

I saw the Sherpas were losing and though I had a few oranges in my pack, I could see the advantage of having more. I was about to offer their price but then I realized I would be intruding into their game. If I paid their price we would lose and, of course, the game was more important than the oranges. So I let it stand while the Sherpas picked up their loads and the Nepalese did likewise. And now we were off with the Nepalese going down and ever farther away while we continued up the slope. Now the conversations changed completely. The Sherpas doubted that they would ever see these men again so that the insulted individuals would not have to be faced personally. Lhakpa Diring started this new conversational mood.

"You are fools! Wait till you see what happens in Namche." The answer came without a pause."We will see some stupid Sherpas who will pay anything."

There was a long pause now as if the Sherpas wanted to wash off the offending words. Then, as if to change the subject and offer one last weak position of agreement, a Sherpa called to the Nepalese who were now reaching the limit of conversational shouting. "Once more! Forty oranges, one rupee." This was sheer asininity for no one was going to go down the slope for a few oranges. But it was all part of the game.

The faint answer came up the valley breeze. "We will see your women in your houses!" Now there was another long pause and zigs and zags went by. Lhakpa Diring was fuming. Finally he put down his load and stood on the edge of the path overlooking the vast valley where now, once again, the Nepalese porters were mere specks far below. He took a deep breath and cupped his mouth with his hands and bellowed at the extreme of his considerable voice. It was one long and drawn out "Jaaa-taah!" It echoed through the hills. We all burst out laughing. It was a fit ending. "Jantah" with a nasal "n" is a significant term of insult and it fit this occasion very well and it gave the needed relief to Lhakpa Diring. It can be loosely translated as "You pubic hair!"

Those Crazy Climbers

Mountain climbers are a special breed. They come from all walks of life. I am not sure if there isn't some compelling instinct, not only among humans, but also among all terrestrial mammals, to climb up high to see what there is to see from mountaintops.

Ernest Hemingway remarked about the leopard carcass that lay on top of what is now the Leopard Point at 18,000 feet on Kilimanjaro where the African hunting dogs have been seen wandering around the crater at 19,000 feet. What compelled these creatures to climb? H.W. Tilman in his wonderful book. *Snow on the Equator* tells of a Cape buffalo skeleton among the rocks at 15,000 feet on Mount Kenya and I have noted the carcass of a coati mundi in the crater of Citlaltepetl (Pico de Orizaba) in Mexico at 17,800 feet. They presumably fell to their deaths on their own obscure expeditions.

To go farther afield, butterflies sometimes are caught by a slope and keep flying upwards and, if the slope ends in a relatively pointed top, keep flying in circles over the summit. Sometimes dozens of butterflies can be seen hovering in this way over a relatively sharp peak. Why can't they judge the precarious nature of this attraction for the heights? Why can't some people do the same? Various flies that have wide distributions use mountaintops as meeting places. Such flies ascend a slope and when it comes to an end at a summit, they wait for others of their species to join them. Thus, over a wide area, males and females are drawn to each other by the slope of the land and can find each other where the slopes end at the top. So it seems that mountaintops can even have sexual motivations attached to them. I have not witnessed this among human climbers, however, but I would not hazard an opinion to suggest that it could not happen. People, especially males and females who unknowingly meet on mountaintops, can sometimes, so I have heard, be very friendly.

Judging that climbing itself may be innate or genetically distributed among people, I can suggest a test for this. Some people choose window seats in an airplane and some do not. It may be as simple as this. Some people look down at the ground and some do not. When the pilot announces an altitude resembling the summit of Mount Everest, do they search the scene below? The whole view is enormous and wide geographical features come into sight. It is like a map that is not a diagram but a piece of reality. If one is unacquainted with maps, the scene is a blur and uninteresting. If one is a geographer of sorts, the scene is fascinating. Rivers meander just where they are supposed to meander. Lakes, such as Michigan, are shaped as they should be with their fringes of construction. The Chicago and Milwaukee are just as they are arrayed on maps and the Rift Valley of Africa looks like a Rift Valley. Why is the amazing opportunity to be high over the earth and see its wonders so often ignored? Perhaps the reason I like climbers is that climbers have studied maps and relied on maps and should be able to under-stand geography. It is mostly climbers or would be climbers who search the lands below and look for the distant ranges of the skyline from an airplane window. This places them above the ordinary.

But an airplane view is far from the view from a summit and I squirm at the idea that some of those cabinmates of mine, lolling in their comfortable seats or dozing over a magazine, can have such a choice view from on high thinking, to be sure, in a distant way, that they may be on top of a mountain. Mountaintops are not for the frail nor are they, as the Bible says, for the weak in spirit. Mountaintops take time, desire, hard work and a challenge. Mountaintops have winds and coldness along with a distant view. Mountaintops allow a sense of space that makes it necessary to identify the hollows and summits of the horizon. Mountaintops are goals achieved with dreams. Mountaintops are not offered without some suffering, a suffering that is the pleasant necessity for appreciation. Mountaintops afford mountaineers the wonderful opportunity to reach out above mere joggers and physical exercise enthusiasts to add the geography of intimacy with the rocks and ever-changing perspective of our jagged world. Mountaintops give substance to adventure. The people of mountaintops are special.

The literature of mountaineering is rife with near misses and sudden death. I think of the description of an event on K2 where two roped teams were trying to cross a wicked slope and one climber fell and dragged his ropemates down the slope. Somehow the two ropes of the two groups tangled and one roped team held the other team by a precarious crossing of their separate ropes. Now, how to get out of this muddle of crossed ropes with three climbers strewn down the slope and three climbers trying to rescue their fellows? Patience and fortitude proved sufficient. It is not so much the accident as the heroism, and it is not so much the heroism as the seeming insanity that several climbers should be trying such a dangerous and obviously crazy attempt to climb a mountain in a storm. This is the epitome of mountaineering which is an asininity and sin if one follows the edicts of our safety specialists but the anticipated sequel of being in high places that is accepted by mountaineers as a fair possibility. It is merely a challenge to their training, ambition and their sheer faith that they will win somehow.

Accidents with climbers must be placed against their normal dedication to training. They go out and try to lift themselves up a rock with one finger on a nubbin of surface. They practice and practice and read every description of failure and insert the facts in their minds so that they will not repeat it. They hold to a dictum of safety and then they proceed to test that dictum and then challenge the roots of its protocol. They go off on solo adventures on impossible cliffs and show off their courage and ability of an ultimate variety that far exceeds that in other so-called "sports." Successes are sometimes spectacular and once in a while for some dramatic reason the event is televised to a public that cannot possibly understand the philosophy that has slowly grown around the subject.

But deaths also happen and are often ignored by newspapers and television for the events that may transpire when a body falls 3,000 feet are not really the stuff for photographers. I am reminded now of some accidents that occurred by sheer misadventure when the climber after all the training and dedication had allowed for confidence stood up on a cliff and simply forgot that the tie to the ice-screws had not been made. This happened to an experienced climber on the north face of Mount Everest. The one that haunts me is the climber on a cliff in Yosemite who, trying to rappel to a ledge of sorts, underestimated the length of his rope and just as he was to find a foothold, the rope gave out and whipped around his body. His partner saw this happen and witnessed the horrible event and noted the falling climber's last words. Consider now the years of careful training, the checks and balances of safety that had become a part of procedure, the fulminating motivations of success and confidence and then some blatant oversight. All these must have whizzed through that unfortunate climber's brain as he fell the half mile to the rocks below. What did he say? It was a loud obscenity that expressed the absurdity of his frustration.

Actually I am not a dedicated and supermotivated climber for I have been tainted by the biological drives to catch bugs and watch birds. I realized my tempered enthusiasm for cliffs and ice best when after a long haul up a glacier from 14,000 feet to 18,500 feet in the Rolwaling Himalaya, I found myself in the throes of an altitude headache that survived a long and sleepless night. In the morning, sometime quite early before the sun had touched the surrounding peaks, I awakened to some strange sounds outside of my tent, mutterings and slapping noises that did not fit the peaceful environs of a camp on the ice of a glacier. I groaned with my affliction and I could not have removed myself from my sleeping bag for any lure. I had a head like a chunk of clay that some fool artist had tried to model all night and my inclinations toward ambition were highly tainted by ennui, what the Mexicans call "mucho flojera."

On that morning I would have much preferred a beautiful coral beach like that at Funzi Bay near Mombasa. But I managed enough exertion to roll over and peer out of the little tied entrance to the tent where, through a crack, I could view the outside world and see what was sounding so strange. What I saw out there in front of my tent overwhelmed any vague notions I may have had about my own vigor and superiority. I was amply reminded that I was not 20 years old any more and that I preferred a soft air mattress to the hard ground and that old notions of a toughness and a leathery response to environmental challenges had passed me by. What I saw was a climber, one of the best in the world, heroic and acclaimed, conqueror of some of the highest peaks the world had to offer, standing outside, absolutely naked, with bare feet that met the snow, plantar surface to freezing ice, swinging his arms and breathing lustily in some strange yoga cadence. He was exercising and cajoling his arterioles to threaten some metabolic boil as he greeted the prospect of the sun. It was bitter out there but the thought of nearby peaks and the opportunity to climb controlled his mind. No greater love and ambition could man ever have. I turned over to go back to sleep hoping that my head would heal. Those crazy climbers!

I have experienced the fairly normal dangers of climbing, such as a head-sized rock bouncing back and forth between the walls of a *couloir*, coming down at 100 miles per hour, and then after its random crashing from one wall to the other, just missing me. Such things that offer death but are simply frightening produce wild laughs from Sherpas. How funny it is to not be dead! And though I have had a half a mountain of rocks fall around me, such episodes are mere minor affairs and never really make the pages of alpine journals. If you die or are maimed in some way you may get a sentence of requiem. So my own personal tales are derived from the accounts of others and what I may have witnessed after the fact. I therefore select some episodes that have a distant biological motif.

During our expedition to Makalu we were the first to explore the vast Barun Valley that led up to the glaciers that emanated from the East Side of Mount Everest. Our status of being first was soon challenged by a New Zealand expedition led by Sir Edmund Hillary who was accompanied by his friend George Lowe who had been instrumental in getting Hillary and Tensing to the top of Mount Everest the year before. The New Zealanders opted to set up their base camp some distance up the Barun Glacier where they could explore the northern approaches to Makalu but our group had close contact with these pleasant intruders into our domain. One day we noticed that a group from their camp were slowly coming down the glacier carrying a man on a stretcher. He was brought into one of our tents and our able physician Bruce Meyer was called upon to help. The patient, Jim McFarlane, had frozen his hands and feet some days before.

Freezing hands and feet are quite common and a number of my friends are walking around with fingers and toes missing. But this was something massive and so I shall report on how it happened. McFarlane and Brian Wilkins had been exploring the upper reaches of the Barun Glacier when, although they were roped together, one of them fell through a crevasse and dragged the other man down with him. They fell about 60 feet to a ledge. McFarlane was more injured so Wilkins with some remarkable technique with an ice axe cut steps and wedged his way out. He hurried back to camp and notified Hillary but by then it had become dark. Nevertheless, Hillary, with two Sherpas, rushed up the glacier and found the hole where the climbers had fallen through. Hillary called to McFarlane and heard his voice. He therefore decided to have himself lowered on a rope held by the Sherpas. But he couldn't quite reach McFarlane so he opted to toss him a sleeping bag where he could spend the night on his small ledge and keep relatively warm. Rescue would have to wait until daylight. When the Sherpas tried to haul Hillary back up, the rope had cut into the ice of the crevasse edge and so, in the darkness, the Sherpas heaved Hillary against the ice of the rim. This merely squeezed Hillary's chest and probably cracked a rib. Nevertheless, after much yelling, the Sherpas loosened their pull and Hillary, with some leeway, managed to get his ice axe over the rim and, in spite of his injury, hauled himself out. All this happened at about 19,000 feet. This fellow had guts.

The next morning with more help, Hillary looked down the crevasse and found to his horror that McFarlane in some dazed state had merely placed the sleeping bag across his abdomen. His hands and feet were unprotected. It took some time to get McFarlane out for he could not help himself and he was carried back to camp on the back of a Sherpa. Someone wrapped his hands and feet with gauze bandages, a stretcher was constructed out of tent poles, and a team started carrying him out towards our camp.

Bruce had McFarlane sit in a chair. I stayed to see if I could help. Slowly the temporary bandages were removed. Around and around the long strips of cloth were unwrapped from one hand and, near the end, a blackness on the hand showed through the gauze. Bruce pulled away the last section and it seemed to stick for a moment. The physician gave a gentle tug. The bandage came away with the last joint of the little finger stuck to the gauze, a phalanx, a little black piece of dead flesh with a white fingernail attesting to its identity.

It was soon obvious to Bruce that all the fingers were dead. They were all black and loose. Bruce wiggled them a little and now a whole finger broke away without resistance revealing the shining bone of a metacarpal condyle to which the finger had once been joined. Another and another followed. There was no blood or oozing of liquids that might have been expected. The fingers simply fell off leaving shiny spots on the hand to show a vacancy. I felt some squeamish rolling in my stomach but the patient merely looked down at the dismemberment of his body and made some innocuous comments such as "that seemed looser than the other." The gory movies designed to shock teenagers could not compare with this real scene. I hope I am not giving Hollywood any ideas.

This went on without variation. Both hands and feet offered up their digits like leaves falling from a wintered branch, and the floor of the tent was fairly strewn with curled, black and crinkled fingers and toes like some random twigs on the forest floor. McFarlane made no sounds of anguish. He was perfectly conscious; he was merely resigned. But I wonder what screaming thoughts must batter the brain to watch those things that have always been part of you, things you accept as integral to your life, things you take for granted as essential, simply fall off to the floor. Surely there must be an overwhelming sense of awe at the prospect for a life, all of the life that's left, that will be vastly different from then on.

This all happened in the days before helicopter rescues and so McFarlane was carried out of Nepal, 100 miles or so, on the backs of Sherpas. All I have heard, subsequently, is that he carries on his profession as an engineer in New Zealand and still climbs mountains. Mountains get into the blood. Those crazy climbers!

Apparently as a result of the chest injury he received trying to rescue McFarlane, Hillary subsequently suffered an attack of pneumonia at a high camp. Pneumonia at high altitudes is a very dangerous affliction. Altitude pneumonia can strike during the night and the anoxic victim may not awaken the next morning. This happened to Oscar Cook in the Andes, one of the climbers who was going to join our expedition to Makalu. It is a relatively common occurrence and seems to come without warning. One of the major causes of death and debilitation among Indian soldiers during their high altitude confrontations with the Chinese along the Tibetan frontier was altitude pneumonia, and both the Chinese and the Indians have contributed research to try and find out why this occurs. Why do the lungs suddenly fill up with fluid and deny oxygen exchange to the blood? I haven't encountered the most recent explanations in the scientific literature and so I cannot be more revealing, but I know the Chinese physiologists have found what seems to be a test of susceptibility for this frightening occurrence. It seems that if a person breathes normal air and then the air is quickly reduced in oxygen content without the individual knowing it, susceptible people respond in some different physiological way to nonsusceptible people. I don't know the details but this study is now used as a basis for selecting people from the lowlands of China for work in Tibet.

Getting back to Hillary's encounter with pneumonia, I learned of his illness when a Sherpa came running down the glacier with a note requesting the use of oxygen, oxygen that we carried for just such medical use and not as a climbing aid. The Sherpa quickly packed a 50-pound cannister on his back and proceeded to run, uphill, back up the glacier from about 16,000 feet to 18,000 feet, bouncing from rock to rock, until he was out of sight. These men are wonders. Those of us in camp were very worried so we mentioned it in our weekly short wave broadcast to India. Now the newspapers picked it up and the world was worried about Hillary. But in a few days another Sherpa could be seen running down the glacier carrying a small sack. He delivered a note to the effect that Hillary was recovering and thanks for the oxygen. The thanks referred to the sack. In it were pounds of luscious, gooey New Zealand chocolates. The New Zealanders were well aware of our craving for sweet things for we visited them often hoping for just this hospitality since our own candy was in a box that had fallen into the roaring Barun River never to be recovered. Candy for oxygen is a fair trade. Since that occasion, Hillary has had some strange reactions to high altitude and now, in his seventies, I see from recent newspapers that he had to be rescued by helicopter out of a high camp. I wonder if these strange responses emanated from that event on the Barun or if they had some distant connections with the top of Mount Everest. There are all sorts of rumors about climbers who, running out of oxygen near the summits of K2 and Everest, still climbed on and conceivably depleted their brains of oxygen. It is said that their subsequent behavior was abnormal. Hillary obviously had no mental effects but why should such a healthy and vigorous man who was once the finest climber at high altitudes suddenly become sensitive and ill at high altitude?

Another pneumonia event involved another New Zealander climber on a different expedition. I was sharing a tent with Michael Gill in the Rolwaling area of Nepal. In the morning I had to rouse him from a deep sleep and then noticed that he was having trouble putting on his boots. I looked again and the young man's face was an obvious purplish blue that stood out in contrast to his shock of very blond hair. Fortunately, there was some small amount of emergency oxygen handy and so I was designated to hold the oxygen mask over Gill's mouth and nose, and feed him oxygen. It was necessary to conserve our short supply, so I would give him a few sniffs, then let him breathe normally. He would quickly lose his purplish color and turn bright pink with oxygen and then, when the mask was removed, just as quickly revert to purple, pink, purple, pink, purple, pink. This went on for some hours and then he gradually recovered and stayed pink. In the next few days he was out scouting the 21,000-foot peaks around the camp. Those crazy climbers!

Let us now leave the awfulness of high altitude pneumonia where lungs fill with fluid and one can die while sleeping. How about human odors and the human sense of olfaction? Seldom in the travails of travelers are such things mentioned and I would not breach this sensitive area of biology except for some unusual circumstance, as I shall presently explain.

Consider that indoor baths and the necessary plumbing are features of the 20th century and we, today; completely neglect to refer to the smells of individuals and human congregations of the past. Where do we hear references during the sufferings of Valley Forge of the soldiers who smelled to high heaven or even the fragrance of George Washington, the "Father of our Country," who seldom if ever took a bath? Such things were so ordinary and accepted that chronologists simply ignored them. To be sure, we hear of perfumes among the aristocracy, and much of the "Spice Trade," that was originally inspired by an ice-less society for the amelioration of the taste of rotting food, shifted to expensive spicy powders that altered or covered body odors. I suppose that to some degree this was an effort to separate nobility from the "unwashed masses." Movies and TV cannot depict smells except for the occasional fine lady who, when approaching a nasty dungeon, lifts her silk handkerchief to her nose. And I doubt if that really happened for even such dainty ladies were well acquainted with and accustomed to human stenches. I think we should better accept our reeking past and recognize the novelty of our current fetish for our bland and innocuous state.

Lively body odors come naturally to those crazy climbers who go off into the mountains and don't take a bath for months on end. Take the case of a whole expedition of ten sahbs crammed into a tent waiting to open a new bottle of soluble coffee for their pleasure. The cap is screwed off and the bottle is placed in the middle of the table. There is only a second before someone gasps "Look at that!" Now we all saw that the waxed paper covering the bottle under the removed lid was rounded and swollen like some tumorous thing. We were at about 16,000 feet where the air pressure approaches half the pressure at sea level and the air in the coffee bottle was at sea level. We all knew that the bulging thing was about to explode. It was now too much for our physician, Bruce Meyer, who with his medical predilections could not resist such a pathogenic protuberance and he reached out and touched the swollen paper. "Poof" it went and the finely powdered stuff that once used to be standard for instant coffee exploded into a brown cloud that engulfed us all. It settled slowly and insidiously. It settled on everything—faces, hands and clothing. There was a brownish hue that was added to whatever white was left on our skins. That sinister stuff had a way of sticking and staying and it tainted the air of that tent for months. But at least, in the tent, it retained its gentle odor of coffee. Not so on our bodies.

That brown powdery stuff worked its way into all the little creases of the skin. If you looked closely, there were tiny brown lines here and there over the body, behind the ears. along the hairline, those grooves on the wrists and I suppose it bored its way down into the pores and microscopic apertures that connect the epidermis with the dermis. One may wonder why we

173

didn't wash the stuff off. We tried soap and water on hands and face but a whole bath? Not on your life! Even crazy climbers don't like to freeze.

And so it was that this pulverulent stuff lingered and aged on our skins and as time passed, the odor of one's own person, a thing that has one's own individual bias and is well known to those who have traveled to remote cold places, was not quite right. Something was askew. Aromas that my own nostrils recognized from past experience were now affronted with some additional nuance of olfaction. I could smell, along with my normal and acceptable richness, a distant taint of coffee, a combination that was not likeable or, at least, needed more time and experience to get used to.

Human noses have lost their exquisite sensitivity to many odors. Our arboreal ancestors did not need the ground-sniffing nose of a bloodhound. But curiously, we have retained some fine sensitivity for certain molecular arrangements of vapors. We are probably just as good in recognizing skunk odor, for instance (something like one molecule in 36 billion), as dogs, and we are very alert at considerable distances to the wafted mercaptans of a dead body. I think, somehow, we have also retained a fine sensitivity for body odors, especially those that have been stretched beyond normality.

One does get used to natural odors that may, to the unaccustomed, be better defined as a stink. After a while one can often detect a comrade by his smell as if he were releasing a pheromone of identity like any other normal mammal. But add the permeating and rich tang of coffee and let it mix and ripen to promote new breeds of microbes that churn up new enzymatic combinations for the production of novel volatile molecules and then sense the result. Like musk or civet, these new inventions of skin alchemy become the vehicles of strange aromatic compounds.

Fortunately we were all similarly dosed; we all had a touch of this unsavory bouquet for we were all present when Bruce did his thing. Because of this I have wondered what the Sherpas thought of our unsavory fragrance. It should be understood that Sherpas do not take baths for water is not something to be wasted on such nonsense. Sherpas acquire a veneer on their skins that protects them from the severities of the environment and with their abstinence from ablutions, they gain a distinctive, robust odor that may be troublesome to the uninitiated. But this was the first time any Sherpas had encountered an American expedition. We were new to them and no reputation about Americans had spread among Sherpa grapevines. I wonder what generalizations they may have made about our taint. We could all be identified; all Americans they had ever known in their lives smelled as we did. Did they relegate us with those Tibetans of rancid butter fame and prefer us to be downwind? I think, perhaps, that they came to the conclusion that those crazy American climbers drank too much coffee (which we didn't) instead of tea because it was obvious to them that it was much easier to drink coffee for all you needed was to spoon a little into hot water. Tea, on the other hand, came in little small bags that were the very devil to open and the tea from several of these miserable bags had to be opened and pinched into the hot water to get a decent pot to drink. The Sherpas had never seen tea bags before.

On another expedition one of the members seemed to insist upon baths. He had not graduated into the necessary acquiescence to human odor. He constructed a rock wall at considerable expense of time and energy and started a fire using juniper boughs that burned for hours. This heated up the surrounding rocks and when it was all just ripe, he covered the enclosure with a plastic tarpaulin that was held up by a long stick. Now one could crawl into this contraption and pour water on the heated rocks and the steam would saturate your naked self like the saunas of the Finns. I was persuaded to try this once and standing in the hot steam, the accumulated veneer on my skin came loose and dribbled in little brown streamlets down my legs. I scraped more of it off with a handy twig and then had to leave because someone else was eager to begin his own affair with this compromise with civilization. When I dried off and felt the cold again my skin was like that of a newborn babe, but now the cold permeated my new softness and I found new places to itch. That wonderful oleaceous veneer of the epidermis, that extra coat of discarded keratinized cells that allow for thriving populations of commensal and symbiotic bacteria, had gone forever, lost in those brownish rivulets that coursed down my legs. I am not advocating bathlessness. That is impossible in our urban society where advertisements constantly remind us of perfumes and smell-negating devices whose lack of use would surely damn us to hell and deprive the advocators of their required profits. I am not advocating bathlessness where the skin protects us against the elements and leaves us comfortably odorous. Bathlessness is for those crazy climbers.

My friend, the late Professor Ludwig Immergluck, a distinguished psychologist, used to call to me as we passed on the crowded campus, "Let us talk sometime. Sicology is part of Beeologee!" This is what some people claimed was a Viennese lilt in his speech but which I suggest was a refinement of Kissingerese. I think Immergluck had it right and so, with Psychology as part of Biology, let me delve into the behaviors of climbers. When climbers gather in an effort to go to some peak, climbers who have not climbed together before offer a curious response. Some of them set off across the lower hills like rams after ewes to the next camping spot that is supposed to be about six hours distant. They arrive in about three hours and the first to reach the predesignated stopping place lies down in a comfortable place to await his rivals. It is a game of sorts to show off agility, purpose, sheer muscular, vascular and respiratory superiority. Early arrivals are supposed to inform all others that they have some inner strength, some deep purpose, some exceptional ability to be on that final summit team.

If several nationalities are involved, this unannounced competition grows fierce. The French, some member among the French, must beat that outspoken German who arrived first on the previous day. I judge from experience that Italians, Greeks and Spanish climbers seem to reflect the casualness of their Mediterranean heritage and fail to chase after this golden fleece of nonsense while the more northern Europeans and Americans are trapped by its guile. I prefer the Mediterranean winds that blow on an expedition. I am influenced by an occasion where, coming last as is my wont, I encountered a climber of a foreign designation standing on a prominence along the path that overlooked the valley and the distant hills. I had heard him for some minutes so when I approached I was prepared. He was belting out some of Verdi's finest arias to the valley below with a few Nepalese porters watching in bewilderment. I joined this wonderful man who taught me that an operatic aria, or my alternate, a Tibetan chant, is the best way to express appreciation for a magnificent view (for those who do not know a Tibetan chant just sing, slowly, on a constant note, "Sola Maneeee" and end with a grunt that could sound like "Om" which is the holiest of all sounds"). I joined with him on Rigoletto and what I knew of Puccini arias. We sang in harmony which must have been a consternation to the pre-Renaissance qualities of the minor themes of Nepalese songs that these hill men knew.

These peripatetic efforts to arrive first and their inferred lesson of superiority are generally avoided by those climbers of success and experience. They can rest on their own laurels. And so, I sometimes came into camp with a known and recognized climber as the last dragging remnant of the expedition. Whereas the recognized climber was never questioned as to his physical capabilities. I, as a mere biologist, was subtly exposed to innuendoes about my condition. "Gad you're last again! Have any pains?" I have responded to such barbs with questions about whether or not they had seen that wonderful tree or that huge monitor lizard or the Nepalese Gurkha that told of his experiences in France during World War I. These speedy guys scarcely noticed anything as they raced up the hills. I found it advisable to be last for if any hotshot got behind me there was the dire possibility that he would be a major inconvenience. Once, after I had passed a devotee of the physical who had been delayed with some sort of problem with his gear, I heard a distant call from far down the slope, "Look at this thing! Its incredible!" And so I had to retreat down a steep path to see, like a doctor called by a dying patient, what was so remarkable. I was confronted by a climber pointing at a giant yellow grasshopper with blue stripes that was, indeed, spectacular. The only thing was that I had already collected a full quantity for they were all over the place in abundance and this blind man had finally opened his eyes to the wonders of nature. Those crazy climbers!

High altitudes sometimes promote high emotions, and small quantities of alcohol or innocent drugs can produce exaggerated responses. During a time of depression (the reasons for this are given below) Bruce gave me some little green capsules that were supposed to be mood-altering in their effect. They contained desoxyn which today might be called an "upper." They not only altered my mood, they drove me out to the glacier stream where I proceeded to spend the day tossing rocks into it in an inane and totally useless effort to see if I could dam it up and produce a lake. Little quantities of rakshi, a Nepalese distilled liquor that could have been brought in by our mailmen who periodically went off to deliver our letters, would sometimes set the Sherpas into violent episodes of anger. I once saw an ice axe that can be a very lethal weapon go flying through the air and just miss another Sherpa who was accused (some six months earlier!) of making eyes at the other Sherpa's wife.

The exaggerated effects of drugs at high altitude should be noted by the pharmaceutical industry. What a place to test their new concoctions to see what the extreme responses might be! I am sure there would be an ample supply of climbers who would be willing to act as guinea pigs provided the sponsoring commercial enterprise could supply the cash for an expedition along with other amenities. There would have to be some restrictions to prevent some hopped up individual to try his hand at the nearest peak, but having them toss rocks into the glacier stream to see if they could dam it and produce a lake might be a logical test of their sanity.

Without drugs or alcohol some desperate arguments started among climbers who had always been friends and, unfortunately, some of these antagonisms remained long after the expedition. A friend on another expedition remains to this day absolutely livid about another climber who refused, in very bad weather, to go up a mountain and help rescue another member. I had an argument with another member of an expedition who refused to let me have three cups of sugar for a long journey I was to make across the mountains. He was as stubborn as a mule and I was loud and insistent. He won. I still resent that man even though it should have been obvious to me that I could have purchased some raw sugar from a Nepalese village which, eventually, I did. That event has also taught me to be more reflective on the consequences of a disagreement and how asinine some things seem to be in retrospect at lower altitudes or with the attenuations of time.

There is an unappreciated level of stress that accompanies the members of an expedition. One of my friends actually acquired ulcers. I don't think it is the anticipated dangers of the peak for, if anything, the exciting stages of actually climbing after so much preparation is a relief. It is the continual give and take among climbers who are thrust together very closely and where little peculiarities of personality induce exaggerated responses. Under ordinary circumstances these idiosyncrasies would be unnoticed but under the trials of an expedition, they can grow out of proportion. How can you understand the growling derision that arose concerning a nice fellow who simply wore his Texas ten-gallon hat too much?

Nello Pace, our distinguished physiologist from Berkeley, made some studies concerning stress. In those days the role of the several corticosteroid hormones produced by the adrenal cortex were still being elucidated, and Nello was comparing our stress hormones with his various other studies, such as soldiers in the front lines in Korea and a group swimming across the English Channel. He was continually after our blood and urine and, after a siege of long days on the slopes, he would appear at your tent opening holding a syringe and a bottle. No protestations of being exhausted ever worked against the onslaught of "Nello's Needles." Syringe and bottle always won. I once put a red and yellow flag (representing blood and urine) over his laboratory tent. The results of those tests, now lost in all the newer discoveries, showed that we compared to front-line troops (or actually, the troops about to go into the front lines who had more stress) and that the Sherpas showed much less in the way of abnormal levels of hormones. I think corticosteroid levels could explain why minor cuts and abrasions did not seem to heal very fast and sunburned skin took too long to tan.

To get back to bona fide Biology, let me close with a tale of an event that occurred near the base of Makalu. It is generally known that travel across the mountains exposes one to different foods, different habits, different things of all sorts, as well as to different postures. Somewhere among these differences lies the reason for the frequency of episodes of hemorrhoids among climbers. I became a sufferer, a sufferer of some exquisiteness, to the extent that I found sitting down was uncomfortable and required some positioning when all there was to sit on was some rock. At camp, our crude benches gave me trouble and I have to admit to giving out a few groans. Now on top of this, one night I got a siege of coughing, a not too uncommon symptom of breathing heavily in the high, dry air. The coughing was so severe that I felt concerned that some antiperistaltic wave could mess up my sleeping bag. So I leaned out to one side and that was the wrong thing to do for in this position, a massive heaving of my chest produced a sharp and immobilizing pain. I had pulled a costal ligament somewhere back where the ribs articulate with the vertebrae.

The next morning the pain in my back was there with a vengeance and I found to my considerable consternation that now I had difficulty standing erect. Now I could not stand or sit down. There was some moaning in all this, enough to catch the attention of our compassionate physician, Bruce Meyer, who felt obligated to cure my syndrome of ennui and self-pity. He was, furthermore, fresh from a residency as an orthopedic surgeon without much experience in private practice and he saw the occasion of my despondency to enhance his art. So, unbeknown to me, he had some of his medical instruments sterilized in a pressure cooker (the temperature of boiling water alone is not hot enough at 16,000 feet) and offered me, still innocent of his intentions, a pill of sorts that would help to dull my world of pain.

It was late morning. The sun was shining and in the sun I was relatively warm. I was instructed to take off my clothing which I did without any sense of apprehensive anticipation and then, like that innocent sheep that was led to slaughter, I was led to a large rock where I was positioned at an uncomfortable angle and not too gently held in place by some other conspirators. Bruce stuck a big needle into my rib area and that insertion of novocaine helped the pain in my back. But he was more interested in my older and more persistent ailment that was lower down. He started his chipping away of this part where there was no obvious anesthetic and it was clearly indicated to me that I would not be very comfortable.

Bruce proceeded slowly, testing my reflexes of withdrawal and listening for my sounds to see if the pain was sufficiently excruciating. And then it happened. The sun went its way behind the clouds. In the shade it chilled immediately. This is a phenomenon of high altitudes that requires experiencing the event for belief. And now, a brisk breeze set in and, horror of horrors, some snow flurries visited the scene of my discomfort. I saw those flakes fall near my immobilized nose that was being held down close to the giant rock that served as the operating table of this primitive medical adventure. They touched and melted on the rock just as they were touching and

179

melting all over my bare and immodestly arranged body. I heard Bruce behind me now complaining about the changed events. "Damn my hands are
cold!" he was saying. He said it again and I sensed the irony of his com-
plaint. Here he was lamenting the chill on his precious hands while I was
completely naked on a rock that was getting colder and colder as the wind
whipped at it. But at any rate, the freezing air made the surgeon hurry and
not be too concerned with the esthetic quality of his production and I did not
have the patience to wait for some anal masterpiece of stitch work. At last I
was hauled off to my tent and I climbed into my sleeping bag to shiver
myself to sleep. This sort of an affair wounds one's psyche and in this case
my psyche was also where I sat down.

Much later, near suppertime, I emerged and went down to the larger
tent (the one that smelled of coffee) where we squeezed in for meals. I sat
down in my quiet corner. My friends who had often listened to my tales
about the wonders of the Himalaya with some feigned disbelief, now noted
my subdued state of silence. "You know," said one. "That was the highest
hemorrhoidectomy in the world—a thing for Guiness. There's another tale
for your collection." "Yes," I answered "It certainly was high. It was way up
there." "And" said another, "you could write a book about all this. What
would you call it? 'Hemorrhoids in the Himalaya'?" This brought on some
laughter and a lack of appreciation for my wounded state. I had to answer. "I
prefer, if you want, 'Piles Among the Peaks.'"

Bruce Meyer (our physician) and Nello Pace (our physiologist) taking blood from my arm for analysis of cortisone levels under stress.

There is a sequel to all this that needs comment. First it should be understood that with two physiologists, Will Siri and Nello Pace, and one physician, the afore-mentioned Bruce Meyer, on the expedition, we were doing

180

Will Siri, the leader of the 1954 expedition.

all sorts of physiological experiments. The promise of this effort had allowed donors to our very sparse coffers of cash to help with our financing which were so low and precarious that on our return to India we were actually borrowing from our Sherpas. One of our many schemes to pay for the expedition was to make a movie of our adventures and we finally did get a movie out, "Ten against Makalu," that made its way around some theaters and was actually quite good. So it was that some years after we returned, a previous student of mine, and now a teacher in San Francisco, came to me with some excitement saying that he had recently seen our movie. It had been shown at his school and was making its way around the country. He was high in his praise. He went on to specifics and pointed out how well the physiological experiments were presented, being, as he said "marvelously displayed." Now my eyebrows started to go up. I had not seen very much about our physiological experiments in the movie. What could he be talking about? Could he have seen some other movie and was being confused? And then he said "And that hemorrhoidectomy was out of this world!" That did it.

Now I tried to hide my widening eyes for I didn't want him to see my utter surprise and complete astonishment. If I gave a clue to my thoughts he could wonder how I, a member of the expedition, did not know about the movie. As it was, I did not know about the movie he was talking about. Those rascals, those scoundrels, those knaves and villains, those crazy climbers had filmed the whole operation with me spread out on the rock without my knowledge. They had then included this episode in another movie about the medical and physiological efforts of the expedition. Thus they had justified the inclusion of the world's highest hemorrhoidectomy that exhibited, across the country, my own worst profile. It is not everyone who has such a chance to be seen in such a primitively intimate way. Furthermore, my face seldom appears in the movie, either movie, but I am, presumably better known from a different angle. There is an extension here of one of those advertisements that American Express used for so long. Someone with a well-known name but less known appearance would extol something like "You may not know my face but ..."

L.W. Swan in his youth and vigor.

Willi Unsoeld who gained fame by climbing Everest West Ridge.

A Tale of Philately

Philately has been for me the opening up of the world, an introduction and finishing course in geography, a lifting of the curtain on a host of other subjects. It has been an intellectual challenge and a stimulation of the mind. All this may not convince anyone who has not found this treasured activity and therefore I write about my efforts to promote an expedition stamp or label with some doubts about it being universally interesting. In the world of philately, however, it is something quite out of the ordinary.

Back in 1954 there was a desperate problem of financing the Makalu expedition. The prospect of starvation became a compulsive goad to further the development of imaginative solutions to counteract the chill winds of poverty. I remembered that somewhere around 1924 one of the Mount Everest expeditions had used a special stamp for its mail that was supposed to bring in money. That particular stamp today has become a classic and envelopes carrying that label sell for a pretty penny. So, to carry on that old tradition, I made a pen and ink sketch of Makalu from the south, a depiction that had some imaginary aspects to it and where parts of the mountain had to be obscured with clouds for, aside from that magnificent photograph made of

183

the Everest Range during the 1933 flight over Everest, there were no available photographs of Makalu from the south, the side we would be on. Down in one corner of the sketch I drew a small spider suggesting Hingston's discovery and a possible ambition of mine. I rather think that the other members of the group were not prepared for the idea that a spider should symbolize their efforts but, on a whole, they remained silent.

I had the sketch reduced to stamp size and it was engraved. I chose two colors, some to be printed in red and some in blue to allay any latent feelings about this being either a Stanford or Berkeley affair. It was printed on gummed paper but I could not afford to have them perforated. I have tried for my own purposes to perforate them by carefully cutting the edges with pinking shears, going over the edges twice and so I have instituted a new and curious perforation called PKS 13 (Pinking shears 13 to an inch) that will surely endear me to philatelists who like such detail. I had about 500 of each color printed. The number was a sheer guess for I had no idea how popular the cover would be. Having the stamp, I then had to advertise and make sure that our chief sponsor, the Sierra Club, approved of the effort.

I visualized a grand scheme. The envelope would be made of native, Nepalese Daphne paper, a rather crude but attractive paper that is made as a village industry in many parts of Nepal out of the bark of Daphne bushes. This would certainly give it an attractive primitive charm. The label would be affixed to the upper left hand corner of the envelope and be hand canceled "Carried By Runner" for, after all, our mail would have to be carried by some of our hired Sherpas who would periodically jog from our Base Camp to Jogbani on the plains of India to pick up our correspondence. To add to this, I also contemplated another hand stamp that would function as our address namely "Barun Glacier Base Camp."

The postage stamps to be used would be most unusual if not unique for, in 1954, Nepal was not yet a member of the Universal Postal Union (UPU) and therefore its own genuine stamps were not legitimate outside of Nepal and India. In other words, stamps of Nepal would not be legitimate for postage to the United States. The UPU required that all stamps carry some international language and that Arabic numerals indicating value be prominently displayed. Nepalese stamps carried only native script and numerals. Generally, mail sent from Nepal to other parts of the world simply carried Indian postage. All this made Nepalese stamps rather rare and interesting from the point of view of their primitive design and manufacture. Therefore, to legitimize our mail, I decided to include both Nepalese and Indian stamps on each cover, something that normal Nepalese citizens or even officials of the country did not do. Why pay twice for a letter if once would do? Whereas, our expedition label was not an official stamp, it did approach that category for we would have a post office on the Barun Glacier (and I would be post-master!). So it would seem that the expedition cover would carry two sets of very appropriate postage stamps and a third that was somewhat legitimate. I did not know if such a cover existed in all of philately.

I advertised in two philatelic magazines telling it all. The cost I estab-lished at one dollar per cover. Since I would be paying double postage plus the cost of envelopes and I would be hand addressing all of them, this seemed cheap, too cheap. Since that time I have learned to be less guileless.

The timing of the advertisement was unfortunate. It had to appear after I had already left for Nepal and so I arranged for requests to be sent to the Sierra Club who would then send names and addresses to my wife who would send them on to me. I had no idea how many requests would come in and therefore no idea of how many stamps I would have to buy in India and Nepal. I did wonder about the security of the mail that may or may not reach us high on the mountain so I suggested to my wife that she make two copies of the list of requests and send them to me two weeks apart just in case one or the other got lost.

When we arrived in Calcutta I hurried over to the General Post Office and found to my delight that they still had some one hundred Mount Everest stamps left, the stamps that were issued to commemorate the climbing of Mount Everest by Hillary and Tensing. These stamps were the first in the world to depict an actual Himalayan peak. I had to purchase many other stamps not only for a possible windfall of requests but also for use by mem-bers of the expedition. All this depleted my cash considerably and the first of a long series of borrowings began which ended up, eventually, on our way out of the mountains by all of us borrowing from our own hired Sherpas, much to their amusement. I put all the stamps in a large book allotting stamps to each member and stamps for philatelic mail and wrapped it all up in two bags of plastic. This was the Barun Glacier Post Office.

In Nepal my problems started. Our route from Dharan to Dhankuta and up the Arun Valley was not exactly a common road. The post office in Dharan was devoid of Nepalese stamps and they had no envelopes made of Daphne paper. I had always assumed that native paper envelopes would be easy to obtain but in the years of my absence these home-made items had been replaced by common, ordinary, died-in-the-wool, manufactured envelopes. I could not find my chosen envelopes anywhere. In desperation I did find some sheets of Daphne paper and calculated that if worst came to worst, I might construct my own envelopes. I therefore also purchased some glue that I was assured was capable of sticking envelopes together.

We went on to Dhankuta, the Capitol of the Province and we were received by the Burra Hakim, the Governor himself. This was the first time any expedition had appeared at his door step and he was not sure what he could or should do. He offered us fruit and hospitality and inquired what he could do for us. At this question there was complete muteness from the sahbs and the Governor was about to go on to other matters so I had to present my voice. "Sir" I inquired in some abject way "Sir, I cannot find any native paper envelopes. Can you tell me where I may obtain some?" After translation the Governor appeared to be quite happy to be of some service and he sent off an aide who soon reappeared with 200 envelopes made of choice Daphne paper. The Governor handed them to me as a gift and pointed out that this was all he had. The Government of Nepal had long since turned to Western paper and prosaic envelopes and so these precious envelopes had been lying on his shelf for years. I was once more abject in my profuse thanks. Now, if the requests were numbered close to 200 I would be in good shape except, of course, for Nepalese stamps. Even the Governor couldn't help me there.

So on we went, up and over the mountains and into the Barun Gorge where the post office was carried in my own pack across that threatening precipice. My precious cargo would go with me. Whatever happened to me, would happen to it. At Base Camp, especially during those days of depression that I have referred to after the surgeon's wicked schemes had been perpetrated, I designed an envelope shape that could be cut out of the Daphne paper sheets just in case I did not have enough envelopes. And now I awaited the names of those people who may have seen the advertisement and had been convinced that it was worth a dollar.

We waited a long time for our first mail. We had chosen two of our healthiest Sherpas to act as our runners and they took their job very seriously. The postman of India is an honored person and perhaps this was true in Nepal. In India, the Dak Walla jogs his way from village to village not only carrying mail to his distant outposts but also carrying news and gossip from the outside world. He is welcomed wherever he goes and the Government recognizes such men as the means by which India is united, where distant villages become part of the whole. Typically, the Dak Walla has bells around his ankles and he carries a spear, a symbolic threat to thugs and tigers, and he can be recognized in addition by his leather sack strapped over his shoulder. Any traffic on the road must give way to him. The jingling of his bells on his ever moving feet tells of his coming. He has priority, and, as I have said, he is honored.

Our own designated postmen had been gone longer than they should but, finally one late night, they came puffing up the path into base camp. They had a tale to tell. Somewhere past Dhankuta where the hill rises far above the Arun valley floor (and where those ladies had preferred my bed), they had been attacked by brigands who had hit each of them on the head and knocked them out. When they regained consciousness they found to their complete consternation that their precious mail had been stolen. They therefore, in agony and haste, ran back to Dhankuta and informed the Governor and his chief law enforcing officer. The word went out for any trace of the villains and our Sherpas helped in this search. Clues came in and finally the thieves were cornered in a remote shack. The law busted in and found our mail scattered over the floor. If they were searching for valuables and consignments of money they should have picked some other expedition. At any rate the mail was recovered, the criminals hauled away and our mail runners continued on their way. They arrived with their heads still bandaged, less for medical reasons than to impress us all with the evidence of their vicissitudes. They arrived very heroically, for, after all they had our mail, and appreciation and awe were amply distributed by all of us.

My mail was there including two large envelopes. I opened one and there were all the addresses and names I had been waiting for, nearly 500 names. I opened the other and it was a duplicate. It seems that both envelopes, although mailed two weeks apart, had come together and both were on that ill-fated journey and both had been inspected by those culprits. I still marvel at my precarious luck. What would have happened if the mail had been lost? But now there were 500 names and the prospect of $500. And my wife said that even more names were coming in and she wondered if there were enough labels. This was a problem. It seems that all the sahbs were demanding labels for their mail. My little philatelic experiment was popular now that we were functioning and even some of the Sherpas were demanding "Expedition Stamps" for their occasional letters back home. One of our Sherpas, Sonam Gompu, a nephew of the great Tensing, wanted a label to put on a letter to his famous uncle and I agreed provided he would donate to me the envelope that Tensing would use as a return letter. In this philatelic enterprise, I now have covers, side by side, sent by Hillary and Tensing. It is such nonsense that makes philately interesting. All this demand had depleted my supply of labels and so I wrote my wife to print some more, 200 in green.

There now followed the necessity of manufacturing hundreds of envelopes from those sheets of Daphne paper. I worked out a system that would roll along smoothly and then I persuaded sahbs who were not otherwise occupied to help me paste them together. Now, as I have so often stated, Sherpas are helpful people; they always want to add their bit to whatever may be going on and here, while I slaved at making envelopes, they watched and decided that they too could contribute their talents. Thus, Sherpas showed up at my tent intent on making envelopes. I showed them how and they responded with their normal enthusiasm. But Sherpas are not really office types with knacks and abilities to fold and paste. Envelopes emerged from under their hands, hands that were never really pristine, that were more like parallelograms, oblate squares and shapes that would defy trigonometry. At first I thought of gently refusing these contributions, these asymmetrical and distorted wonders, and then the true purpose of philately shone through. I had not advertised that the envelopes would be hand made by exotic Sherpas but I could add this unheralded attribute to the covers. Surely the recipients of my gift would or should appreciate the primitiveness and rarity of a crude envelope where wrinkles in the glued, coarse paper were quite standard. The envelopes piled up in a host of shapes and I set in to address them with my pen that, late at night under my candle glow, often froze its ink.

The job was done except of course for the Nepalese stamps. I had left word with the postmaster of Dharan that I would be back and he had agreed that he would obtain an ample supply of stamps. I was trusting him and I knew I shouldn't. But what else could I do. There was something else too. How could I be assured that the Nepalese stamps would be canceled in Nepal, presumably in Biratnagar, and then taken over to the Indian post office in Jogbani and canceled again. With all the honor that goes with postmen, there is also the accompanying miserable salary and so, the posts of India and Nepal are not necessarily the safest. Stamps can be removed and sold again and my huge mailing would have a lot of money on the envelopes. I therefore decided that I would have to accompany the letters and see to it that they made their way through Nepalese and Indian post offices. I myself would be the runner.

Early in June when the climbing was over and we were waiting for porters to arrive from over the high passes, one of the first to walk into camp was a Tibetan refugee, Dorje, which, in Tibetan means "Thunderbolt" (like "Darjeeling" or "Dorje-Ling," the Land of the Thunderbolt). Dorje was clearly not what his name suggested but he was gentle and curious and took a liking to me after I entertained him with some simple magic tricks. I decided that, with Pemba Norbu and Dorje's help, I could leave Base Camp early and have time to collect and wander around a little before the main group headed for the Plains. I have told about our adventures on the way out where the cold Monsoon winds and rain on a sharp ridge nearly saw our demise and how Dorje ate our whole pound of butter one night in a fit of piggery. So it was some days later that we approached the Arun River and its formidable swinging bridge made of vines and miscellany that throbbed and twisted as one tried to cross it.

As we got closer to the great river the roar increased and finally we were at that infernal bridge that swung out across the abyss where the river ran. It was now during the Monsoon so the water had risen about 30 feet since we had visited it last, and its surface was a churning madness of huge waves. It spun past like a long greenish beast that made the whole world tremble with its fierce rage. It was roaring its wild and angry unrestraint. And this we had to cross on those pitiful strands of braided vines. We sat and contemplated our doubtful future. I decided that Pemba Norbu should go first so that I would have some control over Dorje who showed some giant apprehensions about our flimsy route. After all, Tibetans do not encounter such devilish water on their high plateau. Pemba Norbu set out. I noticed that his hands grasped the side ropes a bit more carefully than is usual for Sherpas. He made it across and now it was Dorje's turn. He put his load strap to his forehead and hoisted his basket onto his back and muttered some incantation from the many available to Tibetans. He started out very deliberately and I watched as the various harmonic waves of the rope bridge hit his gait and made him pause. He was having some troubles for he paused too often and for too long and that set the strands moving even more. It was then that I remembered I had made a terrible mistake. My load down the mountain had been getting heavy with collections and miscellany while Dorje's kept getting lighter as we ate our supplies. I had entrusted him with that priceless container of philatelic supplies. They were there on his load that was rocking to and fro over the mad water.

He kept moving and I had hope - but not for long. He reached one of those places where the torque becomes amplified and this increasing rocking motion put him into a near panic. The bridge kept twisting and twisting back and forth and Dorje's body kept rocking one way and then the other until it seemed that the bridge would spill him into the inferno. I watched in horror as the man froze in fear and then reached up to the tump line on his forehead as if to release his load and thus, perhaps, save his life. I yelled but of course he could not hear me in the river's din. I started out on the bridge moving as fast as I could with the hope that my weight or position would take away some of the blind momentum of the bridge and perhaps institute some new variant in the vibrational mode. It seemed to work and now the man seemed to hold his own. He lowered his hand back to the side ropes. I moved up to him and he saw me. That seemed to reassure him and he started out again. He slowly narrowed the gap towards the far side and then he was on the firm earth. I followed. The thought of losing all those letters and seeing them on the brink of a desolating calamity left me weak. I wondered how all those hopeful donors of one dollar apiece would have felt and I wondered, now that they had a prospect of actually receiving their request, how they could know how nearly it all came to disaster. There would be no postmark saying something like "Almost lost in the Arun River by a panic stricken Tibetan." We camped on the shore, a place to collect.

I gathered the contents of the "Barun Glacier Base Camp Post Office" from Dorje's load and returned it to my own heavy pack. There would be no way that such a near catastrophe would threaten the mails again. We traveled on and finally we reached Dharan near the foot of the Himalaya. At the Dharan Post Office (a small mud hut with a table), the postmaster was ensconced on his office cot and yes, he had stamps. But by now it had become dark and there was only a very weak kerosene lamp. Furthermore, I had collected a band of children and all of them went into the post office with me. The postmaster brought out a book with stamps and stamps, gorgeous things with maps of Nepal on them and, altogether, just what I wanted and needed. But, of course, they were all inscribed in Nepali, everything on them was in native writing and I couldn't read their designations very easily. The postmaster could read, but the light was too dim and neither of us could use color as a guide. The blues and greens were identical and in the dim reddish glow of the lantern, oranges, yellows and reds looked the same. The postmaster tried hard and was painfully meticulous but it seemed hopeless. He would state once that a stamp had a certain value and then change his mind and so I would have to recalculate the cost. Finally, I think he got tired and since by now the mob in the post office was even getting on his nerves for they had spilled a bottle of ink very near his supply of stamps, he decided that payment would have to reflect a possible huge loss on his part. I therefore reassured him that I was perfectly capable of adding baksheesh (which, considering our meager finances was a downright lie) and getting on with it. It seemed to me, too, that who would care what the value of the stamps were? Who in some post office in San Francisco would look to see that the orange stamp was 4 annas and the red stamp was 12 annas? I assumed that very few American postal people could read Nepali. I just needed enough stamps to make it look like the postage had been paid. Besides, the stamps were better than I had ever contemplated. I finally had some hundreds of stamps, the whole supply of the Dharan Post Office and, with my army of children, I left contented and hopeful for a philatelic success.

There was another job to be done in Dharan. I had seen what looked like a telephone line, a single wire that swung from little white insulators that were attached to trees. Perhaps we could call some place, perhaps even Calcutta, and get the consulate to send up the money we so desperately needed, the money from the philatelic effort, as well as some cash our wives had scrounged while we were away. We needed trainfare and we had to pay off our debts to our money-lending Sherpas. I went to the telephone office and there was a telephone. I presented my request and a very agreeable young man asked me to write down my message and he would call it to Biratnagar for that was as far as the telephone line ran. I wrote a message, as it turned out, a rather long message for the system to handle. He took it and picked up the phone and rang on a crank and said "hallo, hallo, hallo, hallo" for 15 minutes. Finally he had someone to talk to but he didn't talk as one might expect. He proceeded to spell out each word of my message but not in the sometimes American fashion of "A Able, B Baker, etc." It was a Hindi equivalent "A atcha, B burra, etc." This was a telephone whose critical function was one decibel above silence. It would only work as a sort of telegraph, which, indeed, would have been faster. Incredibly, the message was delivered; it was sent to Calcutta and, even more incredibly, we did get some money. There, in actual rupees was the product of philately. Happiness ruled and the Sherpas, with cash in their fists made for the nearest place where some Nepali concoction of beer might be had.

In time we went on to Biratnagar by a series of dilapidated trucks. After we arrived, I went down to the post office and explained my needs, that I wished to have only the Nepalese stamps canceled but not the Indian stamps. All my requests seemed agreeable, even the suggestion that the cancellations should not be the normal obliterating black smudges that postmasters in that part of the world prefer. Such destroying marks seem to say that never again should this stamp they are blotting into extinction be ever used again. The postmaster then dumped my huge pile of letters on the earth floor of his place and proceeded to bang the very devil out of them with his canceling device. He did not show the respect I wished for my valuable cargo. That done, he called in one of his postmen and my letters were shoved unceremoniously into a large leather bag.

It was explained to this man that he was to carry the load over to the Jogbani Post Office in India about two miles away. The postman picked up the bag, went out of the door and in the style of the ages began jogging off towards India. There was nothing I could do but to jog along at his heels and so the two of us paced our way along the dusty roads through crowds of people who looked at me with all the signs of bewildering wonderment. The mark on my letters that proclaimed "Carried by Runner" was the solemn truth. I jogged my way across the border into India knowing full well that this was a frowned-upon behavior but there was no border guard or eagle-eyed customs officer in this far corner of the world to check my passport. I wondered when they last had some strange foreigner run across the unlined border.

At the Jogbani Post Office I repeated my requests, and the postmaster was as congenial as his neighbor in Nepal. He too spread the envelopes on his earth floor and started to bang the very devil out of them. Finally, it was all done and the handfuls of covers with their odd shapes, the product of my Sherpa envelope factory, were stuffed into a box. They were now beyond my supervision and I hoped some decent percentage of them would find their way back to those mail boxes around the world where some nice person had parted with a dollar to help save the destitute American climbers in Nepal.

I jogged back towards Biratnagar. But I made a slight detour to the nearby train station in Jogbani where I found myself on the brink of the partly civilized milieu that trains bring to far corners of the world. Here there were some bottled drinks, things I had not seen for months. It was common practice some years ago to use the word "pop" as a generic word for a soft drink. That nonspecific word seems to have been suppressed in favor of commercial designations such as "Coke" or "Pepsi" and so forth. However, in India where western terminologies tend to linger long after their demise in more hectic and fulminating places such as the USA, the concept of "pop" was still here in Jogbani. But, to fit the inventive Indian need for private enterprise in some distinct mimicking of our own culture, there were competing "pops" in the train station at Jogbani. One was called "peep" and one was called "poop." I was pleased with both or either or any. I toasted the success of philately with a "peep" and a "poop."

There is a sequel here. Many years later I dropped by a philatelic exhibition in a major San Francisco hotel. In wandering through the various displays that ranged from "Covers of the Mexican Revolution" to "Covers of Post World War I Divisions of Hungary." I suddenly encountered "Covers from Nepal." There on a large board was a whole section devoted to all sorts of varieties of my own precious cover, red and blue stamps—even one in green with different assortments of Indian and Nepalese stamps. Some of them had the telltale shape of hand-made Sherpa fare. Not really! There was a man explaining something to visitors and I drew closer to try to overhear what he was saying. He was telling about the difficulty in deciphering the Nepalese script of the mark from Biratnagar but he could clearly see the Jogbani mark. How could he know? Nothing had ever been published on the matter and, indeed, this writing is the first public account of those marvelous covers. I bided my time and then gently translated the Biratnagar postmark. He looked at me in wonder and then I had to explode with some of the story I have just written. He was really awed but I rather think he preferred to have his collection left as a mystery rather than with its shroud uncovered. I expressed my gratitude for his work and his insight in being able to recognize one of the most interesting covers in all of philately. I think he won some sort of prize there.

Nepalese stamp

Finally Tibet

Darjeeling lies at the end of the road from Tibet. It is here that the long mule trains carrying salt or borax or clothes or rugs would finally unload after months of marches across the high plateau. I used to watch these caravans led by wild-looking men in fur caps and strange woolen boots that were soled with yak hide as they came up the road near my school. To me, in time, Tibet would become the land beyond the high peaks far to the north, a place too far away for my schoolboy resources. I envied those occasional travelers and expeditions who had entry permits and who had the money to travel the long road through Sikkim to the frontier at the Natu La or Jelep La passes that led to that forbidden land.

This was the environment of my youth where Tibet and its wonders were nearby and its secrets cast a real spell. People in Darjeeling still felt the throb of the 19th century search for Lhasa when, after the discovery of the sources of the Nile, the enormous tales of Livingston, Burton and Stanley, the world looked for another great geographical goal. Lhasa, deep in the heart of an unknown land of mountains and more mountains and vast and desolate high altitude plains, fit the imagination of explorers and they set off searching. They were always rebuffed before they fulfilled their dreams but the writings of men like Sven Hedin, who described the immensity and the impossibility of the endless bleakness, brought the world to listen. Prior to these dauntless men there had been the obscure explorations of the "pundits," the trained native observers of the Great Trigonometrical Survey of India who had marched the plateau tolling their beads which numbered their strides and had measured their altitudes by secretly testing their boiling tea water with thermometers and finding its temperature. From these men whose exploits are revealed to us in Survey accounts, the first accurate descriptions of Lhasa were made. From them we heard how travelers would bow low when they first caught a glimpse of the golden roofs of the Potala, the fabled palace of the Dalai Lama in Lhasa. The story of the pundits needs to be told so it can become, in textbooks, the epitome of geography and the study of the world.

It was not until 1904 that westerners had their first opportunity to see this hidden city. It was then that a British brigade was sent up to Lhasa to quell some problems of the Empire. Later, in 1911, when the Boxer Rebellion in China brought confusion, the Tibetans were able to extricate themselves from immediate Chinese dominance and were able to declare that they were a separate nation. And now, British representatives were allowed to remain in Tibet, single men in isolation from the rest of the world, but observers who could report on the unusual affairs of the country. Later still, with the Everest Expeditions, which traversed southern Tibet because Nepal and Kathmandu were still off limits, the expedition scientists gave their scattered accounts of the geology and biology of the land. With few exceptions, all others were excluded.

Occasional Americans did visit Lhasa but their routes were fairly confined to travel by the high road to Darjeeling. A few American fliers saw Lhasa for a few days after their plane crashed along the Tsangpo River but they were hurriedly shipped out so as to not cause an international problem during time of war. Just after the war and before the reoccupation by the Chinese, Lowell Thomas and his son were able to visit Lhasa, but shortly after this the country became closed to all save a few observers from Eastern Europe.

In the early 1950's when China once again dominated the plateau, the new regime did not seem willing to open the land, and I feared that even the religious protectionist zeal of the Dalai Lama would be exceeded by the exclusionist attitudes of a Communist Government that, from all stories, had much to hide in its ruthless control over the people of Tibet. Therefore, on those occasions when I was able to see that land of red hills and distant

195

lakes far away on the northern horizon, I never held any real hope that, in my lifetime, I would ever visit the interior of the land or witness the splendor of the Potala.

When Richard Nixon made contact with China and sat face to face with Mao Zedung and Cho Enlai, I saw a glow on the horizon. When Chinese scientists came on visits I had some chances to inquire about Tibet, but it seemed that that frontier of China was even forbidden to the majority of Chinese. A visiting delegation of Chinese scientists appeared at the California Academy of Sciences in 1978 and I offered myself as a host and so reached some conversation with the leader of the delegation. A translator expressed my desire to reach Tibet for I explained that I had viewed Tibet from the south. The words came back in Chinese which I could not understand but even before the translator started to interpret the answer to me, he had a big, enthusiastic smile on his face. I was told that the Director assured me that I would soon have an opportunity to see the Himalaya from the north. The translator went on with his own thoughts now and told me that this was a notable invitation and that, perhaps, Tibet was to be opened and that I just might have the opportunity to visit that forgotten world.

Some time prior to 1980 I sent a letter to the Academia Sinica, the Chinese Academy of Sciences, for I had heard a rumor that they were going to have a Symposium of some sort and then, in the Fall of 1979, a letter arrived. I was invited to attend a Symposium on the Qinghai-Xizang (Tibet) Plateau to be held in Beijing in May 1980. More than that, there would be a post-symposium tour of Tibet under the auspices of the Academia Sinica. This last offer was absolutely unbelievable. Could it be that I might be able to visit Tibet? Surely there must be some catch. Surely something would go wrong. Surely some casual event of international relations would keep me from a lifelong dream.

The preliminary accounts of the Symposium were rather vague and I had little notion of the nature of the research that was to be presented or who might be attending. I flew to Beijing in late May and was driven to the Jing Xi Guest House, a remarkable hotel that had lately been vacated by the military leadership of the country. Now the Symposium agenda became apparent. There were over 100 foreign guests and perhaps as many Chinese scientists who had some relation to research conducted in Tibet for the last 20 or 30 years. The vast majority of foreign scientists were geologists and other varieties of physical scientists. As a biologist I was in a distinct minority but I was in good company for two of my associates were S. Dillon Ripley, Secretary of the Smithsonian Institution, and George Schaller, the incomparable observer of animals and who was, at that time, beginning his studies of the Giant Panda in western China.

The papers were presented day after day for a week. It was remarkable. Some 30 years of research in Tibet by the Chinese scientists, none of whom I had heard of or met before, were now made known to the world. Intriguing gaps to my knowledge were being filled minute by minute. For instance, I had known of Tony Hagen's discovery of Pliocene deposits near the Tibetan frontier in Nepal. The Pliocene should contain fossils that coincide with the origin of man and I had held an inference that there should be similar deposits in Tibet and that fossils of this age might throw some light on the environment of Tibet at that time, perhaps even reveal something about human fossils in a place that I have long maintained should, on zoogeographical grounds, be the cradle for our family. One of the very first papers described hyenas, giraffes, rhinoceroses, and so forth, from Pliocene deposits located now at 17,000 feet, indicating, without a doubt, what I had suspected, that Tibet was a savanna at the very time that mankind originated.

It was a week of intense learning and I reveled in this huge accumulation of interpretive information, but my mind was very much on the prospective visit to Tibet itself. At the end of the Symposium we were politely requested to wear tie and dress up and then we were bussed off to the Hall of the Peoples, a place where not every tourist is privileged to visit. We entered this huge building where the doors were guarded by stately officers and as we entered we were faced by a reception line. There to greet us was the Chief Minister of China, Deng Hsiao-ping, along with other leaders of the country. He met all of us and later, at a fantastic banquet, we had an opportunity to speak individually and informally with him. It was all very remarkable and the whole affair indicated how important this Symposium was to the Chinese. I cannot imagine such an equivalent affair occurring in the U.S.A. where a miscellany of scientists could meet and converse freely with the President and his Cabinet. All of this was a formal display that signaled the opening of Tibet, the unveiling of the forgotten land, an offering to the world to visit Tibet, an incredible break from the past, a landmark for new opportunity. The American Press missed this opportunity although it was highly acclaimed in Asia.

Between meetings, some of us had a brief visit to the Beijing Zoo where the pandas were in some abundance. On our tour with the Director we were taken to a place where the general public was not admitted and we were shown a most remarkable animal, a Bactrian camel. This two-humped camel is a common feature at zoos but the individual creature that we saw was a wild camel, a young specimen that had been found in the distant Kun Lun Range on the northern border of Tibet that had been abandoned by its herd. It had been found by a wandering party of exploring Chinese scientists and brought to the zoo. Its presence confirmed the existence of wild Bactrian camels in the remotest part of Asia. That it was here at all seemed incredible to me for it represented proof that these creatures were still extant. There have been many suggestions that the wild and original Bactrian camels from which the domesticated types have been derived had all been eliminated.

This individual camel, the only known representative of its species as it once existed, was a lithe and prancing creature that was far from the heavy and steady creatures that we generally visualize as Bactrian camels. Here was a camel that, during the long history of mankind, had avoided the genetic manipulations of domestication and stood before us showing the original morphology of camel-like animals. It was not unlike the wild guanaco from which the llamas and alpacas, the domesticated South American camelids, had been derived.

The time to move on to Tibet eventually arrived and we flew off to Chengdu. On the way, from high above the earth, I calculated that a distant and vague line of snow was actually the dim outline of the Amne Machin Range, those strange mountains that were once claimed to exceed the height of Mount Everest. The intrepid explorer and botanist Joseph Rock who, seeing the amount of snow on the peaks, added to the perception that they were exceedingly high first photographed them. There are, as we know now, no such legendary mountains and the arguments of Leonard Clark, who managed to reach them some years ago and tried to convince the world that they were indeed the highest mountains in the world, have fallen some 8,000 feet short. Nevertheless, just to see in the distance the hazy outlines of this remote range that I knew only from maps, and a great deal of contemplation, was a permeating thrill.

At the airport we were faced with several Russian-built planes, all of which were headed for Lhasa. The first planes were filled with young mothers carrying babies on their backs, and I was told that they had all come down here to lower altitudes to give birth. It fit the words of the physiologists who had garnered information that some new and fascinating forms of altitude troubles had plagued many Chinese who were assigned to the high plateau. Birth, it seemed, was better pursued away from the thin air.

By good fortune I was able to obtain a good seat. I had to be able to see the valleys and rivers below and find them on my maps and time their arrivals to establish the speed and route of the airplane. As the configurations on my maps matched the rivers and mountains below, I was able to calculate the speed and direction of the flight and could anticipate to a few seconds our prospective position and estimate what mountains might come into view. I knew which of the many deep valleys we were flying over and marked the crossing of the main streams of the Yalung, Yangtse, Mekong and Salween. I noted that we flew just north of where Ronald Kaulback had explored back in the 1930's and I could recognize some of the geographical features he had described in his book, *Salween*, that told of the last and only recent western visitor to this land this far north. Far to the south there were also some of the ranges and valleys that had been explored by Joseph Rock, an American botanist whose collections of seeds from the area have added so many flowers to our gardens, and whose accounts of his travels were marvelously displayed in a series of *National Geographic Journals* during the 1930's.

Since I knew where I was and could match my view with what I saw on the latest maps available to Americans, I felt certain that there were peaks far above 20,000 feet in places where nothing that high was indicated. Even a recent Chinese map, that had been derived from U.S. satellite photographs, shows no equivalent peaks. Where else in the world is the earth's surface so little known and so versatile in its form? It was all a most emotional experience to me.

Beyond more than half of the flight, I calculated that, far off to the south, we might be able to see the eastern rampart of the Himalaya, the giant peak of Namcha Barwa, but the spot where I envisaged it to be was covered with clouds. I watched that pile of clouds and then as we moved, it became apparent that there was snow amongst the towering clouds and finally the peak emerged from its distant curtains over a hundred miles away. Its consort peak, Gyala Peri, showed itself to indicate the route of passage of the Tsangpo River and the position of the great gorge of this river that cuts its way between these great peaks. We were seeing from the north a peak so remote and isolated that no reasonable pictures of it existed. The great botanist Kingdon Ward had searched the gorge as far as he could go, but being directly under the slopes of the peak, he did not appreciate its form and left us no photograph of the peak in its whole setting.

As my calculations suggested, we abruptly turned south. We had been flying at near 31° N. and we had to move south to land in the valley of the Tsangpo River, south of Lhasa. I assume we had been traveling on a radio beam from Chamdo on the Mekong, a place reported by those 19th century explorers and which we flew directly over, for I could see houses scattered on the slopes of the gorge. The plane turned and the view revealed the great snow-covered peaks of Northern Bhutan that few westerners, such as H.W. Tilman, had viewed at close range from the south. My view from the north could have been unique. I waited as we moved west and then, as I expected, the distinct outline of Chumolari appeared, that stupendous 24,000-foot mountain that rose up high enough for me to see it from my home in Darjeeling so many years before. We came down very fast into the valley of the Tsangpo River and I saw it as it had been described so many times by those earlier explorers, a highly braided stream and a wandering river across a broad valley. My token altimeter now rapidly started to rotate from a cabin pressure of 3,000 feet to 11,500 feet and the wheels were down to touch the Tibetan earth. The great alluvial fans that were green with crops went by the window and then I was in Tibet.

A vehicle drove us toward Lhasa and after nearly an hour of driving, I anticipated that we must have been approaching the city. We turned a corner and there, just as the pundit explorers had described, far in the distance before any houses could be seen and far beyond any indications of the city, there, far against a blue sky, were the shining reflections of gold, the gilded roofs of the Potala. Lhasa at last. Like my Sherpas of the past I had to utter Om! Mani Peme Hum!

The guest house was in full view of the Potala and I spent an hour examining it with my binoculars. That night a few lights remained on in this huge palace and I wondered who might still be living there. I was eager for our visit there on the following day, but we spent the morning examining a place that could be even more remarkable although less well known. This was the Jo Yang monastery where crowds of Tibetans, to my surprise, were worshipping at the shrine. There was the clear indication that the forbidding attitudes toward religious freedom that had so characterized the Chinese dominion in recent years was now relenting. And just as I had read for so many years, here were the faces of Mongolians, the costumes of distant Ladakh, the crude skin robes of the nomads of the high Chang Tang and the signs of people who had come from the Takla Makan Desert and beyond. The Jo Yang was still the magnet for Tibetan Buddhists, the holiest place in all of Central Asia.

I put some miscellaneous coins in an offering bowl and added all I had in the way of American quarters. A lama was smiling at me as if to indicate that he was glad to see me. I imagined he saw a distant foreigner representing the arrival of new times, a symbol of a new era in Tibet, an indication of some relent in the recent malevolent suzerainty of the Chinese. He gave me a kata, a thin scarf, an item that now hangs over the upper roller stick of my

Tibetan tanka, a strange painting, that I acquired, long ago, from some Tibetan refugees near the Nangpa La as they came over from Tibet. There was
a strong pulse to my emotions when, after so long, the pungent odor of
burning yak butter stimulated my memory. It was a significant reminder that
this was not all a dream and that I was, yes, actually in the land that had
haunted my aspirations for my lifetime.

Tibetans outside the
Jo Yang Monastery.

In the afternoon we visited the Potala. We entered by the back into an
enormous room with ceilings that must have been 70 feet high, and we were
immediately among the graves of the ancient Dalai Lamas. These chortens
with their square bases and round domes had the flattened openings that indicated the presence of human remains. The earliest tombs were relatively small
and they progressively became larger for more recent Dalai Lamas until the
chorten of the 13th, and penultimate Dalai Lama reached 20 feet or more
above us. This was the tomb of the Dalai Lama who had opened Tibet to the
west, a man of international distinction who was in Tibet when I was growing
up. I well remember the announcement of his death. His tomb was totally
guilded in shining gold and there may have been a ton of it on the tomb. It was
encrusted with precious gems and beside this monument to priceless riches
there was a model monastery made totally of precious pearls, thousands and
thousands of pearls glued together with abandonment to any price.

I was witnessing one of the most secret and holiest places of Buddhism.
I never dreamed that I would have this improbable experience. I walked up
and down the narrow and steep stairways and down the long hallways where
there must have been a mile or more of paintings on the walls, lifetimes of
work for art historians and the interpreters of occult portrayals. I was with
many others of our group and we finally reached the highest level and I

stood in a courtyard where the golden roofs of several structures marked the summit of the Potala. The abundance of gold at this and other great buildings of Tibet is beyond belief. Not only are there figures covered with gold foil but devices and figures of various sorts made with gold plate and even made of solid gold. There were tons and tons of the stuff. The tombs of the Dalai Lamas themselves could fill some vaults in Switzerland and the whole could rival Fort Knox. I could not help but wonder where it all came from and how much wealth was spent upon death and religion. There was a strong symbolism in all this shining glitter of riches in a country that was once so poor and filled with beggars.

I could dwell on tales of Lhasa and compare what I have read of the old and what I saw of the new. I could continue on and on about the fantastic paintings that covered the walls of the monasteries and the Potala and I could go on further into the plight of the lamas and of politics and the new agriculture, but the high plateau and its crossing come next. We spent a day traveling up to Yangbaijan, some hours north of Lhasa where there are hot springs, and we saw the beginnings of a program to tap the hot springs for energy to power Lhasa. The springs were interesting, but I was far more impressed with the fact that I was immediately on the slope of the great Nyenchentangla Range, the Transhimalaya of Sven Hedin. Just ahead was the towering giant of this range that reached above 23,000 feet. It was just a few miles away that Sven Hedin, on his most successful approach to reach Lhasa, had been caught and turned away over 80 years earlier.

The springs at Yangbaijan were at about 14,000 feet and as I wandered around the place collecting from a stream, I heard Dillon Ripley's shout "Look!" Dillon was not usually given to such loud outbursts so he had my immediate attention. He was pointing up the stream and seemed most excited. "Look! Look! An ibisbill." And there it was, one of the strangest birds in the world that makes its home in high Central Asia. I had read how the early naturalists on the Mount Everest expeditions had seen this bird and how they marveled at its presence for it is rare and seldom seen. It has a beak like an ibis, long, stout and curved and at first glance one might think it was an ibis that had strayed from some tropical land. But its legs give it away; they are a bit thin for an ibis. But who would know except a bird anatomist that it was a close relative of the avocet and stilt. I am not sure if Dillon Ripley, who is probably the greatest authority on Asian birds, had ever seen one of these in the wild. From his enthusiasm, it would seem he had witnessed a flying dinosaur or some such thing.

Going south from Lhasa, we crossed the Tsangpo River by a new bridge, and on the main road from Lhasa to India, we climbed the winding road to the Kamba La, a pass of 15,700 feet. As soon as the cars stopped on the summit, I was out and digging around under the rocks looking for anything that could live in this bleak world. I was immediately surrounded by the younger Chinese scientists who watched my every move and inquired what I was doing and what I was collecting. They were intent on learning everything they could and picking up any hints that I might give as to what I considered unusual or particularly interesting.

The feature of this pass was the large and showy red flower of *Incarvillea younghusbandi*, which reminded me of the past presence of Francis Younghusband, a leader of that 1904 British skirmish up to Lhasa. Younghusband had been an explorer of Central Asia and subsequently a key figure in obtaining permission from the Tibetans to launch the first expeditions to climb Mount Everest. This flower was most unusual and I had never encountered it further south in the Himalaya. Its flower was fully two or three inches across and yet its leaves were very inconspicuous. Except for the large flower, it was a typical alpine plant that hugged the ground, and its leaves were frequently totally hidden and covered with windblown sand so that the bright flower emerged directly from the soil. It existed only on a few such passes south of Lhasa and its form indicated to me that it was insect pollinated by some special insect that also lived only in these remote localities.

Beyond the pass was the exquisite Yamdrok Tso, a blue wonder of a lake that had formed when a contributory stream of the Tsangpo had been dammed by faulting and the thwarted waters had backed up the several valleys of the source streams to create a lake with a strange shape. This amoeboid shape stands out on the maps of Tibet so I had long been acquainted with its existence. And now here it was, and from the high pass its strange, almost crablike, form could be appreciated. At its shore, at an altitude of over 14,000 feet, I ran out on the mud flats and slapped my net and scooped up the frogs that were abundant. They were *Altirana parkeri*, a ranid frog that some taxonomist from past years considered sufficiently different from the standard genus *Rana* to give it a different genus. These, as with most of my collections, would be the first specimens from Tibet in American museums. Each fly and miscellaneous midge, each tadpole or worm, each spider or minute crustacean, would be unique or most unusual in any American museum.

On the lake there were relatively few birds, and although we may have been there at an odd hour, or the birds had congregated elsewhere, the impression I gained was that the water bird populations were clearly reduced. There were, for instance, no bar headed geese and I knew from the old explorers that this lake was famous for their presence. I had a clue here for my wonders about the population of this bird which I have discussed earlier.

I was impressed as we rode on our small buses that we were actually far from the ancient Tibet where days were marked in long marches that could have gone on and on for months. Here we were, in the comfort of vehicles, covering in one day what it took those old explorers and the caravans of old Tibet many weeks to traverse. We were not so committed as they were. We were fortunate, but I knew from my own long marches across Nepal that this convenient travel of speed removes one from the realities of the land and makes it all too easy. And with this ease comes superficiality and a failure to sense the wonder and hugeness of the land. I can say now that I have crossed Tibet. That could be a fact, but I know that I did not sense the land like Bonvalot or Przewalski who spent years on the trail.

On the other hand, I did see the dark-blue, unhazed skies, and I did feel the crispness of the high air and I did experience the endless rolling hills that had been featured in the writings of old. And so, as it always has been, you cannot go back again, and remorse about change is a useless pursuit. I watched the old Tibet from afar and sensed it in the words of others; I have experienced the new Tibet and the two are far apart. But, with all its changes it is still Tibet. With camera-arrayed tourists haunting the streets of the once forbidden Lhasa, where trucks and paving are scattered across the land, it is still Tibet. Nevertheless, with this acceptance of the changing world, the inevitable alterations of time seem least comfortable upon this ancient land that somehow demands that it should stay medieval. Of all the places where I have difficulty in accepting modernism and the intrusion of the centuries, I find the hills of Tibet most difficult to sacrifice for the needs of time.

We spent some days in Shigatse, and there was an opportunity offered to travel for some miles along the valley of the Tsangpo to where the river leaves its wide and wandering course and gathers itself together and plunges through a gorge, a gorge that had never been seen by westerners. On a day's journey several of us drove down to this point where the road ends and the river disappears into its unknown zone. Along the way the broad valley indicated to me that this area around Shigatse was at one time a huge lake which, at the time I was there, I thought may have been caused by a dam of sorts in the gorge below. I have since altered my opinion and have considered the possibility that a lake of this sort may have resulted in a change in direction of the flow of the Tsangpo. This would appear on the surface as a wild and impossible conjecture. What river in the whole world has stopped its flow in one direction and turned around and flowed in the opposite direction?

In the sand dunes along the side of the Tsangpo, I saw the telltale tracks of a lizard, and soon I had captured some of these fascinating animals that I immediately knew as the rare and seldom captured *Phrynocephalus theobaldi*. This gentle lizard, not too unlike the common "horned toad" of the U.S., is admirably adapted to live in sand dunes for it has strange sand-excluding scales around its eyes. A.F.R. Wollaston, during the 1921 reconnaissance of Mount Everest, had collected a number of these lizards and reported them as high as 17,000 feet. Among lizards this places them second only to *Leiolopisma ladacensis*, a skink that was found at 18,000 feet in northern Nepal. Inasmuch as none of these lovely little creatures had ever been obtained alive, I managed to carry a few back with me to the United States where I donated them to the California Academy of Sciences. What worried me in this accomplishment was not their entry into the United States for I had permits for them, it was the many customs examinations and body searches that I encountered on my way out of Southeast Asia. In India itself there were innumerable "baady saarches" which in Hong Kong are "Bonny sorches" and which in Japan are "Borry sauches." Each time I was patted and rubbed and when they encountered my little box of lizards, they did not look inside and scare themselves, they merely rattled the box back and forth to scare my precious lizards out of their wits. In tropical Bangkok I had to go out at night around the lights and collect insect food for them and commiserate with them in my hotel room about the unfortunate heat and humidity. Most of them survived these difficulties but, at home in the Academy, they gradually lost weight and eventually all of them died. There is something about our artificial environments that does not satisfy these pleasant animals.

On the way to Shigatse we had passed through Gyantse, a place that was well known to me as the type locality of a snake that was first described as *Natrix baileyi* but has now been removed from the common water snake genus *Natrix* and placed in its own distinctive genus *Thermophis*, meaning "hot snake." Colonel Bailey was the British Resident at Gyantse for many years and, it seems, a native collector had brought him this snake which was said to survive near some hot springs near Gyantse. I doubt if Bailey ever saw the snake alive.

This snake species represents the only snake of the high plateau and the reason for its survival is most remarkable. It would appear that with the uplift of the plateau, and the accompanying climatic changes which must have been intensified by the Pleistocene glaciers, that all of the snakes except this species were eliminated from high Tibet. That it survived must surely be associated with its environment, the neighborhood of hot springs. In the annals of zoogeography, *Thermophis baileyi* stands out as a spectacular example of a relictual creature that, as with the aquatic Scutiger frogs, reminds us by its existence that Tibet was once (and not too long ago) a land of warmth with an agreeable climate.

In Shigatse I now started inquiring among the most knowledgeable Chinese scientists about this snake, but since there were no herpetologists among them they could not give me first-hand information. They told me, in no uncertain terms, that none of the few small bubbling hot springs in the vicinity of Gyantse would be an appropriate place to look for snakes. For not only had they not seen any but that whatever hot water there was, was now used for bathhouses.

They told me that the only place they had heard of snakes in a hot spring was at Yangbaijan, and this sounded very reasonable. Back in Beijing we had been entertained by a movie about Tibet and in this presentation I had seen some brief footage of a snake swimming in warm water; this could very well have been made at Yangbaijan. I now regretted I had not spent more time at those hot springs searching, for it now seemed logical that the snake could have come from there. I do not know if Bailey's record is in error or if there may be several localities of this interesting snake. If there are several localities, the snakes from several hot springs would make a most challenging taxonomic study.

After Shigatse we drove west to Lhatse, a military outpost that few if any westerners had visited. Along the way we drove along what is known as the "ophiolite belt" which derives its name from the presence of rocks that have been so exposed to friction that their surfaces resemble the skin of a snake and hence, "ophiolite." The friction that has produced this slippery looking surface had been the collision of continents, for this belt of strange rocks indicates the zone of contact between the subcontinent of India and the old Laurasia that we know today as the major portion of the Asian continent. We saw the pillow lavas, a form of extruded lava that is produced in the form of rounded pillow-like formations where lava is extruded deep under the sea. We were driving along in what must have been a great cleft in the bottom of the Tethys Sea that once was a great ocean that separated Laurasia in the north from Gondwanaland in the south, a time when there were two massive continents, a southern Gondwanaland and a northern

Laurasia. The Mediterranean Sea, the Black Sea, the Caspian Sea, which is really a lake, and a series of other remnant bodies of water remain as reminders of that ancient sea. The geologists, as they drove along this amazing piece of ancient evidence, noted the great "exotic blocks," some a mile or more on a side, which had been removed from their normal places and, by some huge forces of continental collision, had been thrust on top of other, younger rocks.

From Lhatse we turned south and started the long slow climb up to the Gyaco Pass (Maphu La of older maps) at 17,250 feet. Along this remote road we saw some huge flocks of sheep, many hundreds of animals covering acres of the near barren hillsides. There were also large herds of yaks. They were surviving on the sparse tundra vegetation and their effect on the land must have been devastating. Grazing animals at lower altitudes, if given time and opportunity, can destroy the covering plants effectively and animals grazing on alpine vegetation are much more destructive. These high altitude plants grow very slowly and some of them may take 30 years to add two inches to their size. They can be damaged or even killed by simply being stepped on, and so, overabundant grazing animals in a place like Tibet can leave the hillsides barren and hopeless. Recovery in centuries would not be an optimistic hope. Overgrazed brown lands at high altitude are like geological formations that last for the ages.

It is not only the grazing animals in abundance that destroy the land. Humanity needs fuel for comfort and cooking, and so today, most of the original shrubs of juniper have been taken for burning and even the once plentiful woody shrubs, such as the widespread Caragana bushes, are gone from many of the slopes around human habitation. Now, the low growing *Sopophora morcroftiana*, a plant with profuse blue flowers, is being collected for fuel, but these shrubs are dug up by the roots for the roots are thick and woody. As a last hope for firewood this plant is thus being destroyed without hope of regrowth or recovery.

One could believe that Tibet, with its vast expanses and relatively small population, might be immune from the destruction of the land and the search for fuel that so characterizes parts of India and much of the continent of Africa. In reality, Tibet with its fragility may be even more threatened for, in terms of support for its rural and nomadic populations, it may have been saturated with people long ago. The Chinese with their organization, their public health and medical support, their economic programs for the Tibetans that tend to concentrate people have inadvertently added even greater stress upon the land. The prospect appears to be that the Chinese will have to import more and more food and fuel which, in Tibet, where such things may have to be transported for thousands of miles by truck, will be inordinately expensive. Even as it stands, it appears to me that the maintenance of Tibet is a growing strain upon the Chinese economy, and the prospect of growing high yield crops, although in part successful, together with the value of Tibet's ores and mines, will not be sufficient to bring this plateau land out of the category of an economic drain.

All along on this trip across the plateau I shared a small bus with some zoologists. The two mammalogists, Richard Mitchell and George Schaller, were outnumbered by the ornithologists, Dillon Ripley, Peter Jackson (representing the International Union for the Conservation of Nature) and K. McClennan (of the World Pheasant Association). Mary Ripley, in addition to helping her husband with the birds, shared nets with me in collecting insects. Whereas I appreciate birds and mammals and insects, I find myself on such a trip refusing categorization and so, rather generously, classify myself as a Tibetologist.

Since mammals were few and the old descriptions of herds of kiang (wild ass), antelope and chiru, another antelope, are hopelessly out of date, the bird people became the dominant members of the party. We were continually stopping to put binoculars on a distant blue speck far in the valley below or making guesses at what a disappearing dot on the horizon might be. Many of the birds were inconspicuous, finch types, which even caused Dillon Ripley some hesitation. I generally call such things "L.B.J's" for "Little Brown Jobs," and leave their precise identities for some other occasion. I was happy to stop for the shouts from the ornithologists of "Stop the car!" It gave me an opportunity to get out and brush for insects or to wade off into the mud to catch frogs or whatever my net would find. I was seldom the perpetrator of that fateful call "Stop the car!"

However, just after we left the high pass at 17,250 feet where we had spent more than half an hour and the others seemed satisfied with the long stay and were ready to move on, I had to yell out. Now I got some dark looks when it was apparent that no strange and wonderful bird was to be seen. No, I wanted to stop the car because down the slope, some distance, there were two small ponds that were not even pretty. But this stop I had to have and so I argued for just 10 minutes of their time. There was something in those ponds. They were dragging at me like a magnet.

I jumped out of the bus and ran down to the first pond and when I got to it I realized that wading in was hopeless. It just did not seem to have the right look. So I started off for the lower pond that I knew would take more

208

than 10 minutes to get to and get back. But here the feeling was right. I knew there was something in there. I waded into the muck around the sides and reached out my net and dragged it through the water. All it caught was a great mound of mud. Again and again I tried with similar results. I waded out further and tried and when the net came back and I started to finger through the mud in the net I knew I had been successful. I saw a small piece of white that disappeared again into the black mud and so I carefully ran the mud through my fingers.

I wondered what the impatient others were thinking as they must have seen me down on my knees in deep mud poking my way through the net. And then I had a slippery little thing in my hand, and then another. They were small fish. They were, I knew, some species of loach that live on this high plateau, a representative of the genus *Nemacheilus*. I also knew that the pond was at 17,000 feet and that I had just captured the highest fishes in the world. Long ago in 1932 the distinguished biologist, G. E. Hutchinson, during the Yale expedition to Ladakh near western Tibet, had collected some fish of this sort at 16,250 feet. That record had remained until now.

I will explain some more about why I was so impressed with these little loaches. How did they survive? There must be ice over their pond for most of the year and, furthermore, how did they get to that little isolated piece of remnant water that came from the snowfields above? There was no stream leading from the pond that would offer a route in. Could it be that those little fish and their ancestors had always been here or had been in this general locality since the mountains were lower and there was a different arrangement of the pond and a stream? Could they have been raised up here with the mountains? Fish in strange places are often explained as having been brought in on the feet of birds or some such thing. Fish being lifted by mountains seems just as reasonable to me.

Coming down from the high pass, there was something good and something bad. The bad was the weather. Along this descent I had expected to get a view of the north face of Mount Everest but the monsoon clouds had come up from India and had enveloped the peak. The lower northern slopes could be seen and they suggested something very big up in the cloud cover but Mount Everest and her consorts, Changtse, Pumori, Gyachung Kang and Cho Oyo were hidden. Somewhere, not too far away, I also knew that Makalu was hiding. I had seen Mount Everest from the west and south and east and points in between, but I was denied this northern view with all the historical inferences that came from those early expeditions.

The good was the visit to some diggings near 17,000 feet where fossil giraffes had been found. These were the telling traces on the bleak and barren hillside that this part of Tibet, perhaps only four million years ago, was a warm and productive savanna. It was an exhibit of the rapidity of earth movements and the forces that thrust both the Tibetan Plateau and the Himalaya up to form the highest ramparts of the earth.

At Xezar we learned that the road down through the gorge, to Kathmandu, had been closed by landslides, and there was a possibility we would have to go back to Lhasa. I was willing to tie my suitcase on my back and walk for I did not want to miss that gorge. Fortunately word came that crews of workers had cleared enough of the way to let our buses through and so we continued our journey.

The road now led west and the streams we crossed were the tributary waters of the Arun which, not too far away, swarmed under that long swinging bridge. As we approached Tingri the "Stop the car" call went off. There were bar headed geese in the field. They were quite far away and when we cautiously tried to approach, they flew off. They were primed and suspicious. This locality was almost due north of Mount Everest. I conjectured they were some of a flock that had come this way by flying over the summit of the earth and, perhaps, descendants of the geese that flew far above me on the Barun Glacier and made their way here over the pinnacle of Makalu.

We continued past the town of Tingri, a cluster of white houses on a hill above the plain. I had heard of Tingri often. It was the main trading post in Tibet for the Sherpas, and just to the south, hidden in the rounded lower slopes of Cho Oyu, the great peak west of Mount Everest, was the Nangpa La, the pass to Sola Khumba and the land of the Sherpas. Twenty years earlier I had been up there somewhere.

The road now turned north and made a great circuit almost as far as the Tsangpo river again, and then after some more high passes we descended toward a gorge, the route through the Himalaya. We stopped at the town of Nyalam and I could not help but remind my associates that we were the second group of westerners to see this place that hangs below the enormous peak of Shishipangma, the Gosainthan of the Nepalese. A.F.R. Wollaston had visited Nyalam once before, in 1921, when on that first reconnaissance of Mount Everest. He had, without the express permission of the Tibetan authorities, taken off to the west and managed to get this far. He had looked down the gorge we were going to go through, but that way, toward Nepal, was closed to him.

Now, south of Nyalam the great Himalaya are split to allow a river to spill through. A quiet stream on the plateau now gathers water and starts to roar and churn its rapids and hurtle down a spectacular chasm. Our road followed perilously along on the slope above the stream and soon we encountered the landslides that had threatened our passage. We slid around on the mud and squeezed between the huge boulders that had been pushed aside for our passage and went on down the gorge. The road started to hug the side of cliffs while, as we went along, the river was left farther and farther below. It was like that day in the Rolwaling but here I was in a vehicle. My window on the outer side of the bus allowed me to look straight down into the colossal abyss and the wheels of the bus seemed hardly on the road.

I had heard that the Chinese were great builders of roads and now I could see where the reputation had come from. Some cliffs had simply been blown away to leave a flattened edge, and where this did not work, the cliff was blown out to leave a great groove in the vertical precipice. The groove became the roadway. In some places where the road dissolved its way into the rock, it did so to avoid a waterfall, so that when I looked out my window there were three sides of hewn cliff and on the fourth a wall of water.

We stopped often for photographs and I found that I could not get the full length of the opposite wall of the gorge in my camera viewer and had to resort to a 28mm wide angle lens. Such a lens gets close to focusing a photographer's toes while at the same time recognizing the zenith. I saw a waterfall of sorts, a narrow stream that may have been a temporary feature of the monsoon, falling straight down the opposite wall of the gorge for perhaps 5,000 feet, something that exceeds the great Angel Falls of Guyana. This was a gorge!

The road led down by zigs and zags and twists and turns, hovering on the edge of nothingness or sliding into the vertical rock to get enough space for wheels. In this way we reached Zham, a new town around an unfinished hotel. As we passed a small warehouse I noticed heaps of toilets that were only partially unwrapped from their crates and I knew the hotel had not been completed for our arrival. In the future I can see this hotel at Zham offering tourists an opportunity of a lifetime and also cutting into the tour business in Kathmandu. Consider that from here, a long day's ride up the spectacular gorge could lead to a prominence where the north side of Mount Everest could be seen and where the giant Shishipangma (26,291 ft.) is guardian to the gorge.

The Zham hotel at about 7,000 feet is low enough to be relatively warm and at night myriads of insects were out around the electric lights. I spent many hours picking up creatures that I knew from similar altitudes in Nepal and Darjeeling, but some were new and all could have that exotic label "Zham, Tibet." Some Chinese helpers found a snake for me. They had no container for it so one of them had sacrificed a boot lace and had managed to tie up the animal with a series of ingenious loops. It was brought to me, twisting and turning in its trap, on the end of a long stick as if it was the ultimate cobra. It was a gentle harmless thing that turned out to be *Trachischium guentheri*, a first record for either Tibet or Nepal.

We made some tours back up the gorge for more photography and collecting and on our final day all the scientists, Chinese and those from the all the other countries, got together in a review of our findings and experiences. I should think this was the first international symposium on Tibet that was held in Tibet. I hope there will be more.

On the final morning we drove down to Friendship Bridge, the border of Nepal. Here we would meet buses that had come from Kathmandu to pick us up. We said our goodbyes to the Chinese, men and women we had learned to enjoy and appreciate. We all stood in the middle of the bridge and then we separated, the Chinese remaining where they were on the edge of their great nation and the rest of us, walking backwards, waving and calling to them as we moved toward our buses. It was an emotional moment. I thought as I left how much those people had worked for us, the months of work that had gone into the preparations for our visit, the enormous dedication they had to this cause of opening their new land for the world to see. It was a gamble of sorts to take these unknown foreigners across a plateau of many obstacles and leave them safely at this bridge. They had won and I, for one, was deeply appreciative.

We were soon on our way over the 80 miles of winding road that separated us from Kathmandu. We passed Barahbise and I looked up into the cloud-capped mountains for somewhere up there I had camped that night when the sheep came to call and collapsed my tent. Perhaps Sophia Loren was still up there collecting sheep dung.

In those days this area we were driving through was seldom visited. Now it was the main road to China. The hillsides were decimated and goat trails on scrubby hillsides showed the red earth where forests had been. The river, which at Friendship Bridge had been a torrent with glacial gray colors, turned brown and then showed streaks of red. By the time we reached the junction of the Indrawatti and the Sun Kosi, the whole broad stream was red like one of those lateritic roads so common in the tropics. I was watching great chunks of the soil of Nepal being washed down to India where it would settle out and form its sandy dams that would change the course of India's rivers and flood the land.

I was also watching the fertile earth of Himalayan hillsides, the hold of life that the forests require for their existence, the future welfare of Nepal, slide in red, like blood, away from the wounded hills. Once more there was the token of too many people making too many demands on the innocent earth. A 20-year lapse between that long walk in 1960 and this comfortable ride in 1980 revealed, as no written obituary can, the rape of the Himalaya, the demise of Nepal's wealth of forest, the death verdict of the needs of too many people.

A few days later I flew out of Kathmandu and as the plane reached quickly out of the monsoon clouds I saw the ghostly form of Gaurishankar with its summits pointing into the blue. I had camped below its cliffs with my knights, and Old Bloody had sensed the spell of redness reflected from the snows that hovered above us. And then the Rolwaling summits appeared and my memories grabbed me again and placed me on that small summit where the yeti tracks had baffled me. Far away to the east, the clouds parted and there was the great white-turreted mound of Kangchenjunga, the peaks of my youth. In center stage was Mount Everest reaching its pyramid above the walls of Nuptse and Lhotse and telling all the surrounding peaks with its soaring that it was the mightiest of all.

But my eyes were chiefly on the hopelessly beautiful Makalu standing in its frame of cumulus. There I could see that long slope to the north where I had collected those highest plants in the world, and there was that awful snow face where my friends had seen the avalanche roar over the entrance of their snow cave, and there was Tutse defining the limits of the Barun Valley where even now its Yosemite-like cliffs were covered with rhododendrons and untouched by man. It was a moment for me and, as usual, I was saying things to myself with "oohs" and "ahs" and making sounds that came out as little groans of pleasure and wonder. Beside me on the adjacent seat was an Indian businessman and he heard some of these groans of delight and per-haps thought that I was in some pain. "What is it?" he asked. I turned to him with my eyes wide and at the end of a long strand of emotion. "Look! Look! Mount Everest! Makalu! Kangchenjunga!"

"Ah!" he exclaimed, as if with a sense of relief that I was not dying in the seat beside him of some sort of plague, "Thank you, but I have seen it before." I then knew I was back in the "real"world where there are other values and the glories of the world can be mundane.

Monsoon

This is a story of the greatest conflict on earth. A battle between the giants, a war between the largest mass of moving air on our world, the Monsoon, and the mightiest bulwark of the earth, the Himalaya.

The beginning is a scene of blue ocean and great rising billows of cumulus clouds. It is the Indian Ocean where much of the world's weather begins. It is here that the water temperature rises to approach the bath-like warmth of 90° F. and above the waves the warm air holds its full capacity of moisture and turns heavy with its load. Rains begin around April and water pours back into the sea. Unique among the world's great oceans, the Indian Ocean is not free at its northern boundary for it is limited there by the huge mass of Asia that holds the water to the south. There is no such limit to the Pacific or the Atlantic. On the Pacific, the open ocean allows the Trade Winds to flow freely toward the southwest above the equator and northwest below the equator. This normality is sustained unless some unusual event, such as the destroying El Niño, changes the pattern.

The "cells" of rising and falling air that rotate vertically over the Indian Ocean, thrusting themselves around with the growing heat, reach out beyond their center to impinge on Africa and Madagascar and extend eastward to beyond New Guinea. Here, perhaps, any irregularity of the Indian Ocean may influence the equatorial Pacific and may start the erratic flows of water and air that characterize the El Niño events. The meteorologists who wonder about storms in San Francisco and droughts in Australia are more and more interested in what may be the nidus of it all, the unusual relationship between the Indian Ocean and the Asian landmass.

In the Indian Ocean, the Trades are hampered each year. Reverse flows of air are the norm rather than the exception because the huge land that bars the north becomes heated or cooled more than what would happen to free water. And thus, over Central Asia the rising heated air lowers the pressure of the atmosphere and this "hollowing" of the air stands in contrast to the filled and heavy air over the Indian Ocean.

Furthermore, the major part of Central Asia that sends its heat aloft is the vast Plateau of Tibet, a giant thrust of land that divides the skin of air that covers the earth and stands to impede any latitudinal shiftings of the atmosphere and so, as eastward moving currents strike this mighty barrier they must move around to south or north. There is, in the wake of this giant intrusion into the moving atmosphere, a sort of ripple of turbulence that carries far out into the Pacific and sets a pattern, perhaps, for some of the climatic features of North America. The Tibetan upland with its coldness in winter can vary greatly on how much snow it accumulates and, if there is much snow, there is less heat absorbed and therefore less rising of air and there is less in the way of a reduced pressure.

If there is less snow, then the pattern supports a strong difference between Central Asia and the distant Indian Ocean. Incidentally, the vegetation of Tibet, a factor that may ameliorate the effect of snow cover, may, in this crucially sensitive balance between atmospheric pressures of ocean and land, have an influence that is not yet appreciated. Can it be that the cutting of woody shrubs for fuel and the grazing of too many sheep in this delicately fragile land of Tibet have an effect upon the crops of Nebraska? It must with more surety have some influence upon the great accumulations of humid air that piles up over the Indian Ocean.

The final effect is the growing negativity over Tibet and the rising heaviness of the air over the ocean. What happens is that the southern, wet air moves inexorably toward the low pressure over Tibet and, as if the whole earth had tilted, it rolls and rolls towards the growing vacuity that governs the lands of Asia. This moving air that is filled to the brim with its load of water is called the Monsoon. It is a unique feature of the earth where a great

215

land mass beckons the air from a vast warm ocean. The Monsoon becomes the greatest wall of moving air in the world.

Let us now shift the scene and look at the plains of India. It is May. For miles the seemingly endless fields of rice hold nothing save the brown and withered stalks of the previous harvest. The ground itself, the once wet alluvium, seems as withered as the stalks of rice with its baked cracks of gray dessication. The sun burns and the shimmering heat cooks the land and all its varied plants and animals. I think it was Shakespeare who said, "Now, too hot burns heaven's eye."

Out in the sweltering villages of Bengal, still centuries from air conditioning, the torrid air governs all behavior. A pariah dog lies stretched out in the tenuous shade offered by a tree that holds its last leaves untrembling in the fixed air. The dark skins of farmers contrast with their whitish dhoties that are pulled up around their loins to expose as much of their bodies as possible. They too rest in the shade of a leaf- stressed tree. Man and dog alike with their languid inertia act as behavioral thermometers, instruments measuring the heat of the oven of India before the monsoon. And as the days proceed the local air, like the ocean far away, fills with vapor. This, with the baking air, adds it quota of stress so that long strands of sweat pour out of parched skin. The humidity destroys the patience that is so necessary for life. And at night when the sun has gone there is no remission from the pervading grasp of the stagnant and sweaty air with its surfeit of heat and moisture. The whole world seems to wait and cry out for relief.

In the city, in Calcutta, the incessant sun drives the people to the shady sides of the street and here and there where there is a water outlet, a tap along the street, people congregate and wet their faces and clothes. It is hot. It is May. It is before the Monsoon. Shift now to a scene where a newspaper in Calcutta is lifted from a rack and the headline in the English language fills the front page with big black letters. It says, simply, "Monsoon Sighted in Colombo." There is not much else. The headline is enough. Some days later there is the similar prime announcement, "Monsoon to Arrive in Madras." And then, in due time there is the overpowering statement, "Monsoon Due Tomorrow."

Let us now look at a lad up on the roof of a higher building of Calcutta. It is not really the kite season but kites may fly at anytime in this part of the world when breezes blow. He lets out his munja, his cutting kite-string that is designed for kite fights by being lightly coated with a fine dusting of ground glass that sticks to the string after it has been run through a fine paste of boiled rice. The kite flies in a steady wind and is joined by others, blue, red and dappled, all wishing for a contest in the air above the city. They streak across the sky in the hot afternoon dipping and lancing at one another, and trying to rise high above each other's string, hoping to cut a munja with a fast and daring dive. And then a strange thing happens. The kites sag in unison and drift and oscillate and sink. There is no wind. It stopped very suddenly. But then it rises again and now it changes in direction and the kites, like high vanes in the air, rock sideways to the new tune of the wind. They move until they reach a full half circle away from their previous line of flight and now they gain a new current of momentum in the opposite direction. Before they flew away from the sea, and now they fly toward it. The reversal took only a minute or two.

Now look! The kites tighten their strings and pull towards a huge wall of clouds that seem to reach to eternity. The sun touches the summit of the wall with light but as the eye descends the ramparts of this fortress of clouds, the colors shift to darkened hues that hover near the deep indigo that borders the black. There is a spraying of lightening now that flashes randomly over the growing darkness and then a distant rolling thunder. The kites, in unison, are rapidly pulled in. The city awaits the storm.

And then, Boom! And the rain comes. Bang— and the rain comes harder. Flash—and now the air is filled with water. The pervading sound is the roar of rain on roofs and streets and, as the puddles grow into moving sheets of water on the land, the surfaces dance with the infinite pelting of rain. The striking drops leave a hazy grayness over everything. It is raining. This is rain! This is the wet air gone mad in its relief to rid itself of its burden. This is rain! This is roaring, churning unbelievable rain! The Monsoon has arrived.

But, now look! In all this roaring downpour people start coming out of their houses and working places. They run out into the rain. Some have bared their bodies except for loin cloths and some are fully dressed. And some even have business suits on. Like a motly mob they stand out in the rain and raise their arms and seemingly, almost figuratively, they cup their hands as they lower their arms. It is as if it was all a form of worship that signifies a great and abundant thanks. The Monsoon has come. The Rains have arrived. India is saved!

The vast front of the Monsoon sweeps up from the Bay of Bengal and pours its substance upon the land, and some 300 miles inland, to the north-east of Calcutta, it reaches the flanks of the Khasi Hills that rise abruptly from the flat plains of the Brahmaputra drainage. On the upper edge of the escarpment lies the town of Cherrapunji and, perhaps from some local peculiarity of the shape of the hills, it is Cherrapunji that receives the fullest wrath of the storm. Consider that here at the rim of the Khasi Hills, the first uplift of the land that has faced the inexorable rolling of the Monsoon, the mighty thickness of moisture laden air is shoved upward as if a mighty wheel had encountered an immense rock in its path and sent a shiver up through its rim and hubs. There is a sudden lift in the front and a sudden cooling and the vapor, the gas of moisture, seemingly explodes into drops of water, the rain. It proceeds to pour.

Look now at the surge of water from the sky. Look at the rain gauge and see how the meniscus rises right in front of the eyes, look at the people with their woven mats over their heads and the sea of black umbrellas. Look at an elephant that stands out in the falling water as if it were in its bath at the nearby river. A stream issues from the tip of its tail and the sheets of water that plunge off its broad back show small ripples like the beginning of a lake. The big animal turns and heavily lies down in the storm kicking its legs in bliss. In all of this response to falling water, a visitor must have a central query, an underlying curiosity about why and how in the name of sanity, anyone in their right mind would live in such a place.

There are a thousand scenes from this rainiest place on earth (Cherrapunji) where, in 1860, the incredible record of 1,041 inches fell, 86 feet of water, and this was only in the four months between June and September. A calculation from this would yield an approximate average of over 8 inches per day or something like one third of an inch per hour. In temperate lands, 8 inches on any one day would make headlines while here, this was the average water arriving day after day. But of course, even in 1860, it did not rain all the time and so, back then and now during lesser rains, great downpourings occur and, sometimes for several days in a row, the gauges will record over 40 inches of the Monsoon's water each day. This is something like 4,500 tons of water per acre in a day, a figure which only points in wonder at the huge capacity of the air to carry moisture.

Beyond the Khasi Hills the mighty Monsoon finally reaches the mighty Himalaya and the real battle begins. Rains pour on the lower slopes but not with the intensity visited on Cherrapunji. Exposed slopes may accumulate 300 inches while behind a rise there may be only half as much. But it rains and as the air is lifted higher the clouds envelope the forested slopes. At 7,000 feet the mists swirl in Darjeeling and it rains. The drains along the roads fill and sweep down the hill and, as the waters from culverts combine, a great torrent is finally let loose to roar down the mountain and finally reach the valley in a surging brown river. At night when the rain adds an incessant patter on the roof the sound is sometimes broken with a roar, the booming of a distant landslide where the earth has soaked up more water than its strength will hold. During the days and days of rain, life continues as if nothing had changed but now there are wet clothes around the fireplace trying to dry.

The Monsoon continues northward and higher and higher reaching toward the great peaks. It is now a cold and shivering rain that meets the high forests where the rhododendrons are still in bloom. Here, as it did so long ago on that high exposed ridge south of Makalu, the pouring may come as if in waves that pulsate and drum the ground with a rhythm that sets a dozen species of primulas to nod and dance to the throbbing tune. Here, too, the impeyan monal and tragopan pheasants scurry beneath the bushy rhododendrons to add their iridescence to the reds and maroons and blues of littered, fallen petals. Higher still the cloud-filled air sweeps on but now the moisture freezes and it snows. And here also the wind twists and blasts at the cliffs and covers them with deep blankets of snow.

But now the air is getting thin. At 18,000 feet there is only half the air that presses at sea level and higher still there is even less, so that at the top of Mt. Everest only a third of the air remains. At such heights the air cannot hold its vapor and the top ridges of the Himalaya squeeze out all save a last remnant of water, a mere dribble that escapes across the high passes into Tibet. It would seem that this greatest wall on earth had won against its adversary, the rolling Monsoon. But the battle is not over yet. The Monsoon has only thrust its lance. The wounds have not yet been felt. There is much more to come.

In the morning after a snow storm, with a warming wind, the valleys are greeted by the booming sounds of avalanches. Huge, white sides of the peaks give way to gravity and shoot down the slopes. Much of this falls upon the accumulations of years of piling snow, snow that is now pressed into ice, the stupendous glaciers. It is these rivers of ice that are the main tools of the Monsoon in its rivalry with the mountains. These slow and grinding monsters with their accumulations of sand and rock are the giant chisels that carve the peaks. The inexorably pushing glaciers cut at the rock and grind it and undercut the cliffs and sculpt the chasms and mold the uplifted land.

Look now at the white crests of the Himalaya as they rule the horizon. Enormous, fluted pinnacles, great buttresses, spires like colossal cathedrals, monstrous slabs of rock and ice fill the sky. They seem like eternal masters of the world shining their white shields down on the encircling lowlands and beckoning any challengers to test their supremacy. But, in reality, that is not the case at all. The glory of the towering peaks is actually the ancient sculpture of the Monsoon. The higher and haughtier the crags rise into the sky shows only how much the Monsoon has cut down. The jagged ridges, the stupendous cliffs, the reaching summits are merely what is left and, their beauty not withstanding, the peaks, like worn and ragged teeth, show the wear and tear of an old and persistent battle. Yes, the mountains, the great Himalaya itself is losing the conflict and, in spite of the colliding continents that impel the mountains and drive the land upward, in time, the Monsoon will rub and abrade and wear with its timeless tools and, leave not a rack of any ridge behind.

The winning Monsoon is, however, a generous victor. Its waters pour down from the peaks and roar into the canyons and carve the valleys. Waters upon waters coalesce into giant rivers that pound the basement rocks. The churning waters carry the sediments from the glaciers and add their complement of powdered rock to a browning stew of grinding fluid that cuts and cuts some more. And then the down slope slackens and flatness supervenes and the current slows. The load of the rivers is dropped along the lower beds or slowly pushed out from the base of the mountains upon the vast plains. It is here that the sediment finally falls and as the waters reach over the walls of silt they have deposited, the flat land is flooded. And so the finely ground load of the rivers is distributed far and wide as the streams and rivers and floods make their sometimes random way back to the Ganges and thence back to their cradle of the Ocean.

The generosity of the victorious Monsoon is in the sediment that it donates to the flat plains for this is a fertile thing, the alluvium of life.

This sifted, powdery stuff is the rich clay that holds minerals and the necessities of growing plants. It is the mother of rice. It is why rice grows in seemingly endless fields and dominates the landscape of mankind. It is why rice grows and feeds its billions of people. The Monsoon does not only donate its water for irrigation and the needs for living cells in all living things, the Monsoon supplies the land that makes food, the land of plenty.

But look at the clayish soil! It used to be the Himalaya! Reach down and cup some of this formless earth and look, look closely, and see the minute flecks that make the stuff. Look at this one and that, and though they have no identity, consider that these dull scraps are the finely slivered remnants of a distant cliff, a far spire, or a towering summit, a piece of Makalu. And, perhaps, there is a speck here that derived from a great peak that is no more, a huge monolith that once stood higher than Everest itself. The great plains of India, the soils for the life of the land, the gifts of the Monsoon, are the rasped ruins of mountains that have gone, the shadows of ancient battles between the giants of the earth, the Monsoon and the Himalaya.

I should perhaps stop here but there should be an insert into this drama. For instance, envision a scene of a flood where a village is perched on some high ground surrounded by water. It is here that man and animals congregate to avoid the water. It is here that the trees are sometimes festooned with snakes. In such places the toll of a snakebite may be high and it is reported that some 20,000 people die in eastern India from the venom of cobras, kraits and the deadly Russel's viper. Aside from this is the argument that has been made to have a mass extermination of snakes in the interest of saving human lives, an argument that fails to sense its consequences. Snakes are the first enemies of rats, and rats, in India and elsewhere, are a leading destroyer of food and the economy. If the snakes went, the delicate balance between starvation and life would tip dangerously toward the former. It could well be that famine would devastate the land and kill more abundantly and cruelly the people of Bengal. And so it is that the magnificent cobra with its warning marks of eyes on its back, a snake that is maligned in the presence of the mongoose and which, when not on the defensive with its hood raised, can attack and kill the contaminating rats - or mongooses -like no other animal. It is perhaps very wise that the Hindus revere the cobra, the snake that normally avoids humankind, as the descendant of the great Nag that helped to churn the milk that gave all life to the earth.

There is also my own need to insert myself into this drama of war between the Monsoon and the Himalaya. I should like to witness again the huge walls of clouds and the water-filled air and the pelting rain. But now I would like to stage this event and prepare to photograph and study it, to find a place, or places, where its biological effects are most dramatically displayed. And behind this hope and wish is the realization that no place on earth shows such a contrast with time, no winter to spring explosion of a temperate season can compare with the suddenness of change that accompanies the arrival of the Rains.

I should like to find a bungalow, a site near the lower forests of the Himalaya where the vista is to the south and across the Plains, and where the Monsoon can be seen coming in all its glorious fury. It could be near Tindaria below Darjeeling where once I witnessed the rebirth of the land by the magic of the storm. It could be in the foothills of Bhutan or further east in the unknown Himalaya of Assam. I should like to arrive early in May, during the heat, for it is in May that life prepares for the arrival of the Monsoon. It is in May that the insects form their swarms and the moths build their mosaics on lighted windows. It is in May because May is the time for reproduction and the laying of eggs. The eggs will hatch when moisture arrives and leaves grow and food is abundant for larvae.

I should like to see again those patterns of moths covering the glass and photograph and collect the myriads and look closely and know them by their names and behavior. And watch again when some huge beetle drones in from the darkness and smashes into the window sending the moths scurrying. I should like, once again, to hold the jeweled scarabaeids, the squeeking, long-horned cerambycids and the shiny stag lucanids and keep what I can alive and bring them back with me. I should like to revel, once more, among the crowded butterflies and know what they are and find their haunts and the plants they feed upon. And photograph their beauty. I should like to know the trees again and try to reach back and sense the intense love I once had for their presence and know them and name them and wish for their survival.

I would search out some old friends like the giant *Rhacophorus maximus*, the emerald-green frog with enormous fans for feet that could leap from high on a tree and sail out on its spread webs and glide for many feet in the air. I could find the marvelous Draco lizards with their hidden wings between their front and hind legs that could also glide for long distances in the air and twist their tails to guide their flight. And, if I could be lucky, I might find that incredible snake *Chrysopelea ornata* that flattens its body and somehow springs into the air and sails out of the trees. I wish that this flying snake in its unknown haunts and unknown behavior would grace my presence.

Once, so long ago, I was searching among a clump of those huge bamboos looking for anything, but especially for the immense bamboo weevil with its extended and hairy front pair of legs—a thing that is over three inches long. Just then, as my kukri knife split a bamboo section, there flew out a number of fluttering things that swept past my head. I had no idea what they were and my first impression that a dozen moths had escaped did not seem right. They flew too fast and they didn't quite fly like moths. It was much later while I was reading about bats that it came to me. It seems that the flatheaded bat, or bamboo bat (*Tylonycterus pachius*), lives in bamboos. It is perhaps the strangest of the whole strange order Chiroptera and it seems to be the smallest mammal on earth, even smaller than the pigmy shrew that is usually quoted to be the smallest mammal. It is unique in having a skull that is much flattened and entirely different from other bats. And what should be the function of the flat head and body? It seems that this little thing finds cracked sections of bamboo and, perhaps waiting for the wind to stir and bend the stalk and therefore stretch open the crack a little, it slides into the hollow bamboo. Is this true? I should like to find out and hold and wonder about some of these phenomenal animals of the Himalaya.

There are so many things to watch and wait for and then, as the Monsoon approaches and the pouring rain drenches the land, I should like to see the growth of the plants that shoot up and turn the dull shades of the dry season into the glossy green that veils the forest with the coming of the water of life. Can it be that some bamboos grow three feet in a day? And with the rain new things arrive. The wet forest resounds with the calls of many species of frogs, huge worms come near the surface and the snakes seek out their food after a long dry spell. A dozen bat species form the crowd of swooping things that mill around the lights at night. And every so often a large moth flies too close. There is a soft whap as a bat hits and then the huge wings of the moth, now bodiless, flutter down to the ground.

All this and more I should like to see again and, perhaps, revel in wonder like the youth who knew little about it all. But this same youth felt the charm of surging life and sensed its power to hold a love for living things that would last a lifetime. I should like once again to ride that trolley down from Ghum to Sukna, fifty miles of rollercoaster through the changing zones of life and into the land where insects light up the trees of the tropical forest. I should like to see, again, the rose-colored purple sunset from Kurseong, the peaks in twilight far away and the lands beyond the skyline that lure my heart along.

THE HOAR OF TIME
(Dedicated to aging teachers)

On a foothill of Himalaya,
Rising up from India's plains,
From air that browns with dust and murk
Now suddenly a snow range reigns.

The north horizon bursts with peaks,
White giants of the world loom high,
Like obelisks and granite spires,
Draped with ice their glaciers lie.

In all their huge array of might,
As if with shields aligned with spear,
Here nothing stands against their height,
They challenge all to bow in fear.

Their phalanx though is aptly used,
For here there is a battle fought,
The greatest war the world has seen,
A thing that books and time forgot.

Like a far field east of Macedon,
Where Persian faced the Greek,
The clashing swords, the blood on sand
Left one to win the other weak.

Here older foes contest the land.
The hugeness of Himalaya's strength
Sets war upon a flimsy thing -
The air itself! How can it be?
Does wind have lances it can fling?

The highest wall on earth cries hold!
The largest moving mass of air,
The monsoon knows of no such threat
And rolls on north without a care.

The slopes that rise beneath its cloud
And higher where the air grows thin
Snow and ice assume command.
And now the battle cry is out!

Avalanche and glaciers roar.
The rock is cut and ground to dust,
Year after year and more and more.
Until at last there comes a time
When valleys furrow into cliffs
And few great peaks persist with age.
Look! Those whitened monoliths that rise
Are merely remnants on a stage!

Obelisks and spires white,
Like age-old teeth have worn to bone,
They raise their heads but for a while
But ice from wind wears down the stone
The proud white line of majesty
The crowning row of earth's aretes
Are just a sepulcher of time.
The mountains lose; the wind defeats.

The monsoon is benign in this.
The raging streams that carry silt
Flood out upon the plains and give
Alluvium like a massive quilt
That grows the rice that feeds mankind.

Pick up some piece that looks like mud -
From Bengal or from Bihar -
Look closely at this dirty muck.
Look! A tiny grain that shines of quartz.
Detritus from an ancient peak?
An Everest lost? Or its cohorts?

And so I look around my friends,
Where more and more the white allows
The hoar of time, the snows of age
While valleys furrow into brows.

Like ice eroding rock we stand
Daring wind and cold,
Challenging our timeless quest,
To teach some thoughts to youth with zest,
To leave our lights where dimness falls,
To live a while 'till Gabriel calls.
Persistent time will roll its dice
But we'll make muck turn into rice.

Routes of 1954 and 1960 Expeditions

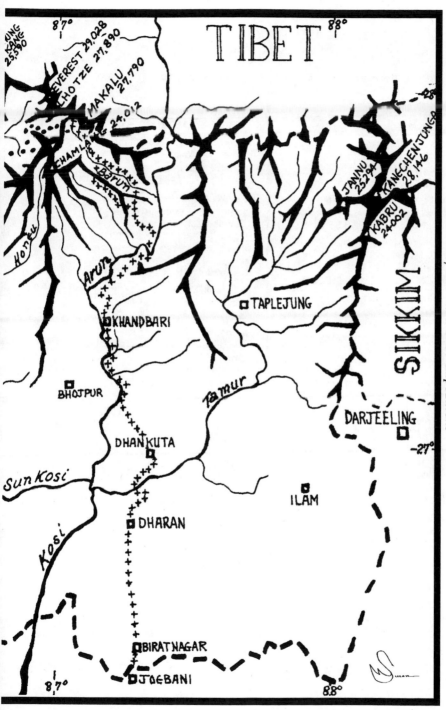

Routes of 1954 and 1960 Expeditions

OTHER TITLES PUBLISHED BY
MOUNTAIN N' AIR BOOKS

ADVENTURE GUIDES

Cross Country Northeast
   John R. Fitzgerald Jr.
   ISBN: 1-879415-07-0 $12.00

Cross Country Skiing
   in Southern California
   Eugene Mezereny
   ISBN: 1-879415-08-9 $14.00

Great Rock Hits of Hueco Tanks
   Paul Piana
   ISBN: 1-879415-03-8 $ 6.95

Mountain Bike Adventures...
   MOAB, Utah
   Bob Ward
   ISBN: 1-879415-11-9 $15.00

The Rogue River Guide
   Kevin Keith Tice
   ISBN: 1-879415-12-7 $15.00

ADVENTURES, LITERATURE

A Night on the Ground,
   A Day in the Open
   Doug Robinson
   ISBN: 1-879415-14-3 $19.00

Baja Fever:
   Journey's into Mexico's Intriguing
   Peninsula
   Greg Niemann
   ISBN:1-879415-19-4 $19.50

High Endeavors
   Pat Ament
   ISBN: 1-879415-00-3 $12.95

On Mountains and Mountaineers
   Mikel Vause
   ISBN: 1-879415-06-2 $12.95

Rock and Roses - Second edition
   Mikel Vause, editor
   ISBN: 1-879415-28-3 $19.00

ADVENTURE, LIT. (CONTINUE)

Roughing It in Gold Country
   William S. Pierson
   ISBN: 1-879415-21-6 $18.00

Thinking Out Loud Through the
   American West
   Pete Sinclair
   ISBN: 1-879415-20-8 $18.00

The View From the Edge: Life and
   Landscapes of Beverly Johnson
   Gabriela Zim
   ISBN: 1-879415-16-X $17.00

COOKING AND EATING

Cooking with Strawberries
   Margaret and Virginia Clark
   ISBN: 1-879415-26-7 $10.95

The Nose Knows: A Sensualist Guide
   to Eating Joints in the Greater Los
   Angeles Area
   Lloyd McAteer Battista
   ISBN: 1-879415-23-2 $13.00

HIKING AND HIKING GUIDES

Lori Saldaña's Backpacking Primer
   ISBN: 1-879415-13-5 $12.00

Best Hikes of the Marble Mountain
   and Russian Wild. Areas, California
   Art Bernstein
   ISBN: 1-879415-18-6 $16.00

Best Hikes of the Trinity Alps (CA)
   Art Bernstein
   ISBN: 1-879415-05-4 $17.00

Portland Hikes, 2"~ Edition Art
   Bernstein and Andrew Jackman
   ISBN: 1-879415-22-4 $18.00

So... How Does the Rope Get Up
   There, Anyway?
   Kathy Myers and Mark Blanchard
   ISBN: 1-879415-17-8 $10.00